SPECULATIONS ON BLACK LIFE

Bloomsbury Studies in Black Religion and Cultures

Series Editors: Anthony B. Pinn and Monica R. Miller

Bloomsbury Studies in Black Religion and Cultures advances innovative scholarship that reimagines and animates the global study of Black religions, culture, and identity across space and time. The series publishes scholarship that addresses the mutually constitutive nature of race and religion and the social, cultural, intellectual, and material effects of religio-racial formations and identities. The series welcomes projects that address and foreground the intersectional and constitutive nature of black religions and cultures and privileges work that is inter/transdisciplinary and methodologically intersectional in nature.

African Spirituality, Politics and Knowledge Systems
Toyin Falola

Black Transhuman Liberation Theology
Philip Butler

Innovation and Competition in Zimbabwean Pentecostalism
Edited by Ezra Chitando

Religion and Inequality in Africa
Edited by Ezra Chitando, Loreen Maseno, and Joram Tarusarira

SPECULATIONS ON BLACK LIFE

The Collected Writings of William R. Jones

Edited by
Darrell Jones, Monifa Love, and Anthony B. Pinn

BLOOMSBURY ACADEMIC
LONDON • NEW YORK • OXFORD • NEW DELHI • SYDNEY

BLOOMSBURY ACADEMIC
Bloomsbury Publishing Plc
50 Bedford Square, London, WC1B 3DP, UK
1385 Broadway, New York, NY 10018, USA
29 Earlsfort Terrace, Dublin 2, Ireland

BLOOMSBURY, BLOOMSBURY ACADEMIC and the Diana logo are trademarks of
Bloomsbury Publishing Plc

First published in Great Britain 2023
This paperback edition published 2025

Copyright © Darrell Jones, Monifa Love, Anthony B. Pinn and contributors, 2023

Darrell Jones, Monifa Love, and Anthony B. Pinn have asserted their rights under the
Copyright, Designs and Patents Act, 1988, to be identified as Editors of this work.

For legal purposes the Acknowledgments on p. xvi constitute an extension of
this copyright page.

Series design: Maria Rajka

Cover photo courtesy of the William R. Jones Papers, FSU Special Collections & Archives

All rights reserved. No part of this publication may be reproduced or transmitted
in any form or by any means, electronic or mechanical, including photocopying,
recording, or any information storage or retrieval system, without prior
permission in writing from the publishers.

Bloomsbury Publishing Plc does not have any control over, or responsibility for, any
third-party websites referred to or in this book. All internet addresses given in this
book were correct at the time of going to press. The author and publisher regret any
inconvenience caused if addresses have changed or sites have ceased to exist,
but can accept no responsibility for any such changes.

A catalogue record for this book is available from the British Library.

A catalogue record for this book is available from the Library of Congress.

ISBN: HB: 978-1-3503-3874-6
PB: 978-1-3503-3878-4
ePDF: 978-1-3503-3875-3
eBook: 978-1-3503-3876-0

Series: Bloomsbury Studies in Black Religion and Cultures

Typeset by Deanta Global Publishing Services, Chennai, India

To find out more about our authors and books visit www.bloomsbury.com and
sign up for our newsletters

CONTENTS

Notes on Contributors	viii
Foreword Peter J. Paris	xi
Acknowledgments	xvi
INTRODUCTION: SEEING THROUGH THE DIFFICULT: WILLIAM R. JONES AND HIS SPECULATIONS ON BLACK LIFE Monifa Love	1

Part I
(BLACK) HUMANISM

Chapter 1
BLACK POWER AND UNITARIANISM: A PERSONAL VIEW ... 9
    William R. Jones

Chapter 2
THEISM AND RELIGIOUS HUMANISM: THE CHASM NARROWS ... 18
    William R. Jones

Chapter 3
THE CASE FOR BLACK HUMANISM ... 27
    William R. Jones

Chapter 4
RELIGIOUS HUMANISM: ITS PROBLEMS AND PROSPECTS IN BLACK
RELIGION AND CULTURE ... 38
    William R. Jones

Chapter 5
OPPRESSION, RACE, AND HUMANISM ... 56
    William R. Jones

Chapter 6
IS FAITH IN GOD NECESSARY FOR A JUST SOCIETY? INSIGHTS FROM
LIBERATION THEOLOGY ... 64
    William R. Jones

Part II
PHILOSOPHICAL THEOLOGY

Chapter 7
RECONCILIATION AND LIBERATION IN BLACK THEOLOGY: SOME IMPLICATIONS FOR RELIGIOUS EDUCATION — 79
William R. Jones

Chapter 8
THEODICY: THE CONTROLLING CATEGORY FOR BLACK THEOLOGY — 88
William R. Jones

Chapter 9
THE RELIGIOUS LEGITIMATION OF COUNTERVIOLENCE: INSIGHTS FROM LATIN AMERICAN LIBERATION THEOLOGY — 97
William R. Jones

Chapter 10
PURPOSE AND METHOD IN LIBERATION THEOLOGY: IMPLICATIONS FOR AN INTERIM ASSESSMENT — 119
William R. Jones

Chapter 11
MORAL DECISION-MAKING IN THE POST-MODERN WORLD: IMPLICATIONS FOR UNITARIAN-UNIVERSALIST RELIGIOUS EDUCATION — 138
William R. Jones

Part III
THE POLITICS OF RACE

Chapter 12
POWER AND ANTI-POWER — 155
William R. Jones

Chapter 13
RELIGION AS LEGITIMATOR AND LIBERATOR: INSIGHTS FROM THE UNDERCLASS FOR PUBLIC POLICY — 159
(A Worm's Eye View of Religion and Contemporary Politics)
William R. Jones

Chapter 14
HYPOCRISY, BIBLIOCRACY, AND DEMOCRACY: IMPLICATIONS FOR GAYS AND LESBIANS IN THE MILITARY — 172
William R. Jones

Chapter 15
THE DISGUISES OF DISCRIMINATION: CIVIL RIGHTS, 1954–65   179
   William R. Jones

Chapter 16
TOWARD A NEW PARADIGM FOR UNCOVERING NEO-RACISM IN
AMERICAN INSTITUTIONS   183
   William R. Jones

Part IV
CRITICAL REFLECTION ON JONES'S WRITINGS

Essay 1
THE DEBATE THAT SHAPED A FIELD: WILLIAM R. JONES AND
DEVELOPMENTS IN BLACK THEOLOGY   191
   Anthony B. Pinn

Essay 2
NEO-RACISM AND THE SHORTCOMINGS OF RELIGIOUS LIBERALISM   196
   Jamil W. Drake

Essay 3
EXPANDING THE ALTAR: TRANSGRESSING AND TRANSFORMING
CONVENTIONAL BOUNDARIES IN BLACK LIBERATION THEOLOGY   202
   Brittany L. O'Neal

AFTERWORD   209
   Darrell Jones

Index   211

CONTRIBUTORS

Jamil W. Drake is assistant professor of Religion at Yale Divinity School. Drake specializes in American religious history with particular interests in twentieth-century African American religious cultures; religion and politics; and religion and popular culture. More specifically, he is interested in questions around religion and racial identity in the United States. He is author of *To Know the Soul of the People: American Folk Studies and Racial Politics of Popular Religion, 1900–1940*, which tells a story of how the study of race and religion became a central topic in folklore research and the developing social sciences. His research explores how the use of "folk religion" played a fundamental role in the process of classifying cultural behaviors that contributed to defining Black lower- and working-class communities in twentieth-century America.

Darrell Jones, the son of William R. Jones, is an associate professor in the Department of Dance at Columbia College Chicago. His specializations are Contemporary Dance Technique, Improvisation, Contact Improvisation, Movement for Actors, Conditioning, Pedagogy, with his area of research focusing on mechanisms of oppression and liberatory practices. Jones has received choreographic fellowships from MANCC (Maggie Allesee National Center for Choreography), CDF (Chicago Dancemakers Forum) and has additionally been a recipient of the Wesleyan University Creative Campus Fellow (2017), MAP Fund (2017) and Mid-Atlantic Arts Foundation. He is a two-time Bessie Award recipient for his collaborative work with Bebe Miller Company (*Landing Place*) and his most recent research into (e)feminized ritual performance (*Hoo-Ha*).

William R. Jones received his undergraduate degree in philosophy at Howard University. He earned his Master of Divinity at Harvard University in 1958 and was ordained and fellowshipped as a Unitarian Universalist minister in that year. He served from 1958 to 1960 at a Unitarian Universalist congregation in Providence, Rhode Island. Jones received his PhD from Brown University in 1969. His dissertation was titled "On Sartre's Critical Methodology," which discussed "Jean-Paul Sartre's Philosophical Anthropology" (Lewis R. Gordon, *An Introduction to Africana Philosophy* [Cambridge University, 2008], p. 171). After receiving his PhD, Jones was an assistant professor at Yale Divinity School from 1969 to 1977. During this time, he published his 1973 book *Is God a White Racist?* After leaving Yale in 1977, Jones became professor of religion and the director of Afro-American studies program in the College of Social Sciences at Florida State University (FSU) in Tallahassee. While at FSU, he did innovative work on anti-racism theory, developing what has become known as JOG and JAM—the Jones Oppression Grid, the core of the Jones Analytic Model—a "toolkit" for investigating oppression. During the course of his long academic career, Jones held visiting professorships at Princeton Theological Seminary, Union Theological Seminary, and Iliff School of Theology. Jones received an honorary doctorate from Meadville/Lombard Theological School in 1990. At FSU, he served on innumerable doctoral student committees. He co-directed a graduate student orientation program. He was on the board of two fellowship programs that provided financial assistance to minority students. In the late 1990s, he served on the Commission on Appraisal, and served on the UUA Board of Trustees 1997–1999. Upon his retirement in 1999, Jones was honored by FSU with the title professor emeritus. In 2001, Jones was given the Award for Distinguished Service to the Cause of Unitarian Universalism. His final major contribution to Unitarian Universalist theology was his essay summarizing the JOG and JAM model, "Toward a New Paradigm for Uncovering Neo-Racism," which was included in *Soul Work: Anti-Racist Theologies in Dialogue*.

Monifa Love Asante is a professor in the Department of Language, Literature, and Cultural Studies at Bowie State University. Love Asante is a graduate of Princeton University and the Florida State University, where she matriculated as a McKnight Doctoral Fellow and as an associate of William R. Jones. Love Asante is the author of two collections of poetry, *Provisions* (1989) and *Dreaming Underground* (2003, Naomi Long Madgett Award winner). She co-authored two fine arts catalogs about the life and work of Ed Love and produced "my magic pours secret libations," a fine arts catalog and video of an exhibition she curated of African American and Afro-Cuban women artists. She is the author of the award-winning novel, *Freedom in the Dismal* (1998).

Brittany O'Neal is an adjunct assistant professor at the City University of New York. She teaches in the Africana Studies Department at Lehman College and the Africana and Puerto Rican/Latino Studies Department at Hunter College. She received her doctoral degree in African American and African studies with a specialization in philosophy from Michigan State University in 2015. Her areas of research include Black liberation theology, African American philosophy, philosophy of religion, and the Black radical intellectual tradition.

Peter J. Paris is the Elmer G. Homrighausen professor emeritus of Christian Social Ethics at Princeton Theological Seminary. A world-renowned scholar, Paris is author/editor of numerous books, including *The Spirituality of African Peoples* and (ed) *Religion and Poverty: Pan-African Perspectives*. The recipient of numerous honorary degrees, Paris has served as president of the American Academy of Religion, the American Theological Society, and the Society for the Study of Black Religion. He is also general editor of the Religion, Race, and Ethnicity series.

Anthony B. Pinn is currently the Agnes Cullen Arnold distinguished professor of humanities and professor of religion at Rice University. He is also professor extraodinarius at the University of South Africa. In addition, Pinn is a fellow of the American Academy of Arts and Sciences. He is the founding director of the Center for Engaged Research and Collaborative Learning, and the inaugural director of the Center for African and African American Studies (2019–2022). Pinn's research interests include African American religious thought, religion and culture; humanism; and hip hop culture. He is the author/editor of over thirty-five books, including *The Interplay of Things: Religion, Art, and Presence Together* (2021) and the novel *The New Disciples* (2015).

FOREWORD

William R. Jones, whom all of his friends called "Bill," was the first African American I had ever met who was a member of the Unitarian Universalist Association. Since I was the first Black Canadian he had ever met and we both had the common experience of spending time at Howard University from where he graduated and I had taught for a few years in its School of Religion, we felt an immediate bond. I recall asking him many questions and in his friendly, erudite, humble manner he took great care in answering all of them even while inquiring about how my ancestors got to Canada.

Bill loved Howard where his study of philosophy and religion had been nurtured and his professors encouraged him to pursue the Master of Divinity degree at Harvard University. From there he went on to pursue PhD studies in philosophy of religion at Brown University, where he wrote a dissertation on the anthropology of the French existentialist philosopher Jean-Paul Sartre, a subject far removed from his African American experience. Yet, that work would later prove useful as the foundation for his sympathetic critique of James H. Cone's nascent Black theology. Though only recently acknowledged as such, Jones was one of the few acclaimed theologians in the Unitarian Universalist Church whom Meadville Theological Seminary celebrated when it bestowed on him an honorary doctoral degree in 1990.

Jones began his academic career of writing and teaching during a period of great upheaval in African American theological and religious thought that had been sparked initially by the mid-twentieth-century Civil Rights Movement under the leadership of Dr. Martin Luther King, Jr., president of the Southern Christian Leadership Conference. King's adaptation of Gandhi's method of non-violent mass protests to combat racially segregated bus seating in Montgomery, Alabama, was soon expanded to several other Southern cities with the goal of dismantling such practices not only in public transportation but also in eating facilities and voter registration centers throughout the South.

Gradually King's Southern-based movement morphed into the Black Power Movement which emphasized Black racial pride and self-determination in all matters pertaining to the Black community. Its principal advocates included Stokely Carmichael, president of the Student Non-violent Co-ordinating Committee, and Huey P. Newton and Bobby Seale, co-founders of the Black Panther Party for Self-Defense in Oakland, CA. All of those young Black leaders rejected the non-violent philosophy of Dr. King as they courageously demanded social, economic, and political equality by any means possible. Clearly, their philosophy, rhetoric, and public demands were not only more radical than those advocated by Dr. King but harmonious with the strident demands of the iconic national leader, Malcolm X.

Invariably, theological and philosophical advocates on both sides of the ideological divide raised questions about the relation of God's omnipotence and absolute goodness to the ubiquitous problem of Black suffering. In classical theological discourse that question was called *theodicy*, a philosophical Greek term pertaining to the advocacy of God's moral goodness despite the presence of evil in the world. Both then and now, the aim of theodicy is to answer the question: "If God is all powerful and absolutely good, then why does God allow humans to suffer?" That question has been debated in the Christian churches from the early centuries of its existence up to the present age.

On July 18, 1966, as a response to the hostile reaction of white clergy to the call for Black power, a hastily formed organization named, The National Committee of Negro Churchmen, later called The National Conference of Black Churchmen (NCBC) purchased a full-page ad in the New York Times declaring their support for Black power. It was signed by forty-eight prominent Black clergymen that included Representative Adam Clayton Powell, Jr. Three years later the NCBC issued a statement that defined Black theology as a theology of Black liberation.

Also, in 1969, James H. Cone published his first book entitled *Black Theology and Black Power* and in 1970 a small group of African American theologians and religious leaders founded the Society for the Study of Black Religion (SSBR) as a racially separate organization to engage in the academic discussion of Black religion in order to encourage and support additional publications in the field. Cone's book provided the impetus for such an undertaking and his courageous use of the modifier "Black" for the term "theology" unequivocally signaled the beginning of a new era in theological scholarship. Further and most important, the book's title implied a theological justification for Black power which had caused a virtual blitz throughout the nation's public media. As one might expect, many heated debates about Cone's thought occurred not only within the confines of the SSBR but in theological seminaries and religious judicatories throughout the nation.

Now, Cone was not the only one writing in this new theological genre. In recent years Black clergy, seminary professors, and church leaders had undertaken similar ventures. In fact, at that time, the following authors constituted the nascent lexicon for the SSBR's annual conference agenda: Albert B. Cleage, Jr., Cecil Wayne Cone, Vincent G. Harding, Major J. Jones, J. Deotis Roberts, Joseph R. Washington, and Gayraud S. Wilmore. Sadly, the voices of Black women were not heard in the SSBR until the second decade of its life when a pioneering generation of Black women in theology, ethics, and sociology launched a unique genre of scholarship which they called "womanist" thought; a term they borrowed from the acclaimed novelist, Alice Walker. Its distinctive mission was to study religion through the experiential perspectives of Black women.

In 1973 the discourse surrounding the Black theology of James Cone and others received its most profound criticism from a young colleague within the SSBR, William R. Jones, who in that year published his first book with the provocative title, *Is God a White Racist? A Preamble to Black Theology*. In his introduction, Jones made it abundantly clear that he was not an adversary of the Black theology project but one who demanded an adequate answer to the theodicy question as a precondition for any such undertaking. In fact, the subtitle of his book implied his affirmation of Black theology. Thus, he issued the charge that since neither Cone nor any of the other advocates for a Black theology had provided an adequate answer to the issue of God's moral goodness, their theologies were premature, problematic, and wholly unpersuasive. Accordingly, he claimed that their assertions about God's moral goodness in no way disproved the contrary accusation that God was a racist deity. Most important, he contended that the adequacy of their endeavors necessitated an adequate answer to the theodicy question as a precondition. In order to show his good faith as a friend in the quest for a Black theology, Jones ended his book with an outline of his constructive theodicy as grounded in a humanocentric theism which he claimed to be an adequate foundation for the Black liberation theology he intended to write.

Now, let me hasten to say, however, that both Cone and Jones published their first books at a time when most who now call ourselves "African Americans" were still experiencing various degrees of discomfort with the novel linguistic term "Black" that each of them had used to modify the words "theology" and "power." Thus, it is an understatement to say that both "Black Theology" and "Black Power" implied radical criticisms of the traditional understandings of theology and politics in America. Clearly, their respective books were destined to become primers for the exploration of many new questions and concerns regarding the study of religion in general and that of African peoples in particular.

Now, if the term "Black theology" was shocking to many at that time, the question of God being a white racist was even more so since throughout the first century of their bondage enslaved Africans had shown no interest whatsoever in the religion of their enslavers. It was only after they discovered that the God of the New Testament was the same deity who had delivered the oppressed Israelites from slavery that they willingly embraced that deity as their own. After their conversion to Christianity, however, they never doubted that their God was a divine agent of deliverance and wholly different from the one their oppressors worshipped. Accordingly, they composed countless praise songs which they called "spirituals" of which the following had paramount meaning:

Go Down Moses
Way Down in Egypt's Land,
Tell Ole Pharaoh,
Let My People Go.

Both the so-called "invisible church" during the period of slavery and the institutional Black churches formed thereafter became heirs of that same tradition which inspired Blacks to interpret the whole Bible through the lens of the Exodus event. Accordingly, James Cone, nurtured in the African Methodist Episcopal Church, wrote his systematic theology in that same tradition as evidenced in his claim that God's deliverance of the Israelites implied that God was on the side of all oppressed peoples and supported their desire for liberation. But Jones's devastating critique undermined both Cone's theology and the tradition he had inherited. None of the contemporary theologians or church leaders were able to refute his indictment because of their trust in that traditional wisdom. Jones's dispute emerged from a philosophical critique of traditional and neo-orthodox theologies which Cone drew upon as authoritative sources that were grounded in faith rather than empirical evidence.

Nonetheless, Jones argued that prior to writing a Black theology, Cone should have asked about God's moral nature because so much of white theology had either underestimated or strongly affirmed God's agency in both the establishment and promotion of white racism. Most important, he argued that Black liberation theology merely asserted God's goodness and justice without providing sufficient evidence in support of such a claim. Further still, he argued that all who have grounded their arguments in God's moral goodness as exemplified either in the Exodus event or in the teachings of Jesus have ignored the fact that neither the Hebrew nor the Christian primary sources directly addressed the transAtlantic enslavement of African peoples because it did not occur until many centuries later.

In my judgment, Jones's greatest contribution to Black theology lies in his rigorous philosophical analysis of power as a force to dominate, destroy, or liberate those under its control. In short, he claimed that those who do not understand the power of their opponents will never achieve their dreams of liberation. Thus, theological statements about liberation must be evaluated in accordance with the liberating practices they imply. Claims about God being a liberator of the oppressed must be supported by adequate evidence to that effect. Otherwise, one can rightly assume that God might be a divine oppressor. As a helpful guide, Jones devised an empirical mechanism with which to measure and analyze both the level of oppression and its resistance. The anacronym of the former was the "Jones Oppression Grid" (JOG) and that of his analysis was the "Jones' Analytics Grid" (JAM). At the last meeting of the Society for the Study of Black Religion he attended he led a discussion explicating those grids. He also presented and discussed them similarly as a guest speaker at international meetings in both Puerto Rico and South Africa.

Finally, it is interesting to note that both James Cone and William Jones acknowledged with gratitude the assistance rendered them by a senior Black sociologist of religion, Professor C. Eric Lincoln, who was an important enabler of their respective publications. I also recall seeking his advice before publishing my first book a few years later. He was indeed a trusted senior colleague to young Black scholars.

Finally, it should be noted that through his prolific constructive writings one of the editors of this volume, Anthony B. Pinn, has striven to establish Black humanism as a significant dimension of Black religion. In his endeavors he has been influenced by the *humanocentric* theistic work of William R. Jones while opting for the *humanocentric* nontheistic approach that Jones described as the only other viable alternative. Thus, this book is a well-deserved tribute to William R. Jones's significant contribution to the study of Black religion.

Peter J. Paris
Elmer G. Homrighausen Professor, Emeritus
Christian Social Ethics
Princeton Theological Seminary

ACKNOWLEDGMENTS

While a limited number of names appear on the cover of this volume, the editors want to emphasize that fact that many helped us reach this point. Without their support and assistance this project would have been much more difficult to complete and much less fulfilling at the end.

The role of family cannot be underestimated. Infinite gratitude to Dr. Jones's former wife and son, Lauretta and Jeffery Jones, for their loving support of his vision and this collection.

Thank you to Drs. Billy Close, Fabian Tata, and Lewis Gordon for their insights shared during a panel discussion of Dr. William Jones's impact on the Academy in general and a range of his students and mentees in particular. We are grateful to Drs. Peter Paris, Brittney O'Neal, and Jamil Drake for their insightful pieces published here.

At Florida State, where William Jones taught for many years, we must express our gratitude to Drs. Joseph Hellweg, Jamil Drake, and John Cole. We are also grateful to the Florida State University Special Collections—Katie McCormick and Rory Grennan—for all their hard work in preserving Jones's writings.

We can't forget the support and help offered by Florida A&M Meek-Eaton Black Archives Research Center & Museum: thank you Drs. Nashid Madyun and Will Guzman. And thank you, Murell Dawson. In addition, a big thank you to Carla Peterson and Ansje Burdick of MANCC Maggie Allesee. And much appreciation to Jawolle Willa Jo Zollar and Maria Bauman of Urban Bush Women.

Darrell Jones would like to thank Columbia College Chicago for the generous support of time awarded for sabbatical leave. From Rice University we want to thank Maya Reine, who prepared the manuscript for delivery to the press; and thank you to School of Humanities Dean Kathleen Canning for financial assistance with the securing of permission. We must also thank Dr. Lisa Spiro, Shannon Kipphut-Smith, and Anna Shparberg from Rice University's Fondren Library for their help tracking down copyright and publishers' information for several of the chapters.

We are delighted to be publishing this volume with Bloomsbury Academic, and we want to say thank you to Stuart Hay and Lily McMahon for all their support, encouragement, and hard work guiding the book through production. We must also thank the external reviewers who took the time to review the proposal for this volume.

* * *

The editors would like to thank the following for permission to reprint:

Chapter 2:
William R. Jones, "Theism and Religious Humanism: The Chasm Narrows," *The Christian Century*, Vol. 92 (May 21, 1975): 520–5. Reprinted by permission of *The Christian Century*.

Chapter 3:
William R. Jones, "The Case for Black Humanism," in William Jones and Calvin E. Bruce, eds. *Black Theology II* (Lewisburg, PA: Bucknell University, 1978). Reprinted by permission of the Associated University Presses.

Chapter 4:
William R. Jones, "Religious Humanism: its Problems and Prospects in Black Religion and Culture," *Interdenominational Theological Center Journal* (December 1979): 169–86. Used by permission of *The ITC Journal*.

Chapter 5:
William R. Jones, "Oppression, Race, and Humanism," *Humanist Magazine* (published by the American Humanist Association), Vol. 52, No. 6 (1992). Reprinted with permission of the Humanist Magazine (1992), published by the American Humanist Association.

Chapter 6:
William R. Jones, "Is Faith in God Necessary for a Just Society?" In Gene James, editor. *The Search for Faith and Justice in the Twentieth Century* (1987): 82–95. Copyright © Paragon House, 1987. Reprinted with permission.

Chapter 7:
William R. Jones, "Reconciliation and Liberation in Black Theology: Some Implications for Religious Education," *Religious Education*, Vol. 67, No., 5 (September 1972): 384–8. Reprinted by permission of Taylor & Francis Group.

Chapter 8:
William R. Jones, "Theodicy: The Controlling Category for Black Theology," *Journal of Religious Thought* (Summer 1973): 28–38. Reprinted with permission of *JRT*.

Chapter 9:
William R. Jones, "The Religious Legitimation of Counterviolence: Insights from Latin American Liberation Theology." In Lonnie D. Kliever (ed.), *The Terrible Meek: Revolution and Religion in Cross-Cultural Perspective* (New York: Paragon Press). Copyright © Paragon House, 1987. Reprinted with permission.

Chapter 10:
William R. Jones, "Purpose and Method in Liberation Theology: Implications for an Interim Assessment," in Deane William Ferm, ed., *Liberation Theology: North*

American Style (New York: Verizon, 1987). Used by permission of the International Religious Foundation.

Chapter 11:
William R. Jones, "Moral Decision-Making in a Post-Modern World: Implications for Value Education in Unitarian-Universalism." In Wayne Arnason, ed., *Unitarian-Universalism 1985: Selected Essays* (Boston: Papercraft Printing Co., 1985), 31–52. Reprinted with permission from the Unitarian Universalist Ministers Association.

Chapter 13:
William R. Jones, "Religion as Legitimator and Liberator: Insights from the Underclass for Public Policy." In Richard Rubenstein, ed. *The Worldwide Impact of Religion on Contemporary Politics* (New York: Paragon Press, 1987), 237–57. Reprinted by permission of Paragon House.

Chapter 14:
William R. Jones, "Hypocrisy, Bibliocracy, and Democracy," in John J. Carey, editor. *The Christian Argument for Gays and Lesbians in the Military: Essays by Mainline Church Leaders* (Question, Ontario: Mellen University Press), 37–44. Reprinted with permission of The Edwin Mellen Press.

Chapter 15:
William R. Jones, "The Disguise of Discrimination," *FORUM, The Magazine of the Florida Humanities Council* (Summer 1995). Reprinted by permission of Florida Humanities.

Chapter 16:
William R. Jones, "Towards a New Paradigm for Uncovering Neo-racism in American Institutions," in Marjorie Bowens-Wheatley and Nancy Palmer Jones, editors. *Soul Work: Anti-Racist Theologies in Dialogue* (Boston: Skinner House, 2003). Reprinted with permission of Skinner House.

In addition to the foregoing list, good faith effort was made to contact the publishers of the following materials.

Chapter 12:
William R. Jones, "Power and Anti-Power," *Kairos* (1977).

Finally, the following piece is marked in William Jones's records as being unpublished. In our search, we were unable to locate a publisher. According to Mark Morrison-Reed in a note to *Revisiting the Empowerment Controversy* (Unitarian Universalist Association of Congregations, 2018) it was delivered as a sermon at All Souls Church, Unitarian, Washington, DC, on November 5, 1967. (Records of the commission on religion and race, bMS 1148/4 [5]).

Chapter 1:
William R. Jones, "Black Power and Unitarianism: A Personal View."

INTRODUCTION

Seeing Through the Difficult: William R. Jones and His Speculations on Black Life

Monifa Love

> Think not, as you read these pages, that they were conceived in certainty and ease. Fear and trembling, confusion and doubt gave them birth. And if my words bespeak an irreverent iconoclasm and profane dissent for the sake of notoriety, they contradict my conscious motives. . . . Dear reader, tell me the sign; help me find the plan.
>
> —William R. Jones, "Prologue," *Is God a White Racist?*

This collection of chapters tells the story of a mission. The mission begins in segregated Louisville, Kentucky. It has no conclusion because it has influenced generations of philosophers, theologians, policy makers, artists, social workers, negotiators, criminologists, writers, unionists, community activists, and other seekers of a more just society. The work offered here also reflects William R. Jones's deliberate, grueling, and all-consuming effort to ask the right questions and provide the correct answers to ease the suffering of the downtrodden. As the epigraph suggests, Jones fought for clarity about the human condition in general and Black life in particular. Committed to being as accurate and unambiguous as possible, he fought for every word. His only book, *Is God a White Racist?* led many to misunderstand his motives and castigate him as a spotlight-seeking blasphemer. The title blinded some critics to his courageous examination of the question of theodicy. To question the benevolence of God for people who had anchored themselves in divine love and rescue—when there seemed to be no other anchor—was going too far. Jones responded to the chastisement by seeking more interaction with his critics to consider the consequences of a tradition in which one accepted suffering in this life for glory in the next. He proffered another tradition of Black humanism that celebrated the centrality of the human being in human affairs and decision-making. Jones also listened to oppressed people to help him light a path toward liberation. This collection tenders a chronicle of his seeing through the difficult territory of oppression.

Building Intellectual Curiosity

Born the fifth of six children in 1933, William R. Jones was reared among fundamentalist men and women who believed in making things plain. They also held that they would receive their reward in heaven. They invested in the aphorism, "the heavier the cross, the brighter the crown," as it offered some justification for relentless white supremacy and their ethnic suffering here on earth.

Jones's grandfather ministered to the church he attended as a youth. Still, the preacher's certainty about God's omnibenevolence did not exempt him from the terror he experienced in his last days when he worried that he had not been sufficiently faithful in the eyes of God. His grandfather's final trepidation and suffering made a lifelong impression on Jones, and he recalled the incident often. He saw his grandfather in the vulnerable congregations for whom he would advance ideas about mis-religion and theodicy. The community's investment in redemptive suffering focused its energies on deciphering the connection between faith in God, oppression, moral decision-making, and economic, social, and political (ESP) liberation.

In the preface to *Is God a White Racist?* (1973, 1998), the remarkable text for which Jones is perhaps best known, he recounts an epiphany during his life as a licensed teenage preacher in Louisville and follower of the evangelist Billy Graham. The epiphany was the falsity of absolutism and the power of internal criticism. He came to this apprehension as a consequence of memorizing, selecting, and citing biblical scripture. Depending upon the context, he might interpret one passage literally, another figuratively, or join nonadjacent passages for effect. Although he was highly adept at such work, he recognized its dishonesty. The recognition led to a paradigm shift, and that shift prompted a mission to harness his insights into understanding and eradicating the suffering of Black people.

Initially, he did not have the language to describe this critical awareness or his mission in such terms, but he soon gathered it. A voracious reader and student of rhetoric, he scrutinized arguments for their logic and power to persuade. Despite those who encouraged Jones to pursue a degree in Engineering and his attraction to the systems-oriented field, he earned his bachelor's with high honors in philosophy from Howard University in 1955, where the dynamic faculty mentored him. He received his Master of Divinity from Harvard University in 1958 when the Unitarian Society ordained him. He earned a doctorate in religious studies from Brown University in 1969. In Jones's life as a minister, he devoted his energies to the Unitarian Universalist Association (UUA), a pattern he continued until he died in 2012. His 1969 dissertation, "Sartre's Ethics in Relation to His Philosophical Anthropology: A Criticism of Criticism," bears out his commitment to internal criticism and phenomenology. It also demonstrates the various philosophies he drew upon to develop a multi-angular description of Black life and the possibilities for freedom and help disindoctrinate the oppressed and the oppressors from the anthropology of oppression. He was a visiting professor at Howard from 1964 to 1969, at Yale Divinity School from 1969 to 1977, and in 1977 he became professor of religion and founding director of Black studies at Florida State University. He was professor emeritus at the time of his passing. He also served as an instructor at Iliff School of Theology, the Humanist Institute in New York, Princeton Theological Seminary, Union Theological Seminary, and Samuel DeWitt Proctor School of Theology of Virginia Union University.

Wrestling with Oppression and Religion

Jones spent over sixty years developing a precise and predictive definition of oppression and therapies to reduce its impact. He called it the Jones Oppression Grid & the Jones Analytical Model (JOG & JAM) or "the Grid," for short. The acronym paid homage to the people of South Africa with whom he worked closely during the anti-apartheid movement. It reflects how they expressed their resistance by jogging and jamming through the streets and using their bodies as a counternarrative to one of containment defined by the institutional structures of racial segregation in that land. It also reflects how Black people throughout the Diaspora use movement to control their environments, and the boxer trains to take apart his opponent, round by round.

JOG & JAM aimed to give people state-of-the-art tools to address the global behaviors that led to conflict and human-inflicted suffering. He wanted to reduce oppression theory to a "best practices" technology to train educators, human service professionals, and practitioners. He devoted himself to developing a generic model for enhancing competency in critical thinking, problem-solving, decision-making, and systems analysis on micro and macro levels. He wanted a theory people could apply to address issues of discrimination, social upheaval, and extreme conflict. He aimed to develop an accurate understanding of oppression and its location, status, and value in human culture. Dr. Jones held that because our existence requires us to feed on something, we are predisposed to manipulating people and other beings into serving our needs and wants. He theorized that we use a perceived difference in their status and ours to legitimate our use and misuse. Jones argued that legitimation allows people to view the suffering engendered by oppression as an inevitable feature of reality, like an aspect of the natural world or an element of God's will, thereby, something that has to be accepted. For Jones, oppression was a human behavior supported through physical and psychoemotional violence and a sophisticated network of behavioral controls such as labeling, legitimation, false narratives, institutional structures, and value systems. He distinguished between assimilation, integration, and pluralism and identified the tendency among persons and institutions to establish a single norm to control behavior. He worked as an epidemiologist to pinpoint how the virus of oppression could mutate and become invisible to us, even as we were infected by it; how he would have tackled our pandemic moment!

Jones examined the ways perpetrators of oppression blamed God, nature, and the victims of oppression for the continuance of discriminatory practices. He emphasized how labeling, the visibility/invisibility factor, and patterns of denial displaced culpability for oppression and activated anti-powerism and quietism among the oppressed. He examined the emptiness of spiritual liberation where economic, social, and political sovereignty did not exist. He found us all potential oppressors and lobbied for enlightened self-interest among post-enlightened oppressors.

Jones was relentless in his refinement of JOG & JAM, seeing how oppression operated in policy making, pedagogy, the marketplace, social institutions, and religion. Jones pressed to make theodicy a central concern of Black theology, liberation theology, and religion as a whole. Jones identified two (and only two) types of faith—one that maintained the status quo and ethnic suffering and the other that resisted them. He saw that all institutions and behaviors fell into gatekeeper or way opener categories when examined contextually and through internal criticism. Dr. Jones urged theologians to align their characteristics of God to account for ethnic suffering. He argued that functional ultimacy and individual decision-making made a lie of absolutism.

JOG & JAM evolved over Jones's adult life. He shared his theory of oppression and its dynamics in community and professional workshops. He developed hundreds of slides and various presentations to help his audiences recognize and shed miseducation and mis-religion to see themselves differently. Jones's Oppression Grid and Analytical Model is the outgrowth of his work on Sartre, being, freedom, and responsibility. It reflects his engagement with Black humanism and theology and his conversations with coworkers in the academy, church, and world. Most importantly, it expresses his fierce urgency of now, providing the tools to predict, minimize, and turn away from oppressive behaviors.

Jones took on a grueling speaking schedule to provide more opportunities to interact with different audiences and contexts to strengthen the grid's power. In addition to his work in South Africa, he shared his research in Kenya, Ghana, Korea, Belgium, Spain, Uruguay, Canada, England, and the Caribbean. Jones regularly turned to a different liberation evangelist, Harriet Tubman, to propel his difficult duty. He often quoted her description of the unbearable pleasure of breathing free air when so many were still enslaved.

This Volume

Speculations on Black Life is our effort to complete the project—the collection of his writings—Jones began planning prior to his death. It speaks to Jones's observations, investments, and predictions regarding Black people worldwide.

The collection allows readers to see Jones as a philosophical anthropologist— developing a scientific approach to identifying the universals of human behavior (i.e., oppression) and contributing to our understanding of how we can minimize the impact of our penchant for managing power, resources, and the differences among us in oppressive ways. Although the works here do not spell out Jones's analytical model in its entirety—he was working on such a text at the time of his passing—they help us see the building blocks of the oppression grid.

We have divided the collection into four parts. Part I looks at humanism and Black humanism. It begins with remarks made at the 1967 UUA conference in New York on the church's response to African American uprisings. Also featured in this part are a 1975 article from *the Christian Century* on human freedom and autonomy, a chapter arguing the case for Black humanism from the 1978 work *Black Theology II: Essays on the Formation and Outreach of Contemporary Black Theology* edited by Jones and Calvin E. Bruce, a 1979 essay from *The Journal of Interdenominational Theological Center*, and a 1992 article from *The Humanist*. The part concludes with Jones's 1984 presentation at the "God: The Contemporary Discussion" conference in Seoul, Korea. Throughout the first part, readers can observe how Jones uses concepts identified by the modifiers "Black" and "liberation" as a means of internal criticism and a tool for creating pressure points for opposing oppression. This aspect of his work, along with his press to clarify human behavior, the fallacy of absolutism, and the meaning of freedom, defined his analysis of contemporary Black life.

Part II is dedicated to philosophical theology. In his Value Inquiry Book Series, John McClendon III describes Jones's approach to philosophical theology as transgressive and transformative of the conventional boundaries of Black liberation theology. This part attests to some of the reasons why. It opens with a 1972 article published in *Religious Education* regarding the primacy of reconciliation and liberation in Black theology in light of arguments posed by James Cone and J. Deotis Roberts. It closes with a chapter on contemporary moral decision-making from *Unitarian Universalism: 1985—Selected Essays* published by the Unitarian Universalist Ministers Association. Jones asserted that our relationship to absolutism and power defines ethical decision-making. Although the writings in Part II are engagements with particular theologians and philosophers, they speak to those who grapple with contextualism, morality, and the complexities of individualism and community.

Part III concerns the politics of race. It opens with a 1977 article arguing for a theology of power and an investment in co-equality to support social ethics. A 1981 paper addressing the meaning of the Christianization of Africa follows. It is a response to Walbert Bühlmann's *The Missions on Trial*, and his thinly disguised plea for a confirmation of the benefits of Christian missions in light of critiques by "radical Christians, cold atheists, and black nationalists." Jones's 1987 analysis of religion as legitimator and liberator accompanies his examinations of power, missionaries, and the eradication of ESP oppression. Next is a 1993 analysis of the illusion of moral absolutes and the blaming of God, nature, or the LGBTQ+ community itself for discriminatory and oppressive practices. The 1995 essay, "The Disguises of Discrimination," originally published in *Forum: The Magazine of the Florida Humanities Council*, examines the moral leadership of three Florida persons involved in civil rights and the ongoing need to probe social structures for their support of discrimination. Part III concludes with a 2003 essay, "Towards a New Paradigm for Uncovering Neo-racism in American Institutions" that demonstrates Jones's relevance to our current dilemmas. Jones's analytical model speaks to the many guises of oppression, mislabeling, and legitimation as key tools of exploitation, and the need to be vigilant in the face of reform and change.

Part IV offers critical reflections on Jones's writings. The first is by editor Anthony Pinn who works at the intersections of African American religion, constructive theology, and humanist thought at Rice University in Houston. The second is by American religious history scholar Jamil Drake of Yale Divinity School, and Brittany O'Neal of Lehman College, City University of New York, and author of *Apologia for Black Liberation: The Concept of God in James H. Cone's Black Liberation Theology and William R. Jones' Humanocentric Theism* (2015). The primary archivist of his father's papers and the prime mover behind this collection of selected essays, Darrell Jones provides the afterword.

He promulgated controversial texts to foster speculation and debate about Black life. He used Black folk tales and a cavalcade of liberationist figures such as Frederick Douglass, Nat Turner, W. E. B. Du Bois, Ida B. Wells-Barnett, Carter G. Woodson, Sterling Brown, Malcolm X, and Sarah Webster Fabio. He made the Black humanist tradition visible, which he identified as one of the keys to slipping the noose presented by Whitanity and other oppression-supporting forms of religion. He called upon the folk, humanist, and anti-oppression traditions to confirm power in these various segments of Black existence. He sought to make it plain even as he excavated philosophical language in service of the complexities of freedom. Most importantly, he pursued an approach to foster eternal vigilance against oppression. He strove for work that would be so compelling that users would confront themselves despite their resistance to seeing their roles in oppressive behavior and banish the illusions, hypocrisies, and denials with which we seduce ourselves and others. Jones invited readers and audiences worldwide to join him in contesting, then certifying oppression as a human activity with universal features. This volume is an effort to present some of the key texts shaping this process of interrogation—Jones's speculations on Black life.

Part I

(BLACK) HUMANISM

Chapter 1

BLACK POWER AND UNITARIANISM

A PERSONAL VIEW

William R. Jones

Black Power and Unitarianism: A Personal View

When many Unitarians chart their course in response to Black power, they find themselves between the horns of an agonizing dilemma: they desire to support the Negro's just aspiration for full manhood and self-determination, yet they fear that the means and the ends of Black power contradict the vital core of Unitarianism.[1] They see, in short, no way to be true to their Unitarian heritage and, at the same time, sympathetic to the concepts and practices of Black power.

I feel, however, that the foregoing interpretation of Black power relative to Unitarianism is inaccurate. It is possible, in my view, for Black power and Unitarianism to occupy the same theological house without loss of fundamental principles. Indeed, I would say that if Unitarianism and Black power cannot co-exist in harmony, the future of race relations in our nation is assuredly dismal.

The core of my argument is this: persons who see Unitarianism and Black power to be fundamentally incompatible commit two basic errors: (1) they focus upon an inaccurate interpretation of Black power, and (2) they fail to isolate the fundamental cornerstone of Unitarianism. The alleged incompatibility vanishes, I maintain, when a more accurate description of both Black power and Unitarianism is set forth. And that is the purpose of my talk today.

There are three sections to my talk: Section I will present the aspects of Black power and Unitarianism, which are claimed to be contradictory. Section II presents a definition of Black power which, I feel, is consistent with the elementary tenets of Unitarianism. Section III attempts to show that an analysis of what I take to be the cornerstone of Unitarianism likewise gives the lie to the alleged incompatibility.

Also, by way of introduction, let me make clear that I am addressing myself to the *one* issue I have outlined, namely, that certain criticisms of Black power relative to Unitarianism are questionable. My talk, therefore, does not express my complete view and appraisal of Black power. To give my exhaustive analysis of Black power would demand that I indicate a detailed criticism of Black power, and I do find myself at odds with significant aspects of its theory and strategy. These criticisms, however, must await another occasion.

Further, time does not permit me to discuss my interpretation of the conference in New York: *The Unitarian Universalist Response to the Black Rebellion* (UURBR). Dr. Howlett, you may recall, analyzed that conference in his sermon of October 15; copies of his sermon are now available for distribution. My talk does, however, provide the framework for my evaluation of the UURBR Conference.

I

What are the basic points where Unitarianism and Black power are said to be incompatible? Three primary elements of Black power have been isolated: (1) its explicit racism; (2) its subversion of the democratic process and procedural principles which Unitarians accept in policy making situations; and (3) its concept of power, namely, its elevation of non-moral power above moral power as a technique of persuasion.

Black power, it is asserted, exhibits an explicit racism that contradicts the Unitarian ideal of human brotherhood knowing no division of race or creed. Black power appears to value a sense of belonging to the Black community; Unitarians, instead, exalt the ideal of membership in the universal brotherhood of man. Whereas Unitarians advocate a denomination without racial distinctions, Black power seeks to build racial demarcations into the very structure of the denomination. Moreover, Black power convicts every white American of racism, particularly the white liberal, without saying what conditions would enable one to escape the classification of racist. I take the latter statement to be the meaning of "the impregnable argument" of Black power.

In addition to its racism, Black power appears to abandon other basic Unitarian principles. Some interpreters detect a fundamental difference in theory and practice between Unitarianism and Black power in policy making situations. Whereas, it is said that Unitarians assert the principle of majority consensus freely arrived at in open debate, whereas Unitarians support the technique of rational persuasion in the context of uncoerced dialogue, and whereas Unitarians sanction the principle of agreeing to disagree without hostility toward one's opponent. Black power, by contrast, introduces the principle of decision by the determined minority; Black power advocates the tactic of demanding total and unqualified endorsement of specific proposals without debate or discussion; Black power appeals to persuasion by humiliation, intimidation, and intensifying one's sense of guilt.

Moreover, Black power and Unitarianism appear to support contrasting theories of power. Moral power, it is said, is the bulwark of the Unitarian philosophy of power, whereas Black power appeals to something other than moral power.

When confronted with these alleged incompatibilities many Unitarians conclude that only one response to Black power is proper: to "keep the faith," to hold fast to the principles of Unitarianism—even if it means a parting of the ways with Black power.

II

If Unitarianism and Black power are fundamentally opposed, then I agree that Unitarians have only one choice. They, in the spirit of Luther, should acclaim: "To go against reason and conscience is neither wise nor right. Here I stand, I cannot do otherwise." Further, I would agree that *certain expressions* of Black power are irreconcilable with Unitarians; indeed, I would assert that some members of the Black caucus at the UURBR Conference voiced opinions that I, as a Unitarian, could not and did not accept.

But the alleged incompatibility between Black power and Unitarianism, per se, is, I feel, apparent, not real. Two factors explain why the apparent incompatibility has arisen: various interpreters have, on the one hand, stipulated an inaccurate definition of Black power and, on the other hand, an imprecise description of Unitarianism. We will consider the former error in this section.

An unworthy caricature of Black power results when critics commit the following errors: (1) they take the actions and concepts of *a given individual or group* as supplying the quintessence of the movement *as a whole;* (2) they fail to differentiate between the *practices* and the *theoretical principles* of the movement; and (3) they fail to distinguish between *the means* of Black power and *the ends* toward which it strives.

Note, by contrast, how America has defined itself as a democracy. It has not taken its actual practices, its slavery, discrimination, racism, and injustice—and labeled them "American democracy." No, it has, rather, invoked an ideal, not yet realized—liberty and justice for all—as its self-definition. And though Unitarian practice, admittedly, falls embarrassingly short of its ideal of the brotherhood of man, undivided by race, it is the latter ideal, and not the practice, which is enshrined in the definition of Unitarianism. Indeed, it is the ideal, not the practice of Unitarianism, which is found to be incompatible with the racism of Black power.

What I am suggesting is this: if one employs the same surgical skill in cutting away the practice of certain Black power spokesmen from the theoretical basis of the movement, if one discriminates in like manner between the practice of Black power and its ideal expression, if one differentiates between the expression of a given group or individual within the Black Power Movement and what is common to it as a whole, and if one distinguishes between the means and ends of Black power, then one reaches, I feel, a concept of Black power which is both morally defensible and logically compatible with Unitarianism. In fact, I would suggest that recent endorsements of Black power by such groups as the National Council of Churches, the National Organization of Social Work students, and many of the Unitarians at the UURBR Conference are the result of exactly the type of differentiation I have indicated. I think, therefore, that one perhaps misreads the actual situation when he interprets the acceptance of Black power by many whites as solely or primarily the result of guilt feelings, and, likewise, when he interprets the same acceptance by Negroes as the result of intimidation and fear of being called "Uncle Toms."

What, then, are the theoretical bases of Black power as I see them? The first essential plank is a certain *philosophy of power*; implicit in the movement is a specific view regarding the role, status, and value of power in human life. Consider the following statements which seem to be found in the philosophy of Black power: power is the essential force in human society; power "is the name of the game"; power, not love, "is what makes the world go round." Morality is power; that is, the people who have power define what is right and wrong. Equality is power; equality emerges only when one has the power to demand that certain rights be recognized and the power to enforce the recognition of those rights. Fundamental differences of status in human society are, at the base, differences in the possession of power: the difference between master and slave, parent and child, teacher and student, Black and white Americans, and so on is a difference in the amount of power at the disposal of each. Or consider the concept of self-determination in the light of the same philosophy of power: to determine one's own destiny requires power. The person who lacks power is, precisely, the person who is determined by someone other than himself.

It is from the same concept of power that Black power analyzes the Negro problem in America and proposes a solution. The Negro problem in America was created and is maintained because the Negro lacks that power which is requisite for equality and self-determination. The primary obstruction to the Negro's full manhood is his powerlessness, not his Blackness: and the Negro is powerless because a stronger power, white power, looms over the crucial areas of his existence. Consequently, the only viable solution to the Negro problem is to change the power situation of the Negro relative to the white community. In short, if we are to speak realistically about the Negro's self-determination, then one must speak—and act—in terms of his acquisition of economic and political power, etc.

Having stated what I take to be the essentials of the philosophy of power implicit in the Black Power Movement, we must determine whether it contradicts the Unitarian philosophy of power, that is, the ultimacy of moral power.

The first question to be considered in this context is the following: Does Black power entail violence? Though Black power has become synonymous in the minds of many with "burn, baby, burn" and "turn this town upside down," I would argue that violence, per se, is not essential to the theory of Black power—just as I would insist that the tactics of Bo Conner are not essential to the definition of American democracy or white power.

Consider the following. A paper crossed my desk two weeks ago which was highly critical of Brown and Carmichael, particularly of their call for urban guerilla warfare. You would never guess its source: not the Wall Street Journal, but the Newsletter of the Black Man's Volunteer Army of Liberation, Washington, D.C. My point here is simply this: when one Black power group castigates the violence of another, which view do you designate as Black power?

Yet I will be the first to admit that Black power is a departure from the non-violent tactics of earlier civil rights groups. Black power does reject the primacy of moral force as the sole or primary means of social persuasion. Further, Black power has abandoned specific types of non-violent techniques, notably, non-retaliation when struck. If self-determination means anything, according to Black power, it means the right to self-defense. Or put in other terms, *defensive* violence is sanctioned as a legitimate form of self-determination. I admit, as well, that segments of the Black Power Movement do advocate *offensive* violence, but the latter tactic, I feel, is not common to the movement as a whole.

A second question is crucial for Unitarians who attempt to compare the philosophies of power of Unitarianism and Black power: Did the Black caucus at the UURBR Conference, as a representative of Black power, violate the principle of the ultimacy of moral force in social persuasion? Or, put in other terms, did the Black caucus, as it has been alleged, subvert the democratic process?

I would answer as follows: It is significant that no one accused the Black caucus of offensive violence. The only force employed was an implied threat of withdrawal and its consequent embarrassment for Unitarians. The caucus worked within the confines of the democratic procedures established by the conference. The decisions of the conference which are criticized should be interpreted, I feel, as the injudicious choice of the majority—not the subversion of the democratic process by the minority, that is, the Black caucus.

In the light of the foregoing discussion, we return to our original question: Are the philosophies of power of Unitarianism and Black power inconsistent? At this point, I must say, simply, "I do not know." I am uncertain because an answer to the question requires a precise statement of the Unitarian theology of power. The latter, I submit, is a sorely needed but neglected area of Unitarian theology. Indeed, part of the dilemma Unitarians face relative to Black power is the result of the absence of any clear working principles in this area.

I would say this, however. If Unitarianism defines itself in terms of the ultimacy of moral power, then it is committed, I feel, to a position of pacifism. I would admit, in this context, that the Unitarian who is a consistent pacifist can, legitimately, assert an incompatibility between Black power and Unitarianism. But I do not see how a Unitarian who is not a consistent pacifist can defend the same position. Particularly, I find it difficult to see how Unitarians can, consistently, support the employment of non-moral force in Vietnam and yet, accuse Black power of anti-Unitarianism.

I would also say that those who interpret Unitarianism in terms of the ultimacy of moral power must demonstrate the following before it can be said that Black power abandons the Unitarian philosophy of power: (1) defensive violence or self-defense, (2) appeal to the possible embarrassment of one's opponent, and (3) the rule of the determined minority when the majority accepts the latter's position falls outside the area of moral persuasion.

The next essential feature of Black power I wish to consider can best be described as the Negro's image of white America. In 1962 I made the following statement in a sermon:

> In his fight for equal opportunity the Negro will adopt tactics which will be increasingly aggressive and militant. The gradualist approach will be discarded. Legal compulsion will be insisted upon instead of voluntary compliance. Appeal will be made to the conscience of the white American only as a small arms weapon in the total desegregation arsenal. The Negro sees his quest for full citizenship as a fight, a fight which will be expensive, difficult, and at times violent. The tactics the Negro has adopted in the past and will adopt in the future

are determined primarily by the image he has of white America—what its chief values and motives are; what it likes and dislikes; what actions and arguments will generate sufficient coercive pressure to desegregate American society.

I would suggest that there is a glaring disparity between the image of white America the Negro holds and white America's own self-image. Further, I would suggest that this glaring disparity accounts, in part, for the misrepresentations of Black power. Recently, when I repeated the sermon of 1962 to white audiences I was struck by the following responses: an overwhelming agreement that the Negro's image of white America is accurate; a willingness to accept an interpretation of Black power which does not entail offensive violence; the conclusion that a certain interpretation of Black power offers a viable, if not the best, solution to America's racial problem.

There is time to consider only the following aspects of the Negro's image of white America. First, the Negro sees the white American as one who can be appealed to only by force where the racial issue is foremost. Black power takes as its initial premise for action the conclusion of Dr. Kyle Haselden who, incidentally, is a white Presbyterian minister from the South.

> There has been no significant instance in which the white society motivated by love and mercy has voluntarily relinquished an area of domination over the Negro. On the contrary, every major advancement made by the Negro has resulted from some kind of social and legal coercion. It would be folly to assume that the barriers which still stand between the Negro and his full manhood will topple before a trumpet of justice which is not accompanied by any kind of force. (*The Racial Problem in Christian Perspective*, Harper & Bros.)

The second aspect of the Negro's image of white America I wish to discuss is the following: America is a racist society. Because it is racist, white America, the Negro believes, does not sincerely desire a color-blind society; nor could she desire the latter without the most radical changes in her thought and values. And that change has not yet occurred. Indeed, Black power sees itself as the necessary instrument of that change. That is, to the degree that the Negro is considered to be undesirable and inferior, desegregation will never occur, voluntarily. It may be accepted reluctantly, and under protest—like taxes—if it is compelled. White America, in short, sees the elimination of racism as a grave danger to its way of life. And who will voluntarily receive with favor that which, on its face value, is a threat to one's own interests?

Black power, therefore, concludes that the white liberal who sees an integrated society as his primary goal must realize that Black power is a necessary means to that goal, for integration simply will not come without the force, power, and rehabilitated image the Negro seeks to obtain through the exercise of Black power. Without the muscle of Black power, the last walls of segregation and racism in American life will remain tall, sturdy, and impregnable.

The final essential of Black power I wish to consider is its concern to rehabilitate the category of Blackness, and here we come to the issues of the implicit racism of Black power and its compatibility with the Unitarian ideal.

The racism implicit in Black power is understandable if it is viewed from the following perspectives: (1) as a variety of *anti-racist racism*, to employ the term of Jean-Paul Sartre, and (2) as the most effective *means* for dealing with the Negro's concrete situation and problems.

What is the meaning of anti-racist racism and how does it differ from racism per se? The goal of anti-racist racism is a color-blind society, a society in which racism has withered away. Accordingly, anti-racist racism is to be seen as a means for eradicating racism—just as a vaccine is put into service against the very bacteria from which it is made. Anti-racist racism does not assert the superiority or inferiority of a given race, nor does it defend segregation or separatism as in conformity with nature. Rather, anti-racist racism appears to be the most, or only, effective antidote—*given the concrete problems of the Negro*. That is, if the Negro's situation were different, that is, if he were not an inhabitant of a racist society, anti-racist racism would not be a necessary strategy.

What, then, is the concrete situation of the Negro which dictates the employment of anti-racist racism? It is a situation in which the Negro is a minority in a culture that assigns a negative value to a part of his nature over which he has no voluntary control—his skin color. Further, it is a situation in which the culture is essentially racist and where the elimination of racism is resisted.

Confronted with the situation just described it becomes necessary, from the view of Black power, to rehabilitate the category of Blackness. Where Black was designated as bad, one simply invests it with the opposite quality; one now calls it good and beautiful. Again, given the Negro's concrete situation, Black power raises the following questions and answers each "no." Is it realistic to conclude that a nation will move *directly* from the present situation where Blackness has a *negative quality* to the color-blind society where it would have a *neutral quality*? Is it realistic to conclude that most Negroes can move *directly* from *self-hatred* because of their Blackness to *self-pride* because they have worth by virtue of being individuals or human beings?

I think it should be made clear that anti-racist racism does not mean, necessarily, anti-white. I readily admit that Black power can be a form of retribution for the white man's practice of racism, but it can also be the means for rehabilitating the white American from the practice of racism.

III

In Section II I attempted to show that the alleged incompatibility between Black power and Unitarianism turns upon which description of *Black power* is taken as definitive. In the present section I wish to show that the alleged incompatibility depends upon the specific definition of *Unitarianism* which is invoked.

Some two years ago I spoke here on the topic, *Unitarian Totalitarianism*, in which I outlined what, for me, is the cornerstone of Unitarianism. Today, I still believe that analysis is correct. Let me review briefly what I isolated then as the primary tenet of Unitarianism. The cornerstone of Unitarianism is a theory of individualism, more specifically, that in certain areas the individual is the ultimate authority. If individualism is the hallmark of our faith, what does this imply relative to the ideal of human brotherhood on the one hand and the practice of anti-racism on the other?

It appears to me that individualism is more basic to Unitarian faith than the ideal of human brotherhood; that is, individualism is logically prior to the principle of the brotherhood of mankind. The Unitarian rejection of racism follows, in the final analysis, from its theory of the worth and status of the individual. Consequently, for me, the crucial question as regards the relation of Black power and Unitarianism is not whether Black power contradicts the principle of human brotherhood but, rather, does it violate the Unitarian principle of individualism?

The question, then, becomes: Is the anti-racist racism of Black power inconsistent with the Unitarians ideal of individualism? I would say, No, and make the following points: (1) those who detect an inconsistency between Unitarianism and Black power on this issue conclude, and I think erroneously, that the ultimate ideal for Unitarianism is an integrated society. I, however, will make the astounding statement: if Unitarians are true to their principle of individualism, they cannot demand the goal of an integrated society. Unitarianism is, and should be, the eternal foe of *involuntary* racism, that is, the assignment of persons to rigid groups without their consent and from which they cannot leave when they desire. Involuntary racism does contradict the Unitarian theory of individualism, but can we make the same claim with respect to *voluntary* racism? I would define the latter as a form of ethnicism, that is, the voluntary grouping of individuals because of felt mutual needs and interests. In short, the Unitarian principle of individualism and its logical correlate, the theory of voluntary associations, both demand the possibility of voluntary racism.

Perhaps, my argument will seem less strange when one considers the following: the same principle which underlies voluntary racism is accepted as a working principle by Unitarians in other areas. Transfer the concept of the voluntary grouping of individuals on the basis of felt mutual needs and interests to the area of religion and we have the principle which no Unitarian is willing to reject—religious freedom. In the area of religion, we do not demand that the Jew become Christian; we, in short, allow for a plurality of religious groupings. Moreover, we as Unitarians also permit the plurality of ethnic groupings, that is, voluntary ethnicism. If, therefore, one sees voluntary racism as a form of voluntary ethnicism, then the alleged incompatibility between Unitarianism and Black power, relative to this specific point, vanishes.

There are additional reasons why I conclude that anti-racist racism is not inconsistent with Unitarianism. (2) Anti-racist racism can be interpreted, as I have attempted earlier, as a means to the goal toward which most Unitarians strive: the universal brotherhood of all men, in so far as it is proposed as a strategy for removing a fundamental barrier to that goal—involuntary racism. (3) I would also say that Unitarians have, in fact, already endorsed a variety of anti-racist racism. When Unitarians, and others, consciously employ racial criteria for the purpose of eliminating existing racism, that is, when the conscious effort is made to increase the number of Negroes in various positions, unions, committees, and so on, is it not a fact that anti-racist racism is exhibited? (4) I would also suggest that the degree to which Unitarians permit the *practice* of racism in their midst while affirming the opposite *ideal* establishes the basis for affording Black power the same license. (5) If we reject the option of voluntary racism or ethnicism, then we say to the Negro: "You must become part and parcel of the white society," a society the Negro may reject for reasons other than the fact that it is white. That is, if the Negro refuses to be a member of the white society, whatever his reason, then his separation bespeaks a reverse racism—though the reason for withdrawal may be similar to that, for instance, of the hippie.

My conclusion is the warning of a perceptive young man whose voice, unfortunately, is seldom heard today:

> If we—and I mean the relatively conscious whites and the relatively conscious blacks . . . do not falter in our duty now, we may be able, handful that we are, to end the racial nightmare (in America). But if we do not now dare everything, the fulfillment of that prophecy is upon us: God gave Noah the rainbow sign, No more water, the fire next time." (James Baldwin, *The Fire Next Time*)

Note

1 On the weekend of October 8, 1967, the Unitarian Universalist Association, Department of Social Responsibility, sponsored a Conference in New York City on the subject "The Unitarian Universalist Response to the Black Rebellion." Both Dr. Howlett and Professor Jones, an ordained Unitarian minister, were among those in attendance. At the Conference a "black caucus" developed to which nearly all the Negro members of the Conference withdrew. On the Sunday following, Dr. Howlett gave his reaction to the Conference and invited Professor Jones, who was a member of the caucus, to give his on November 5. The Publications Committee has printed both sermons as its contribution to our continuing dialogue in this area. Copies of this and other sermons published by the Committee are available at 20¢ each.

—[Statement made by] Jean Dulaney, chairman, Publications Committee

Chapter 2

THEISM AND RELIGIOUS HUMANISM

THE CHASM NARROWS

> A sense of uncertainty informs the humanist concept of history. Oppression and liberation are equally probable, and there is no cosmic lifeguard to save humanity from self-destructive choice.
>
> —William R. Jones

Both the title and the rationale for the series "New Turns in Religious Thought" suggest that theology is passing through one of its most agonizing periods, as if it were trying to open a door with the wrong key. Indeed, the cultural conditions and theological climate that make this series timely are also stark testimony to the depth of the uneasiness we feel and the depth of the problem we face. Ours is not a time when theological efforts can be focused on mining and refining a limited number of options. Nor does it appear to be a time for manicuring a model of broad consensus, for a general theological agreement is precisely what we lack. Rather, it is a season for exploration and rejuvenation when, willingly or of necessity, we traverse unknown and unfound theological terrain—if not the entire spectrum of religious options—for possible leads and insights.

No doubt some will regard this series as an unwitting acknowledgment of the desperate state of theology, insofar as it suggests that models of theological importance may lie unnoticed on the drawing boards of unsung adolescent scholars. A further suggestion should not be overlooked. The title of the series speaks of turning points in *religion*, and not the narrower category of theology. Is this nomenclature deliberate? Does it suggest—I trust it does—the possibility of reconnoitering nontheistic perspectives for their potential impact upon the church's present task of self-clarification?

It is against this background of a wider examination of religious models, initiated by a heightened doctrinal uncertainty, that I would enter a new version of *religious humanism* in the theological flesh market.

One must first recognize that there are two basic religious traditions in Western thought: a mainstream tradition of Christian and non-Christian theism, and a minority tradition of humanism. Religious humanism has not, however, successfully established itself as an authentic and indispensable religious perspective. Several factors are responsible for its failure. It has continuously been dwarfed by a larger and entrenched theism. Humanism has always been viewed as a hostile adversary, bent on the extermination of religion in general and the execution of Christian theism in particular. Add to this the absence of a systematic theology/philosophy of religious humanism; unfortunately, religious humanism has not yet found a Barth to articulate its inner logic. Nor can we identify a concrete culture or historical era in the West in which humanism was in command. This point evokes the charge from major critics of humanism—for example Charles Hartshorne—that the absence of a concrete humanist culture is incontrovertible proof that humanism cannot provide a viable ground for an ongoing social system. Further, a question-begging definition that equates religion and theism, along with widespread misunderstanding about the normative principle of humanism, continues to camouflage a basic similarity between humanism and expanding varieties of contemporary theism.

Religious Humanism: Aim and Strategy

Because of these factors, religious humanism is a still small voice. But there can be little doubt that it is emerging today as a major religious force that the Christian faith will encounter directly as a rival and indirectly as a prominent ingredient in the cultural matrix in which the gospel must be proclaimed. I am also persuaded that humanism points to a verity that religion must eventually acknowledge as a given. It is my contention that the central affirmation of humanism, the *functional ultimacy* of the human being—that is, the radical freedom and autonomy of humankind—is materially a formative category of contemporary theology. Growing numbers of theologians are consciously adopting the thesis of radical human creativity to the extent that the difference between religious humanism and such theists as Tillich, Bonhoeffer, Novak, and Duméry is not as great as we may think.

Humanism is not monolithic, and like theism it has its effective and its inept advocates. I would champion a species of humanism that differs significantly from other current varieties of contemporary nontheism. Uppermost in this regard is my concern to advance humanism as an alternative *religious* perspective, as a distinct soteriological system. As the qualifier suggests, religious humanism affirms that the human being is *homo religiosus*; what it attacks is the arrogant presumption that religion is limited to the theistic experience. This stance puts me in opposition to those humanists who regard religion as an illusion, who seek to negate the divine reality as the necessary precondition for affirming the humanist gospel of human freedom, and who interpret the history of religion as only an instrument of oppression and dehumanization. In the final analysis these principles must be rejected, because they cannot be confirmed by humanism's own norms. Moreover, these claims fail to recognize the fundamental pluralism of religion and theism, varieties of which are actually corollaries of the very realities humanism affirms.

The religious humanism I endorse does not attack Christian theism with the critical apparatus of rationalism, science, or positivism; nor does it seek to make these the foundation for the humanist perspective. Rather, it adopts a method of internal criticism to avoid the use of questionable tactics of previous participants in the humanist-theist debate. That is, it employs a variety of means to show that the essential norms of humanism are explicit in certain brands of contemporary theism and implicit in the others which advance a different principle of authority. To accomplish this aim, religious humanism would identify positions already adopted by the Christian theologian; for example, the Kierkegaardian principle of truth as subjectivity, which presupposes the centrality of functional ultimacy. In a similar fashion it would chronicle the development of modern theology to identify a clear trend toward the open avowal of the radical human autonomy that functional ultimacy symbolizes. Finally, it would argue that the Christian will be compelled to adopt the norm of functional ultimacy to avoid consideration of uninviting theological propositions; for example, quietism in the face of suffering, or the notion that God is a white racist. (In my book *Is God a White Racist? Preamble to Black Theology* [Doubleday, 1973] I contend that the theodicy question as revised by liberation theologies will force Christian theism to the position of humanocentric theism, the form of contemporary theism in which the principle of functional ultimacy is most explicit.)

Thus, rather than building its theological superstructure on the ashes of a rebutted theism, religious humanism grounds itself in a principle that obtains whether God is or is not, whether the Transcendent is good, indifferent, or demonic, and whether God is or is not the creator of humankind.

Functional Ultimacy: The Controlling Category

The crucial significance of religious humanism for new turns in religious thought consists in its illumination of radical freedom/autonomy as the essence of human reality and its program to construct a systematic theology/philosophy on the exclusively anthropological foundation of the functional ultimacy of humankind as the theological singular. Any valid exposition of humanism must begin here, for it is on the foundation of this principle and its corollaries—the humanocentric predicament and individuals as co-equal centers of freedom/authority—that humanism establishes its methodological policies and builds its ethics and epistemology.

The functional ultimacy of humanity is not a new concept, nor is it confined to humanism. We are already familiar with some of its essentials as the literal signification of Protagoras's dictum: "Man is the *measure* of all things." Functional ultimacy can also be interpreted as a more radical extension of Kierkegaard's principle of truth as a subjectivity to areas beyond the ethicoreligious sphere. It has affinities as well with William James's category "the will to believe" and Vaihinger's "as if" philosophy. If one corrects the erroneous interpretations of critics, the principle is the core of Sartre's anthropology and also Camus's.

A clear understanding of the humanist principle of functional ultimacy is critical because influential critics grossly misinterpret it or designate a different principle as humanism's operative norm. It is argued, for instance, that humanism affirms the person as an absolute rather than a finite freedom, as being ontologically rather than functionally ultimate. For these reasons, the most fruitful way to extract the meaning of the principle is through a comparison with selected theists in whose thought it is prominent. I call these figures humanocentric theists because the assertion of radical human freedom/autonomy is given a theistic base.

We need to look no further than the normative stance adopted by William Daniel Cobb in the initial article in this series ("Morality-in-the-Making: A New Look at Some Old Foundations," January 1–8 *Century*, p.11). His correlative categories of "man as moral creator" and "a moral universe in the making" seem to be mined from the lode of functional ultimacy. "God," he asserts, "created man with the intention that man should 'make what *God* did not make' and . . . that man 'make what God did not *think* to make' as a consequence of God's gracious self-limitation of his own power in the act of creating man." God has limited his own power "for the sake of giving man 'space' in which to be more than a 'robot' or a 'puppet' in a stage play."

Eliezer Berkovits in *Faith after the Holocaust* advances a similar view as a central motif of Judeobiblical faith:

> Man alone can create value; God is value. But if man alone is the creator of values . . . then he must have freedom of choice and freedom of decision. And his freedom must be respected by God himself. God cannot as a rule intervene whenever man's use of freedom displeases him. . . . If there is to be man, he must be allowed to make his choices in freedom.

Equivalent statements are plentiful in the texts of other theologians who address the issue of the divine reality and human freedom.

With these descriptions of human freedom as background, we can highlight the more universal and radical way that humanism asserts human autonomy. In this connection we must note the role, status, and value that Cobb and Berkovits assign to human freedom. It is human freedom rather than reason that is clearly affirmed as the essence of human reality. Both thinkers award an exalted status to human autonomy relative to history; humanity is regarded as a company-determining power—at least up to the eschaton. Each advances an exposition of divine sovereignty that accommodates the extension of human freedom to such areas as history and to values that once were wholly under the direct sway of the divine, thereby refuting Sartre's hypothesis: "If God exists, man is nothing; if man exists . . ." (*The Devil and the Good Lord*).

Though human freedom is dramatically enlarged, humankind is not deified. Man and woman are still creatures. The extended sphere of human autonomy is not the consequence of our *ontological* superiority vis-à-vis the Transcendent. No, the Transcendent withholds its power, as parents may do to allow their children full freedom and responsibility.

Human Freedom and Divine Sovereignty

It is necessary at this juncture to consider an unsettled issue in humanocentric theism that frustrates a more accurate differentiation between humanism and theism: the scope of human freedom in history. Three options have surfaced. On the one hand, Howard Burkle (in *The Non-Existence of God*) represents the view that is closest to humanism. Adopting the model of God as "persuader," Burkle concludes that the human being is delegated a possibly veto authority. At the ontological level, the level of efficient causality, divine persuasion is not operative; "forbearance would mean non-existence." But once humanity is created and God resolves to relate himself to humankind in terms of persuasion and not coercion, God "would have to be uncertain about a number of details of the future . . . and in some respects unable to accomplish his will at all." Moreover, God "cannot guarantee the ultimate triumph of good . . . the good may remain forever blocked. . . . The creature retains a veto even though he had nothing to do with the determination that gave him being." In sum, humankind is functionally ultimate though ontologically still a creature.

According to the humanocentric theists at the other end of the spectrum, humanity cannot frustrate the good. Cobb, for example, ends on the optimistic note that the moral agent can affirm his moral nature in confidence that "[it] will not only not be lost but will continue to be affirmed and redeemed to the glory of God."

Midway between these polar positions stands Gordon Kaufman, asserting "a cosmic intentionality" that enables "men to hope and believe there is a genuine *possibility* of their reaching responsibility and freedom without destroying themselves" (*God the Problem*; emphasis added). This outcome, however, is not explicitly guaranteed, as far as I can determine.

Humanism and Theism: Points of Difference

We can now differentiate religious humanism from the variety of Christian theism that is its closest kin. From a phenomenological perspective I would identify three general differences: (a) the scope and status of the principle of functional ultimacy; (b) a different concept of soteriology that derives from (c) a dissimilar view about the benevolent character of ultimate reality.

As the statements from Cobb and Berkovits evidence, the difference is not that humanism affirms functional ultimacy and theism does not. In fact, the religious humanist is obliged to establish that the principle is implicit in those forms of theism in which it is not explicitly acknowledged. But even when functional ultimacy is asserted by theists, the principle is not allotted and administered in the more radical way that characterizes religious humanism. Historically, humanism has acknowledged the principle as its *norm*; for example, Protagoras's "man the measure." Though theists may even accent functional ultimacy, their explicit norm has been God Jesus Christ, Scripture, and so on. But here too the humanist is obliged to show that the principle of functional ultimacy is logically prior to the affirmation, for instance, of Jesus as Lord.

There is another significant difference with respect to scope. In those forms of theism where the principle is most explicit, functional ultimacy is brought to bear in the areas of values and less clearly, in history. By contrast, humanism tends to universalize the principle, radicalizing it in the areas of values and extending its scope not only to history but even to the sphere of soteriology.

The other points of difference revolve around the category of soteriology and the concomitant concept of ultimate reality/God. Soteriology, in theism, can be reduced to humanity's conformity to ultimate reality. Once it is established that X is the ultimate reality, the conclusion comes as a matter of course—humanity's highest good requires congruity with God's will or purpose.

Implicit in this concept of salvation is a conviction that ultimate reality is intrinsically moral, benevolent, and supportive of humankind's highest good. Thus, conformity is rationally and theologically persuasive because of the experience of God as benevolent. Obviously, one would hardly conform to a higher reality—for example, the devil—simply because it is more powerful. Rather the Christian temperament would demand a Sisyphus-like rebellion if the morality of the extrahuman transcendent is suspect.

At the bottom of the humanist worldview hovers the opinion that ultimate reality may not be intrinsically benevolent or supportive of human welfare. Recognizing that God's benevolence is not self-evident and that every alleged instance of divine agape can also be interpreted as divine malice for humanity (cf. Camus's inverted interpretation of Golgotha in *The Rebel*), humanism permits but does not dictate a human response of rebellion as soteriologically authentic. Prometheus and Adam illustrate contrasting viewpoints. Adam's rebellion is regarded as the quintessence of sin, whereas Prometheus's parallel refusal is, for the humanist, praiseworthy.

Here, in my view, lies the real difference between humanism and theism. Unlike Cox, who concludes that the theist and nontheist encounter the same reality but name it differently, I perceive a fundamental difference in the primordial experience of ultimate reality. The humanist apparently does not experience the goodness of God/ultimate reality in the self-authenticating way that Edward Schillebeeckx, for example, describes in "Non-religious Theism and Belief in God." Precisely for this reason, the theodicy question continues as the eternal stumbling block for the humanist.

It is now possible to delineate in a more focused way the humanist meaning of functional ultimacy. First, let it be said that humanism, like theism, eschews any claim to humanity's *ontological* ultimacy. In the humanist worldview, human freedom is accurately described as a finite freedom, even a created freedom. The tendency of critics to equate humanism with a more exaggerated view of human freedom misinterprets concrete humanist exemplars. Protagoras speaks of man as the *measure*, thus emphasizing that humanity is the ultimate valuator but not necessarily the controlling agent in history or nature.

An examination of Camus's Sisyphus or Sartre's Orestes in *The Files* also provides an appropriate counter to the critics' errors. Since Sisyphus's efforts are constantly frustrated by a more powerful reality, it is clear that humanity's ontological ultimacy is not being asserted. Likewise with Orestes: the unobscured transcendence of Zeus/God and the creaturely impotence of Orestes are unmistakingly detailed in the whirlwind scene reminiscent of Job. Orestes and Sisyphus acknowledge that divine omnipotence is more or less self-evident. What is decidedly less certain is divine benevolence, and for this reason divine might is an insufficient basis for worshipping the divine or conforming to the divine command. Does not Gen. 3:5 hint at a similar motive for the disobedience of Eve and Adam? They appear to countenance rebellion because they question the morality of the divine command.

The Humanocentric Predicament

The basic point of these humanist heroes is to assert the courage to be without regard to external odds, to symbolize the radical scope of human valuation, and to affirm human choice as the final arbiter of the true and the good for humankind. In the humanist canon, this awesome responsibility is the consequence of the objective uncertainty that defines the human situation—not just the ethicoreligious sphere—in which human freedom must operate. We are faced with a cosmos of equally consistent alternatives; we lack self-evident principles or criteria for selection. Accordingly, human choice must decide not only "what is true but what criteria shall be used to determine the truth, and what standards shall be used in choosing between competing criteria, and what judgments shall be employed in deciding on the standards ad infinitum" (Van Cleve Morris, *Philosophy and the American School*).

Abraham's situation, when he is commanded to slay Isaac, represents the human situation. Forced to decide whether he is addressed by God or Moloch and given the impossibility of demonstrating whose voice he hears, Abraham must assume the mantle of ultimate valuator. He must decide the *source* of the command, and in the final analysis his judgment of the source determines the *value* of the command. If he concludes that the decree is from God, it is morally imperative. If, however, he decides that it is Moloch's voice that he hears, the order must be rejected. But clearly, only Abraham can make this crucial decision.

Likewise with humankind: forced by virtue of our freedom and the existential situation of objective uncertainty, we cannot escape the necessity to be the measure of even that higher reality that created us. There is no way to escape this responsibility short of denaturing humanity, for it is a factor of the freedom that is our essence.

The same sense of uncertainty informs the humanist concept of history. The humanist acts "as if" history were open-ended and multi-valued, as if human choices and actions were determinative for human destiny. But once history is afforded this character, it becomes problematical. There does not appear to be an inevitable historical development, sponsored by ultimate reality, that ensures the liberation of the oppressed or a more humane society. Rather, oppression and liberation are equally probable. Nor is there a cosmic lifeguard to save humanity from its self-destructive choices. This is the meaning of the tragic sense of history in humanism—not that human efforts are doomed to defeat, but that the best-laid plans of one generation may be sabotaged by the actions of the next.

Thus, rather than fanatical advocates of absolute human freedom, religious humanists view themselves as faithful stewards of human finitude and creatureliness. This becomes clear when we consider an important corollary of functional ultimacy: the humanocentric predicament.

Religious humanism questions whether we can shed our human nature and escape the human condition to view reality from an extrahuman or superior perspective. It asks whether we are not confined to the circle of human relativity which dictates that all our claims be prefaced with the qualification, "in relation to human measure." This should be taken not as an assertion of human arrogance or superiority, but as a confession of human limitations. To affirm the humanocentric predicament is to assert that we approach being only through the mode of our existence. It would appear that the incarnation suggests as much. God does not denature humanity in coming to us, but the Transcendent adjusts itself to the human condition. God becomes human.

To adopt the humanocentric predicament also does not require that we deny the existence of knowledge of extrahuman transcendence. No, it is only to insist upon the allowance that the actual character of the transcendent may be wholly other. That is, its view of the good and the true may be diametrically opposed to our own, and what we worship as God may be the devil in disguise. All this is simply another way of accenting the factors of objective uncertainty and the multievidentiality of phenomena.

It is from this perspective that religious humanism would request a clarification of what is meant by an appeal to a transcendent norm as the necessary ground for morality. At the first level, the designation of the transcendent ground, it appears that we encounter Abraham's dilemma in a different form. Are not subjective criteria already operative here in designating the ground as God and not Satan, that God is, and Satan is not?

However, when the human being is designated the role of moral creator, thus affirming human freedom and autonomy, the meaning of the Transcendent in this context becomes obscure. Does it mean more than the claim that the Transcendent is the ground for human freedom/autonomy and the world in which this is exercised? Or does it mean that ultimate reality sponsors, and thus guarantees, the eventual triumph of specific activities? That is, once humanity is given the status of moral creator, does *ontological* priority—that is, the Transcendent—still establish *moral* priority? Sartre's claim: "Ontology itself cannot formulate ethical precepts."

The Future for Religious Humanism

Proponents of religious humanism predict that its formative principle will gain increased importance in religion and theology as various forces are brought to bear on the theological enterprise. As theology wrestles with the issue of theodicy in its revised form of ethnic suffering and quietism, as it formulates a theology of social, economic, and political liberation, and as it accommodates the marked theological particularity that flows from the emergence of ethnic, feminist, and Third World theologies, the acknowledgment of functional ultimacy will accelerate. When Christian theologians expose the full implications of theological postures recently assumed, and when they critically examine humanism without the prism of gross misinterpretations, it will be recognized that the formidable chasm is between the right (theocentric) and left (humanocentric) wings of theism, now between the latter and religious humanism.

As religious humanists survey current intellectual and social developments, they are bolstered by a sturdy optimism. They are encouraged by the fact that the major critics of humanism attack a theory of absolute human freedom which religious humanism does not endorse, on the grounds of the general view of human freedom that religious humanism wishes to advance. Moreover, they are heartened by the formation of the fruits of religion, the practice of the time-honored moral imperatives, independent of the trunk and branches of theistic belief. (Cf., for instance, Donald MacInnis's analysis of the moral climate in Maoist China in the March 12 issue of the *Century*.)

For these reasons, I see the coming encounter and dialogue between humanism and theism not as the occasion for sour-tempered vendettas, but as another of those recurring interludes in the history of the race when the search for truth pits conscientious antagonists on the battleground of human thought. The issue is not who wins, but whether the combat enlarges our understanding of ourselves. And as future generations review the coming clash, the verdict may well be that the adversaries were, unknowingly, not-too-distant relatives.

Chapter 3

THE CASE FOR BLACK HUMANISM

William R. Jones

Apologetics or Theological Construction

There are several ways to execute the assignment that is implied in the topic. On the one hand, the topic calls for the formulation of a systematic theology from a humanist[1] perspective. This reduces to an exercise in theological construction. On the other hand, the topic demands that I justify the possibility, the necessity, and the value of theologizing from a humanist viewpoint, and this reduces to an apologetic enterprise. No doubt the best apologetic in this context is the successful construction of a humanist theology, but for various reasons the approach of this chapter must adopt the apologetic model.

Factors more crucial, however, dictate that the apologetic assignment must precede the constructive undertaking, and these relate to some commonly held, but questionable, presuppositions about the nature of theology, humanism, and Black religion. More specifically, it appears that the current Black theologians want to restrict the title of Black theologian to theists and members of Black Christian denominations.

Accordingly, the humanist theologian encounters several problems that his theist counterpart can avoid (this is even more pronounced if the humanist theologian must legitimate his perspective and approach as a *theological* enterprise). Other theologians may be pressured to validate the Christian character of their work, but their membership in the theological fraternity is not questioned. The response to the death-of-God theologians is a case in point. Though many types of humanism do not require the premise of God's death or non-existence, they are not received into the theological community as the death-of-God theologians have been. It would appear that the different response to the death-of-God theologian and humanist theologian results because a strictly etymological definition of theology is operative. Consider, for instance, John Macquarrie's description of the boundaries of theology, where an etymological definition segregates theology from other disciplines in religion.

> Let us be quite clear at the outset that if anyone wants to construct a theology without God, he is pursuing a self-contradictory notion and is confusing both

himself and other people. He may construct a philosophy of religion (and he may even do this brilliantly), or he may construct a doctrine of man (anthropology) or a doctrine of Jesus (Jesusology) or an ethic or a mixture of all of these, but whatever results from his endeavors, it will not be theology.[2]

In addition to the objection of a John Macquarrie, the humanist theologian must also respond to the charge of a Charles Hartshorne, who affirms that humanism is a defective religion and incapable of supporting the minimal requirement of the religious life. "If religion, or any satisfactory philosophy of life, has as its goal the integration of the personality ('salvation'), then humanism is a very partial and inadequate religion. No matter from what angle the question is viewed, integration by humanism will show itself incomplete and unsatisfactory."[3]

But the most serious challenge to the Black humanist theologian issues from the Black theist theologians. They hurl the same charges advanced by Macquarrie and Hartshorne, but with a decidedly different force and sting. When the Black theologians raise the issue of the religious and theological authenticity of humanism, the issue merges inevitably into another question: Is humanism alien to Black religion? Joseph Washington asked in another context, "How Black is Black Religion?"[4] This, for him, is another way of asking: Is Black religion authentically Black or is it white religion in Blackface?

The Black humanist faces a similar interrogative: How Black is humanism? And the Black theologians insist that he must respond by establishing that humanism is rooted in the Black *church* if he is to receive his theological credentials. The arrogant test of the Black theologians here would seem to require that an orthodox rabbi be graduated from a Dominican seminary to be certified. This view must be challenged.

Clearly the Black humanist is engaged in something other than a friendly debate when he throws his religious views into the Black theological circle. Nevertheless, this is the agenda I must address here: to justify humanism as an authentic expression of Black religion, to develop a concept of religion and theology that accommodates humanism, and to validate that a framework that is closer to the humanist pole of the theological spectrum is viable, if not required, for a Black theology that defines itself as a theology of liberation.

Humanism: Saint or Subversive?

One might think that a nontheist model for a theology of liberation would be highly attractive for contemporary Blacks. It is generally agreed that white Christianity has in the main hindered the cause of Black liberation. Nor does Black Christianity have an unblemished record as a liberating agent. Therefore, because of the failure of white Christianity and because of the checkered success of Black Christianity, it seems only reasonable to consider as candidate models for Black liberation theology other forms of theism or nontheism, if only to supplement Black Christianity.

A quick glance at the extant Black theologies[5] presents a bleak picture for the Black humanist, however. There are yet no acknowledged points of entry for his perspective, as theology, into the theological arena. The available Black theologies constitute a rigid monolithic theism, and it is a theism of a specific variety. Each is a representative of Western biblical theism; each is mainly Protestant. To state the obvious, each spokesman is a Black, Christian, Protestant theologian. It is worth noting that none has yet returned to indigenous African sources for his primary theological materials. To speak of a monolithic theism is not to disregard the real differences between Cone and Roberts, for instance; but they are of one voice in affirming theism to be normative.

If one emphasizes the fact that Black theology is still a relatively new discipline, the prospects brighten for Black humanism's acceptance as an essential part of Black theology. Black theology has not been around long enough to spawn the theological pluralism that informs other traditions. With this understanding of the status of Black theology, one would expect that its present theological monolithism would blossom into theological pluralism as it grows and matures.

The prodigious obstacle to Black humanism that I perceive is, however, not temporal but theological. The evolutionary development of Black theology will not guarantee a niche for Black humanism. Rather, a radical shift in theological perspective must occur before humanism is admitted into the Black theological circle.

I will now examine in detail the presuppositions that control the extant Black theologies and thereby black ball humanism from the theological fraternity.

Major Jones epitomizes the theological monolithism I have in mind when he admonishes Blacks not to "ignore the basic tenets of the Judeo-Christian faith. To do so would be merely to establish a folk religion that would not survive the test of history . . . and the black man will have lost the God who brought him over so many difficult places in the past."[6] Several claims that merit consideration are packed into this statement. Note the conclusion that only the Judeo-Christian perspective can provide a sound foundation for Black religion; only biblical faith will "survive the test of history." From a pragmatic standpoint, anything else is futile.

A second presupposition demands equal attention, namely, that the God of Christian faith has been the Black man's agent of salvation in the past. This conviction also has a pragmatic ring. What Major Jones is arguing is that Black liberation will become a reality only through the activity of the God of our past. Thus, the success of Black liberation demands that we Blacks make and maintain umbilical contact with the God of our fathers.

A similar spirit informs the thought of other Black religionists who describe Blacks as a religious or spiritual people. When one unpacks the meaning of *Black spirituality*, it invariably collapses into a password for Black theism. To say that Blacks are a spiritual people means ultimately that they believe in and worship God, in particular the God of the Judeo-Christian faith.

Clearly this equation of authentic religion and Christian theism forces a theological straitjacket on Black humanism at the outset.

A third presupposition segregates humanism from the Black theological circle. All of the extant Black theologies advance the thesis that the Black church is to be the incomparable vanguard of Black liberation. Joseph Washington has described this ecclesiological strategy as "The Politics of God." Reduced to its essentials, this category means that Black liberation requires the creation of effective and community-based power structures in the Black community to operate as agents of change at the political and economic frontiers. The Black church, according to this strategy, is the logical and most promising institution to form this power base. "Negro churches are the only natural communities universal enough to command the loyalty and respect of the majority of the Negro masses. They alone are so extensive as to form unity in political power."[7] Add to this the conviction that the Black church is "the institutional center" and "the dominant social institution"[8] of the Black community, that the Black church came into being as a vehicle for freedom and equality, that it is the single institution that is indigenous to Blacks and owned and controlled by them, and the rationale is established for the church as the avant-garde of Black liberation.

The connection between this ecclesiological strategy for the Black church and the theological status of humanism may be obscure, but clearly this view of the church's status and mission automatically creates certain limits to what is theologically permissible. Theological continuity must be maintained between the masses in the pews and the Black ministers engaged in the politics of God, at least at the level of rhetoric and symbolism. A program of Black liberation based on the Black church as the avant-garde cannot succeed if the theology from the pulpit is abrasive to its hearers.

At this point the second presupposition assumes control. Since Blacks are inherently religious—substitute here *theists*—the "alien" perspective of humanism will only subvert the theological consensus that is the foundation for communal unity. Thus the Black humanist finds his Blackness under attack on two counts. Given the equation of Black religion and theism, Black humanism is an apostate who desecrates the heritage of his forefathers and blasphemes the sacred memory of all the Black saints gone to glory. Given the understanding of the Black church as the vanguard of Black liberation, the Black humanist is a stubborn obstacle to group unity and, thereby, Black liberation. Politically speaking, Black humanism is acutely counterrevolutionary.

In spite of these arguments, persuasive though they appear to be, the theistic monolithism of Black theology must be challenged, and primarily for the same reason that Black theologians excommunicate humanism—the demands of Black liberation. Let it be clear at the outset that the agenda of Black humanism does not involve the destruction of the Black church. Neither does it value a wholesale denigration of the Black church, past or present. Nor is it concerned with denying the enormous potential of the Black church for the future cause of Black liberation.

All that Black humanism seeks is the admission that the strategy of the Black church as vanguard is based on the *potential* of the Black church as a liberating agent. The Black church, as Washington acknowledges, maybe "the natural" but is not yet "the real center"[9] of power in the Black community. Cone also confesses that the Black church has not always made liberation its reason for being. Rather, the more secular agents of liberation—NAACP, the Urban League, CORE, and SNCC—"were created because of the failure of the black church to plead the cause of black people. . . . The current civil rights protest organizations," in sum, "are visible manifestations of the apostasy of the black church"[10] from its divinely ordained mission to liberate the oppressed.

Because the Black church's history, as Cone and others have indicated, is checkered relative to liberation, Black humanism wants to avoid the "all-the-eggs-in-one-basket" strategy implied in the Black church as avant-garde. The enormous potential of the Black church has been appropriately captured in its description as "a sleeping giant."[11] Black humanism, however, thinks that it is unwise for the fate of Black liberation to depend upon whether the Black church awakens from its slumber or continues to snore, however piously and rhythmically. In this connection, the possibility must also be entertained that the emergence of Black humanism as a formidable opponent may successfully prod the Black church as other secular movements have done, "to be about its father's work."

Black humanism would also accent the fact that the Black church has never corralled the majority of Blacks into its pews. This is not to negate its real influence beyond its altars and sanctuary walls. Nor should it be concluded that the unchurched are less religious than their church cousins. There appears to be a growing number of so-called secular Blacks who find the theology of the Black church hard to digest, and this unchurched flock can hardly be neglected if Black liberation is to succeed.

The Black church and Black theology have not collided with the pervasive phenomenon of secularity; some affirm that the encounter need not and ought not to occur. One wonders, however, if the meeting and necessary dialogue can be delayed much longer. Secularism does not make *homo religiosus* extinct, but it does make problematical the traditional pillars of Black theistic religion. And it does elevate some of the central themes of humanism to first rank.

The Black church faces an agonizing dilemma in its quest to unify the Black community by forging links with these prodigal sons. How can it capture this unchurched herd without sacrificing the symbols and the more fundamentalist theology that enchant the people in the pews and keep them loyal worshippers? Should the Black church hunt for the bird in the bush or tightly clutch those already in hand? No matter how the dilemma is viewed, the imagination that pictures the Black church as the organic center of the Black community is teasingly utopian.

Black humanism seeks its constituency from this large, unchurched group, this secular "congregation" that appears to be multiplying rapidly. Accordingly, Black humanism should not be regarded as a replacement for the Black church, but as its necessary complement for Black liberation.

Humanism: Son or Stranger?

Once the Black humanist acknowledges his debt to the Black church, honors its past labors in the cause of Black freedom, but respectfully declines to further its theistic claims, he must address the charge that his position is alien to the Black religious perspective. Behind the charge that Black humanism is alien to Black religion lies an insidious equation that must be exposed for critical examination: the equation of Black *religion* and Black *theism*. This shibboleth must be openly attacked in order to obtain a more accurate understanding of religion in general and Black religion in particular.

It is often necessary for me to remind my colleagues in the Society for the Study of Black Religion that it is not the Society for the Study of Black *Theism*. Black religion cannot be reduced to Black theism, nor can the chronicle of the Black church encompass the full sweep of Black religion in America. For this reason, the following analysis of J. Deotis Roberts must be criticized:

> The question of existence in reference to God is not the real issue for blacks. This does not preclude the fact that many blacks are nonbelievers. This is often true of "cultured despisers" of Christianity, black intellectuals who equate status with a militant rejection of the Christian faith. . . . It is characteristic of many older black intellectuals who are humanistically oriented and are greatly influenced by the position of Auguste Comte. Add to this the lack of exposure to religious scholarship . . . the sentimental Jesusology of an ill-informed magico-religious upbringing, and one begins to understand why in their intellectual maturity, they have found their "God too small" and their religion inadequate. But the return to religion, often as blind faith in middle life, together with the spiritual strivings of their children, leads me to believe that religion is native to most blacks. Religion in some form or other appears to be an Africanism.[12]

Several points here merit special comment. First, it should be noted that the final sentences make no sense without the equation of religion and theism. It is also characteristic of Christian despisers of Black humanism that they invariably trace its roots to non-Black sources—here Comte. If this is an accurate description of the genesis of Black humanism, the charge of alienation truly gains considerable support.

However, the error of this reading of Black humanism is implicitly affirmed by some of the Black theologians themselves, for they are forced to acknowledge the presence of a nontheistic strain in Black religion. In this connection, one can cite Benjamin Mays's classic study, *The Negro's God*. To provide a comprehensive picture of the Afro-American's "God-talk," he includes a chapter entitled "Ideas of God Involving Frustration, Doubt, God's Impotence and His Non-existence." The humanist element in these materials is easily identified.

James Cone's most recent work, *The Spirituals and the Blues*, tacitly admits the presence of a religious perspective among Blacks that is not, to use his term, *God-centered*.[13] He cites the slave seculars, the nontheist counterpart of the slave spirituals, and the blues as examples of a tradition with a religious dimension outside the Black church and Black theism.

Admittedly, this nontheist tradition is a minority viewpoint in Black religion, but it nonetheless establishes a firm link between Black humanism and the

Black religious pasts. Black humanism need not draw upon traditions that are alien to the totality of the Black religious experience. Humanism is a legitimate part of Black religion, though obviously not of the Black church tradition. In this connection, Mays has correctly noted that Black humanism has not developed primarily as a result of the studies of modern science—and one could also add positivism—or from a conviction about the cruelty and indifference of nature, but "because in the social situation, [it] finds [itself] hampered and restricted."[14] Mays's point is that Black humanism emerges not from Comte, but from wrestling with the horror of Black oppression and the crimes of human history where Blacks are the unwitting victim. Black humanism is not estranged from Black theism because humanism is alien to Black thought. Rather, the theist rationale for Black suffering and oppression is thoroughly unconvincing. Indeed, I have argued that the Black theologians' treatment of Black suffering forces us to ask: Is God a white racist?[15]

The Black humanist must also question the normative apparatus that decides the value of a theological perspective by gauging its conformity to the beliefs of past generations of Blacks, especially if that past is narrowed to the Black church. Continuity with the theological traditions of our forefathers is not the critical factor if one purports to formulate a theory of liberation. Because the overriding purpose of a theology of liberation is to exterminate oppression, it is obliged to establish certain guidelines and patterns that will take priority in theological construction. The theologian of liberation, for instance, must identify those tyrannical beliefs and attitudes, such as quietism, which smother the impulse toward liberation. Only after these inauthentic elements of the tradition have been isolated, sterilized, or neutralized, can the theologian of liberation entertain conformity to that tradition. Otherwise, he runs the risk of unknowingly endorsing and perpetuating ideas and concepts that undergird oppression and, consequently, contradict his explicit purpose.

The same point can be made from another perspective. Because Black religionists are convinced that traditional interpretations of Christian faith are infected with the cancer of racism, again a thorough examination of both white and Black Christianity must precede any advice to ally oneself with that tradition. Once the virus of racism or oppression is detected, the entire tradition must be quarantined, and each part forced to certify that its racist or oppressive quotient is immunized.

Black humanism contends that to emphasize allegiance to either Black or white Christianity prior to a root-and-branch examination of both is to beg the question about the liberating character of each. First, we must know with some clarity where white Christianity ends, and Black Christianity begins. Moreover, God, the heart of Black theism, has not been sufficiently cross-examined to determine the nature of His responsibility for Black oppression. Black humanism asks whether making God's intrinsic justice and benevolence the cornerstone of Black faith is a perpetuation of white Christianity. Black humanism suspects that Blacks' convictions about God, especially His intrinsic goodness and justice, and traditional explanations of Black suffering may be part and parcel of Black oppression. In sum, Blacks today should be asked to conform only to those aspects of the tradition whose proliberation impact has been clearly established.

Indeed, it is necessary to ask: Is this not in fact the operational methodology of the extant Black theologians? It seems that they do not simply read off their theologies from the diaries of their forefathers. Black theology, at least in practice, has not been the recording of "a latent, unwritten Black Theology." Rather, a conscious process of selection and rejection is clearly evident in their approach to Black Christianity. Certain of its features, for example, a "pie-in-the-sky eschatology," have been summarily dismissed because of their quietist implications. It can also be argued that such an approach to the tradition has been taken simply to affirm the freedom of man that Cone insists must be exercised relative to the deeds and words of Jesus himself.

> We cannot solve ethical questions of the twentieth century by looking at what Jesus did in the first. Our choices are not the same as his. Being Christian does not mean following "in his footsteps . . . " His steps are not ours; and thus we are placed in an existential situation in which we are forced to decide without knowing what Jesus would do. . . . Each situation has its own problematic circumstances which force the believer to think through each act of obedience without an absolute ethical guide from Jesus. To look for such a guide is to deny the freedom of the Christian man.[16]

To affirm the freedom of man in this manner is not creeping idolatry; in fact, humanism would affirm that choosing without absolute guides is the given condition of humankind. Actually, I am guilty of a greater idolatry if I presuppose the intrinsic truth and demonstrated value of the tradition. Once racist and oppressive elements are uncovered, the greater idolatry is not to subject every jot and tittle of that tradition to the most unsparing cross-examination.

It can also be argued that I am convicted of idolatry if I do not bestow coequally both revelatory truth and theological significance on my own perspective. To assign to another human perspective, be it Black or white, absolute or definitive importance is to confine God's revelation to a particular human context. The Black theologian will inevitably tumble into inconsistency if, on the one hand, he denies absolute status to white God-talk on the grounds of the particularity of God's revelation, but in the next breath, leases absolute merit to a Black past.

I cannot conclude this discussion of alienation without noting the harsh and unappreciative response of segments of the Black church to Black theology itself. The charge that Black humanism is a prodigal son must be considered alongside the charge of a prominent Black denominational leader, who regards Black theology as racist and not suitable as a part of seminary training.

Humanism and Theology: Some Semantic Problems

I have postponed until now a discussion of the possibility of a humanist theology. Two crucial questions constitute this issue: Is humanism an authentic *religious* perspective? If so, what does this entail for an understanding of the activity of theology?

The first question obliges the Black humanist to formulate a definition of religion that can accommodate humanism. Of course, it is always possible in a situation of this type to advance a stipulative definition that establishes a niche for one's own pet position. But such a strategy is obviously a self-serving method. The humanist's position is strengthened if he can show that a more general analysis of religion incorporates his perspective. I suggest that the concept of *religion as soteriology* captures the essence of religion and furnishes room for the humanist position as well.

Religion, I contend, reduces ultimately to a way of salvation. Its basic purpose is soteriological: "to convince men that they need salvation and then offer them a way to achieve it."[17] In this sense, religion is like the medical enterprise: its activity is always preventive or corrective. That is to say, the raison d'être for religion is the conviction that something is radically wrong with man; something essential to man or to his condition must be replaced or supplemented, or special precautions must be taken to prevent the occurrence of the unwanted condition that demands correction.

Religion differs from other preventive and corrective activities in that it advances its specific program as a matter of *ultimate concern*, necessary not merely for man's good, but for man's *highest* good. The religious enterprise, in short, is placed at the core of the ideal, what ought to be. Not to receive the enriching fruits of the religious life is to place man in jeopardy.

Put in other terms, salvation is defined as the ideal, the proper relation between (a) man and ultimate reality and/or (b) man and his fellowmen. Salvation can also be described as man in possession of his summum bonum. Obviously, how the proper relation is delineated and what the procedure is for reaching it will depend on the particular religion being analyzed.

It should be noted that this analysis of religion employs the category of ultimate reality instead of God; this is done to avoid the question-begging point of departure. The inner logic of Western monotheism makes God and ultimate reality one and the same, but other religions do not establish the same ontological equivalence. Buddhism, for instance, is often described as atheistic, because it does not have a prominent concept of *God*; although there is a vibrant doctrine of *ultimate reality*. Lucretius's ontology is another case in point. Gods are included as part of the metaphysical scaffolding, but the gods are not ultimate reality. This, for Lucretius, is reserved for the atoms and the void.

In summary: I submit that soteriology, not belief in God, is the sufficient and necessary condition for religion, and humanism easily fits under the umbrella of religion as soteriology.

With this understanding as background, I can now examine the category of theology. To make this understandable, it is necessary to call attention to an implication of religion as soteriology. Each religion emphasizes a (or more than one) specific *soteriological singular(s)*, that is, that about which one must properly relate himself if the summum bonum is to be realized. For Western theism, God, *theos*, is the soteriological singular. Thus, God is crucial precisely because of his soteriological significance. In this sense, theology becomes a sub-class of soteriology. The function of theology is to describe, reflect upon, draw implications from, and systematize information about the soteriological singular. Nontheist religions would obviously have a (or more than one) different soteriological singular(s), but the explication, analysis, and/or "talk" about the latter are functionally the same as theology.

The humanist faces an acute problem in semantics at this juncture. What is the appropriate term to identify the study of his soteriological singular; Is it *anthropos*? If he follows the line of the theist and speaks of anthropology as the humanist equivalent of theology, the entire soteriological factor is lost. In speaking of himself as an anthropologist, a humanist would identify himself as a scientist rather than a religionist. Nor does philosophy of religion supply the necessary clarity, for it also does not connote the centrality of the soteriological component.

I can only point to the problem at this juncture. A term is needed to describe someone who advances a precise soteriological system without making God the soteriological singular. Should one burden the category of theology to encompass this position, which the strict etymology of the term "theology" negates? Or should we coin a new term, such as *anthropologian*, to determine the humanist theologian?

The Coming Debate

In this concluding section the concern is to identify for discussion and for debate additional topics that bear on the issue of the possibility and character of a humanist theology. These are issues that I have discussed elsewhere or that require separate and detailed treatment.

The first obligation of the humanist theologian is to nominate the prescriptive principle(s) of his variety of humanism. That principle for me is *the functional ultimacy of man*. That is another way of describing Protagoras's epigram, "Man is the measure of all things," and Kierkegaard's principle of truth as subjectivity. Humanism tends to affirm the functional ultimacy of man relative to values, history, and/or soteriology. This principle, I contend, is not absent from theism, though its import is limited to the sphere of values and/or history. For instance, Cone's analysis of the freedom of the Christian man relative to the ethical authority of Jesus's words and deeds presupposes the functional ultimacy of man. I have also isolated a variety of theism, which I term *humanocentric theism*, where the principle is elevated to a central position.[18]

The next item on the agenda of the humanist theologian is to demonstrate that the prescriptive principle of humanism is utilized by the extant Black theologians. I submit that an analysis of their actual, in contrast to their stated, concept of authority will confirm this point.

Another line of analysis would show that the Black theologians will be pushed toward the humanist pole of the spectrum as they are required to deal with some inescapable problems, most of which are raised by positions they have already adopted. I have argued that Black theologians' own principles make theodicy the controlling category for theology, and that their resolution of the theodicy question, in light of their claims that theirs is a theology of liberation, will necessitate the adoption of the prescriptive principle of humanism.[19] The encounter of Black theology and secularism, I suggest, will produce the identical theological movement.

Humanism, from my vantage, points to a verity that Black religion, especially if it is to be a liberating agent, cannot escape. Whether the religious insights of humanism are accurate can be decided only when a Black humanist theology takes its place alongside the now familiar texts in Black theology. For the self-understanding of both Black theism and Black humanism, I trust that that day will soon dawn.

Notes

1. This chapter does not advance a precise definition of humanism; the determination of the defining properties of humanism requires further analysis and debate. It is the general meaning of secular humanism—in contract to Christian humanism—that is intended.
2. John Macquarrie, *New Directions in Theology Today, Volume III, God and Secularity* (Philadelphia: The Westminster Press, 1967), 13.
3. This is the essential thread of his argument in Charles Hartshorne, *Beyond Humanism* (Lincoln: University of Nebraska Press, 1968), 12.
4. This is the title of an essay in James J. Gardiner and J. Deotis Roberts, eds., *Quest for a Black Theology* (Philadelphia: Pilgrim Press, 1971).
5. When I speak of Black theologians I have in mind Albert Cleage, James Cone, Major Jones, J. Deotis Roberts, and Joseph Washington.
6. Major Jones, *Black Awareness: A Theology of Hope* (Nashville and New York: Abingdon Press), 118.
7. Joseph Washington, *The Politics of God* (Boston: Beacon Press, 1967), 201.
8. Ibid., 207.
9. Ibid., 193.
10. James Cone, *Black Theology and Black Power* (New York: Seabury Press, 1969), 110.
11. I am indebted for this graphic description to Lucius M. Tobin of Benedict College.
12. J. Deotis Roberts, *Liberation and Reconciliation: A Black Theology* (Philadelphia: Westminster Press, 1971), 82.
13. James Cone, *The Spirituals and the Blues* (New York: Seabury Press, 1972), 108.
14. Benjamin Mays, *The Negro's God as Reflected in His Literature* (New York: Atheneum, 1968), 255.
15. William R. Jones, *Is God a White Racist? A Preamble to Black Theology* (New York: Doubleday, 1973).
16. Cone, *Black Theology and Black Power*, 139–40.
17. Winston King, *Introduction to Religion* (New York: Harper & Row, 1954), 286.
18. W. Jones, *Is God a White Racist?*, pt. 3.
19. William R. Jones, "Theodicy: The Controlling Category for Black Theology," *Journal of Religious Thought* (Summer 1973): 28–38.

Chapter 4

RELIGIOUS HUMANISM

ITS PROBLEMS AND PROSPECTS IN BLACK RELIGION AND CULTURE

William R. Jones

I would have preferred to narrow my concern to a description of the controlling categories and inner logic of religious humanism,[1] thus providing the reader with a neatly packaged model to compare and contrast with competing perspectives in Black theology and religion.[2] However, because of the actual circumstances and rank of religious humanism in Black religion, I have found it necessary to adopt an approach that is decidedly more apologetic.

A quick survey of research patterns in Black religion reveals the reason. Religious humanism is a neglected aspect of Black culture. In discussions of Black religion, humanism of all varieties is virtually ignored, and when it is unexpectedly remembered, it suffers the unfortunate fate of being misinterpreted and misunderstood. Its situation parallels the predicament of the hero in Ralph Ellison's *Invisible Man*, who though flesh and blood, living and breathing, is treated as if he did not exist.

Researchers in Black religion characteristically narrow their focus to the history of the Black church and its monolithic theological perspective of Christian theism. Because the Black church is the major institutional expression of Black religion, one can readily acknowledge that its thought and practice should receive preeminent attention. Having said this, however, it must also be allowed that the concern to uncover the rich past of the majority position should not obscure the full content and scope of Black religion. Nor should the effort to honor the Black church and its particular theological tradition obliterate the total spectrum of competing species of Black religion, especially the nontheistic perspective. Unfortunately, this has occurred.

I am confident that future research will confirm that there are two religious traditions in Black culture: a mainstream tradition of Christian and non-Christian theism and a minority tradition of humanism or nontheism. There is unobscured evidence of a tradition of religious humanism in the Black past that is opposed to Christian theism and the biblical perspective. Unable to fit the fact of Black oppression and slavery into normative Christian categories and lacking confidence in God's love and concern for Blacks, these ebony humanists, like Prometheus and Job's wife, refused to honor or worship the divine.

Evidence internal to Black Christian theism, its major antagonist, confirms the presence of this "heretical" viewpoint. The testimony of Daniel Alexander Payne, a bishop of the African Methodist Episcopal Church, is worth noting in this regard.

> The slaves are sensible of the oppression exercised by their masters; and they see these masters on the Lord's day worshipping in his holy Sanctuary. They hear their masters praying in their families, and they know that oppression and slavery are inconsistent with the Christian religion; therefore they scoff at religion itself—mock their masters, and distrust both the goodness and justice of God. Yes, I have known them even to question his existence. I speak not of what others have told me, but of what *I have both seen and heard from the slaves themselves*. I have heard the mistress ring the bell for family prayer, and I have seen the servants immediately begin to sneer and laugh; and have heard them declare they would not go into prayers; adding if I go she will not only just read, "Servants obey your masters"; but she will read "break every yoke, and let the oppressed go free." I have seen colored men at the church door, *scoffing at the ministers*, while they were preaching, and saying, you had better go home, and set your slaves free. A few nights ago . . . a runaway slave came to the house where I live for safety and succor. I asked him if he were a Christian; "no sir" said he, "white men treat us so bad in Mississippi that we can't be Christians."[3]

In the very limited cases where the presence of this nontheistic tradition is acknowledged, it is not labeled "religious," nor is it recognized as a legitimate part of the family of Black religion. This is not primarily the consequence of its status as a numerical minority in Black culture; rather, humanism itself is suspect as something alien to the Black psyche. Both its opponent and champion can agree that religious humanism has not established itself as an indispensable perspective in Black religion, the description of which is required for an accurate and adequate understanding of Afro-American religion. Outside of this volume, one is hard-pressed to uncover a panoramic analysis of Black religion which self-consciously includes the humanist perspective as one of the competing options in Black religion. Religious humanism, in sum, has little standing as an accredited representative of the Black religious experience. Hence, the necessity and purpose of this chapter is to inaugurate the discussion that will hopefully establish religious humanism as an authentic expression of Black religion and culture.

Black Religious Humanism: The Invisible Religion

Though there can be little question about the actual presence of nontheism in the Black past, it is exceedingly difficult to determine the actual extent of this radical religious perspective. In addition to the testimony of Bishop Payne, researchers, such as Sterling Brown[4] and John Lovell[5], call our attention to a musical/literary genre the slave seculars, that also confirms a nontheistic tradition in Black religion. The seculars, often called devil songs, ran counter to the spirituals, the musical embodiment of the Black church and its theistic thoughtforms. Rejecting the biblical promises and the God-centered theology that the spirituals have etched in our collective memory, the seculars ridiculed the God their fellow slaves worshipped and bombast the eschatological and soteriological "good news" of the spirituals.

In Lovell's monumental work on the spirituals, it is important to be reminded of the connection he establishes between the spirituals and the seculars. Though he is concerned to make the spirituals, as it were, the womb for fundamental features of Black literature and culture, he does not trace the origin of the seculars back to the spirituals. Rather the devil songs and the spirituals are depicted as two different traditions existing side by side.

Other materials suggest a two-way movement between the spirituals and other varieties of slave music that exaggerates the difficulty in plotting the exact boundaries and religious consistency of each. In the first published collection of slave songs, we find several revealing statements about the rich variety of musical types and their continuing intercourse.

> We must look among their non-religious songs for the purest specimens of Negro minstrelsy. It is remarkable that they have themselves transferred the best of these to the uses of their churches—I suppose on Mr. Wesley's principle that "it is not right the Devil should have all the good tunes." Their teachers and preachers have not found this charge difficult to effect; or at least they have taken so little pains about it that one often detects the profane *cropping out*, and revealing the origin of their most solemn "hymns," in spite of the best intentions of the poet and artist.[6]

The collectors of this first volume of spirituals also inform us that the spirituals, the theistic incarnation of the slave experience, comprise only part of the Black experience that was fashioned into song.

> Fiddle-sings, "devil-songs," "corn-songs," "jig-tunes," and what not are common. . . . We have succeeded in obtaining only a very few songs of this character. Our intercourse with the colored people has been chiefly through the work of the Freedmen's Commission, which deals with the serious and earnest side of the negro character.[7]

This last confession points to the most formidable obstacle to substantiate the actual extent of religious humanism in Black culture: the biased pattern of selectivity used to compile and transmit the Black religious heritage. We must not forget the fact that the individuals who first recorded the spirituals were white, and most of them were ministers. It is important to recognize the influence of these factors in determining both the genre and the number of songs recorded.

As Bernard Katz perceptively concludes:

> The vast majority of the songs that were rescued from oblivion were the songs of the Sabbath—of church worship. The songs of the rest of the week would have to

creep out of hiding during a time when fewer men of the cloth were around. . . . Thus it is very possible that a great body of songs of secular social comment, too difficult to disguise for white ears, stayed underground . . . and would surface later in the blues and other forms.[8]

These materials highlight the risk involved in extrapolating from the number of extant scholars to the actual range and importance of the theological perspective they represent. Moreover, if one does extrapolate from the popularity of the blues, the acknowledged descendant of the seculars, then the cultural and theological matrix of religious humanism may be a more extensive and significant entity than is suggested by the paucity of seculars in the collection of Black songs.[9]

For all of its deficiencies, the account of the Reverend Charles C. Jones is also significant for unearthing the history of Black religious humanism. That Jones, in this account, is describing the different belief patterns the Christian missionary will encounter laboring among the slaves strongly suggests that we are dealing with a radical criticism of traditional theism that is not numerically insignificant.

> He discovers deism, skepticism, universalism . . . the various perversions of the Gospel, and all the strong objections which he may perhaps have considered peculiar only to the cultivated minds, the ripe scholarship and profound intelligence of *critics* and *philosophers*.[10]

Wilmore perceptively identifies another point that bears upon the history of humanism in Black religion. He notes that figures like Edward W. Blyden enjoyed greater theological affinity with the radical left wing of New England Protestantism—the Channings, Theodore Parkers, and Emersons—who were more "dependable as friends of the Black man than the revival and camp-meeting preachers or the pious clerics of the main line denominations."[11]

Several points in Wilmore's analysis are revealing. He has identified members of Unitarianism, the radical theological movement of that era and which today is basically non-Christian and enthusiastically humanist in its theological affirmations. What Wilmore accents as the basis for the theological congeniality is also revealing—their actions were more pointedly focused toward the liberation of Blacks. What his analysis here suggests is that the radical theological left was a more dependable friend of Black Americans than the orthodox theological tradition. Does it crucify the imagination to infer that slaves, convinced of the biblical and common sense maxim—"By their fruits shall you know them"— would not automatically reject a radical theological position that manifested itself concretely in the practice of liberation?

The Invisibility of the Black Humanism: Causal Factors

All that has been discussed thus far has attempted to make us aware of a competing, albeit minority, tradition in Black religion. Having said all of this, however, the virtual invisibility of religious humanism in Black religion becomes all the more perplexing, and the reasons both for its status as a numerical and a disvalued minority in Black culture must be identified. In this connection a comprehensive treatment would analyze those factors which relate to the status of religious humanism as an authentic (a) religious and (b) Afro-American perspective, and those which accent the impact of (c) the context of Blacks as an oppressed group in America and (d) the particular value and cultural orientation of Afro-Americans. Because of restraints of space and time only a select few of these factors can be discussed here.

To acknowledge the presence of Black religious humanism as a minority tradition in Black religion is to affirm that it has been constantly overshadowed by the larger entrenched theism that continues in the Black church. Accordingly, to explain the virtual invisibility of Black religious humanism, we must focus on several features of institutionalized Black theism and decipher their impact. First, we must accent the fact that religious humanism exists as a philosophical/theological *perspective* and not as an ongoing *institution* like its rival, the Black church. To state the obvious, an intellectual movement that lacks an institutional base has a limited life span.

Add to this the fact that humanism has been viewed as a hostile adversary, intent on exterminating religion in general and Black Christian theism in particular, and it becomes clear why the Black church would not be anxious to nurture a potential serpent in its own household.

If we highlight the connection between socio-economic-political context and one's theological/ethical outlook, we can identify another factor that accounts for religious humanism's status as a *numerical* minority. This, however, does not explain its position as a disvalued minority in Black religion.

There are several different ways of connecting the cultural context and the minority status of religious humanism. Perhaps the most important and most controversial is the question: Is the historic oppression of Blacks in America more conducive to the development of certain forms of theism than humanism? Put in other terms, is there a specific complex of socio-economic and political conditions that are correlated statistically with the respective worldview of humanism and theism?

I must say at the outset that there are inadequate research data to answer these questions confidently. However, I would hazard the opinion that humanism emerges most frequently in a situation that is antithetical to that which defines oppression and especially slavery. That is to say, a context of oppression is most generally connected with conceptual framework of theism. Accordingly, the actual historic situation of Blacks in America is more likely to spawn certain types of theism than humanism.

Several factors lead me to advance this tentative hypothesis. The actual evolution of humanism seems to be associated with a firmly developed urbanized economy in contrast to an agricultural or pastoral one. Humanism, moreover, characteristically draws its adherents from the middle and upper socio-economic strata rather than those near the bottom of the economic ladder.

Because humanism affirms radical freedom/autonomy as the essence of human reality, humanism is most prominent in those cultures where individuals exercise in fact considerable control over their environment and history. The humanist understanding of wo/man comes into being, it appears, as the consequence of this type of experience and the material situation it presupposes.

The evolution of humanism in Greek culture, under the aegis of the Sophists, seems to confirm this tentative hypothesis. Gayraud Wilmore's invaluable treatment of the Black church and its contribution to the radical wing of Black thought and practice also supports this tentative conclusion about the socio-economic context for the evolution of Black humanism. Wilmore identifies a "dechristianizing period" when the religious impulse self-consciously locates itself outside the circle of Black Christian faith. Is it accidental that he identifies this secular nontheistic tradition with the intellectual, upper-level groups of Blacks? Is it accidental that a similar socio-economic context seems to be the base for those Black writers associated with *The Messenger* and its radical critique of the Black church?

At this juncture, it is important to make explicit the precise connection between humanism and socio-economic context that is being advanced. I am not arguing for either a strict relation of necessary or sufficient condition. Rather I am illuminating an empirical generalization[12] about the actual development of humanism that can serve as a hypothesis for examining the relation between cultural context and faith content. What I see is a clear-cut movement toward the humanistic pole of the religious spectrum[13] as individuals and groups move away from or release themselves from the scourges of oppression. Perhaps, a more focused analysis of the contrast between the spirituals and the blues will clarify the point.

According to most interpreters, the blues and the spirituals reflect distinct theological perspectives and socio-economic contexts. James Cone's analysis of their contrasting outlook and existential situation provides a helpful specimen for our discussion.

The blues, also labeled "secular spirituals," gravitated to the nontheistic theological pole. Whereas the spirituals gird the Black slaves to endure oppression with the belief that the God of Israel would eventually set them free, the theology of the blues rejects a god-centered perspective as the answer to the enigma of Black suffering, choosing instead to address Black oppression as if God, Jesus Christ, and the Black church were all irrelevant.

Most interpreters also conclude that the blues surface in a less circumscribed socio-economic context.

> The spirituals are *slave* songs, and they deal with historical realities that are pre-Civil War. . . . The blues . . . are essentially post Civil War in consciousness. They reflect experiences that issued from Emancipation, the Reconstruction Period, and segregation laws. "The blues was conceived," writes Leroi Jones, "by Freed-men and ex-slaves . . ." Historically and theologically, the blues express conditions associated with the "burden of freedom."[14]

Having noted this contrast, the general question I raise here is whether this nontheistic faith content is a reflection of a less oppressive socio-economic environment? In like manner, the growing unchurched population among Blacks triggers the same inquiry.

In discussing the connection between socio-economic context and conceptual content, mention must also be made of the impact of the value structure of Black culture. Is it a reflection of its situation of oppression that Black culture has not been a fertile environment for the cultivation of those intellectual and cultural products, such as philosophy and secularism, that have been historically associated with the development of a self-confident humanist perspective? Though religion has been blessed in Black culture, philosophy has been denied a status comparable to its position in the larger culture. Though there are a heady number of Black theologians, the number of Black philosophers is, by contrast, miniscule.

Methodological and Semantic Obstacles

Other factors affecting the visibility of religious humanism as an authentic expression of Black religion relate to specific methodological and semantic practices. The interpretive grids of most current researchers are ineffective instruments for illuminating the totality of the phenomenon of Black religion, especially the nontheistic component. Hence, to materialize religious humanism from its spectral status, it is necessary to challenge the semantic apparatus and methodological presuppositions that control current research in Black religion.

As a corrective I would advance several interpretive principles. With these principles we can accelerate the resurrection of this disvalued tradition for analysis and critical appraisal; without them Black religious humanism will remain invisible, unloved, and unappreciated.

Afro-American religion must be approached as a multi-faceted phenomenon that comprises the full spectrum of theistic and nontheistic options.

What this principle excludes is a reductionist approach that seeks to shrink Black religion to a monolithic pattern. In that sense, the principle demands that we examine Black religion as a pluralistic phenomenon. This means in methodological terms that the researcher should approach the data of Black religion with the view in mind of identifying discrete philosophical and theological types as background for determining which major points of the religious spectrum are actually represented in Black religion.

Semantically speaking, the principle dictates that we abandon the common, but question-begging, usage that collapses religion into theism, a particular—though admittedly the most prominent—sub-class of religion.

I must make the obvious point. If religion and theism are equated, nontheism, by definition, is excluded as a religious perspective. Add to this the common tendency, especially in the context of monotheism, to equate nontheism and atheism, and the possibility of a research apparatus that illuminates religious humanism is exceedingly remote. Nontheistic positions will either be ignored or mistakingly assimilated into the general theistic camp. The consequence is the same in either case: Black religion becomes a single tradition of theism for research purposes.

Much more is at stake than a recommendation for an accurate terminology. It should be clear to all that the case for Black humanism both as an authentic religious perspective and a valid expression of the Black religious tradition stands or falls on this seemingly innocuous issue about the meaning of theism and religion. In deciding about the parameters of Black religion, one is in fact answering the fundamental question of the essence of religion itself, in particular the logical and phenomenological connection between it and theism.

If the advocate of Black religious humanism does not challenge the equation of theism and religion, s/he also provides grounds for the claim that religious humanism is not authentically Black. This line of argumentation is unavoidable once the following descriptions of Black consciousness are advanced within a semantic framework where religion and theism are synonymous.

> We black people are a religious people. From the earliest time we have acknowledged a Supreme Being. With the fullness of our physical bodies and emotions we have unabashedly worshipped Him with shouts of joy and tears of pain and anguish. We neither believe that God is dead, white, nor a captive to some rationalistic and dogmatic formulation of the Christian faith which relates Him exclusively to the canons of the Old and New Testaments, and accommodate Him to the reigning spirits of a socio-technical age . . . .[15]

> The question of existence in reference to God is not the real issue for blacks. This does not preclude the fact that many blacks are nonbelievers. This is often true . . . of many older black intellectuals who are humanistically oriented and are greatly influenced by the position of Auguste Comte. . . . But the return to religion, often as blind faith in middle life, together with the spiritual strivings of their children, leads me to believe that religion is native to most blacks. Religion in some form or other appears to be an Africanism.[16]

Several points here merit special comment. Unless religion and theism are equated, these statements are meaningless. Moreover, it should also be noted that here theism is not simply advanced as the majority viewpoint but rather as the normative perspective and the yardstick by which one identifies the authentic Black consciousness. Indeed, by defining Black religion exclusively in theistic terms and thus failing to make an allowance for nontheistic perspectives, these statements come close to making the acceptance of theism a defining characteristic of being Black.

It is true of course that researchers in this area espouse a pluralistic interpretation of Black religion. Indeed the major research trend in Black religion has been to attack monolithic and stereotyped interpretations of the Black religious experience and its institutional expressions. Received traditions of the Black church as an Uncle Tom institution, with a sugar tit strategy, have been countered by new interpretations of the Black church as a formidable agency of protest and liberation at all levels of the slave's activity. Research such as John Lovell's treatment of the slave spirituals as protest songs with a this-worldly outlook, parallel this development. However, one searches in vain for the same approach to the humanist dimension of the Afro-American heritage. There is still monumental resistance to attack a remaining shibboleth: Black religion as exclusively theistic.

Because of what is at stake, it is important at this juncture to articulate the inner logic of a pluralistic approach as a means of testing the actual, in contrast to the espoused, theory of researchers. Pluralism, in this context, involves, first, the recognition of at least two discrete perspectives in Black religion; neither can be reduced to the other; and each is regarded as co-valuable in the sense that if either is omitted, the phenomenon under discussion will be incomplete or inadequate.

It is important to identify another feature of an authentic pluralistic interpretation: the numerical distinction between the majority and minority viewpoints cannot be the basis for establishing a qualitative difference between them. Concretely, the fact that theistic worshippers are numerically superior cannot by itself substantiate their status as the normative or authentic Black perspective. If this principle is not allowed, Black theists sabotage their own efforts to challenge those interpretations of traditional Christianity that are alleged to be a grotesque understanding of the gospel.

Again, the problem goes beyond a mere recognition of a nontheistic tradition in the Black past; rather the basic issue is that of interpreting this point of view as both religious and a valid expression of the Black religious experience.

Cecil Cone's recent volume, *The Identity Crisis in Black Theology*, illustrates the approach that is challenged here. His thesis is that Black theology is in an identity crisis because it has failed to identify the essence of Black religion and to make this the exclusive point of departure and source material for theological construction and analysis.

Cecil Cone defines Black religion accordingly: "The divine and the divine alone occupies the position of ultimacy in black religion. Indeed, an encounter with the divine is what constitutes the core or essence of that religion. Such an encounter is known as the black religious experience."[17] This God-encounter, the resulting conversion experience, and the variety of responses to the latter define Black religion for Cecil Cone.

Let it be clear at the outset that the Black humanist does not question the accuracy of Cone's account as a description of Black *theism*. Indeed, the issue would be resolved for the humanist if theism were inserted in each case where Cecil Cone speaks inaccurately of religion. What the humanist resists is the arrogant assumption that the Black religious experience is somehow exhausted by the theistic experience.

We cannot escape the fact that Black religion is reduced to a form of theism in Cone's definition. The rigidity of this semantic apparatus forces him to treat those materials which seem to fall outside the theistic tradition in a most dubious fashion.

Citing the slave seculars and the passage from Bishop Daniel A. Payne discussed earlier, Cone clearly acknowledges the existence of Blacks who were unafraid to question God's intrinsic goodness and, like Prometheus, were willing to rebel on moral grounds. But how does Cone respond to this theological tradition that rejects the almighty sovereign God and the Black church?

From one vantage point his response is simply to note the presence of this minority theological view without relating it to his definition of Black religion or discussing it further. According to another interpretation, Cone assimilates the God-defying perspective into the theistic religious experience! The radical question about God's justice and/or existence becomes the *pre*-conversionist mentality of the Black *theist* facing the absurdity of the slave condition. In this interpretation the slave experience, with its excruciating doubt and despair about God's rule over the world, creates the dark night of the soul. This, however, is erased by the slave's Job-like encounter with the divine. The transformation is complete. The pressure of Cone's equation of religion and theism has magically transmuted the humanist into a converted theist!

The Cultural Matrix of Afro-American Religious Humanism

To resurrect Black religious humanism requires a second interpretive principle that current researchers in Black religion do not sufficiently honor: *The actual origin as well as the current position of Black religious humanism must be seen as a response to perceived inadequacies of Black Christian theism, its theological rival.*

Implicit in this principle is the hypothesis that Black humanism emerges as part of a debate that is internal to Black life and thought. It is not a spinoff of the enlightenment, the scientific revolution, or, as J. Deotis Roberts has suggested, a borrowing from Comte.

Rather, as Benjamin Mays, an eminent representative of Black Christian theism, has correctly perceived, Black incredulity about the divine and agnosticism and atheism

> do not develop as the results of the findings of modern science, nor from the observations that nature is cruel and indifferent but primarily because in the social situation, [the Black American] finds himself hampered and restricted. . . . Heretical ideas of God develop because in the social situation the "breaks" seem to be against the Negro and the black thinkers are unable to harmonize this fact with the God pictured by Christianity.[18]

Whether we encounter Black humanism during the slave period or more recent eras of oppression, it appears as a critic of Black Christian theism, questioning the latter's capacity to make sense of the history of Black oppression and to accommodate the prerequisites of a viable theology of liberation. Substantiating this conclusion about the indigenous origin of Black humanism is the telling statement of the heroine in Nella Larsen's *Quicksand*.

The white man's God.—And his great love for all people regardless of race! What idiotic nonsense she had allowed herself to believe. How could she, how could anyone, have been so deluded? How could ten million black folk credit it when daily before their eyes was enacted its contradiction?[19]

And this, Helga decided, was what ailed the whole Negro race in America, this fatuous belief in the white man's God, this childlike trust in full compensation for all woes and privations in "Kingdom" come. . . . How the white man's God must laugh at the great joke He had played on them, bound them in slavery, then to poverty and insult, and made them bear it unresistingly, uncomplainingly almost, by sweet promises of mansions in the sky, by and by.[20]

Any assessment of the relation between Black humanism and traditional Western humanism must incorporate this understanding of the genesis of Afro-American nontheism. Though Black humanists and those humanists who trace their lineage to the enlightenment or the scientific revolution are akin in attacking the superstructure of theism, their criticisms develop from radically different socioeconomic contexts. Accordingly, the question of God is posed in quite different ways.

Scientific humanism poses the problem of the divine in terms of the coherence between the natural world and the supernatural realm. This query leads often to the denial of the divine reality, that is, a form of atheism. Black humanists, in contrast, ask the question: *An Deus sit?* because of the crimes of human history, and this emerges frequently in the form: Is God a white racist? a question that is absent from scientific humanism.

The radical theological questions that Black humanism raises grow out of the context of Black oppression. They cannot be reduced to the protests of a brainwashed Black who has been seduced by white Western secularism. They are not imported, as it were, from the outside. Thus, it would appear that those who attempt to connect Black humanism with non-Black sources, for example, Comte, are still handcuffed by the equation of theism and religion. Having equated the two, and having affirmed that Blacks are a spiritual people, that is, faithful theists, nontheism by definition would have to come from outside the Black community.

A Liberation Theology: The Black Humanist Perspective

To understand Black humanism of the past and to clarify the present agenda and interaction with the Black church, it is necessary to identify yet another interpretive principle that is suggested by Helga's vehement protest. *Black Humanism must be interpreted as a specific strategy for liberation that issues in a particular theology/ philosophy of liberation.* For the Black humanist, this dictates a specific theological method which becomes part of the critical apparatus for assessing Black Christian theism.

Before we outline this theological method, the intended interaction of Black humanism with the Black church must be made clear. The agenda of Black religious humanism does not call for the destruction of the Black church. Neither does it involve an absolute disapproval of the practice of the Black church, past or present. As with its interpretive approach to Black religion, Black humanism endorses a pluralistic program for the mechanics of liberation. Though Black humanism regards the Black church as a "sleeping giant" in terms of its potential as a liberating force, it also recognizes that the history of the Black church is checkered relative to liberation and further that the Black church has never successfully corralled the majority of Blacks to be its congregation. For these reasons "black humanism thinks it unwise for the fate of black liberation to depend upon whether the black church awakens from its slumber or continues to snore, however piously or rhythmically. . . . The emergence of black humanism as a formidable opponent may successfully prod the black church, as other secular movements have done, 'to be about its father's (and mother's) work.'"[21]

In this sense Black humanism should not be looked upon as a replacement for the Black church but rather as its necessary complement. Black humanism seeks its constituency from the rapidly growing group of unchurched Blacks, many of whom find the theology of the Black church unpalatable and an untrustworthy account of their religious history. This large unchurched group, the Black humanist concludes, cannot be ignored if Black liberation is to succeed.

Though the Black humanist seeks a cooperative and complementary relationship with the Black church in the struggle for liberation, s/he nonetheless cannot avoid challenging it and its theistic theology at several significant points. This must be done to legitimate Black religious humanism. But more importantly, Black humanism is forced into a critical or gadfly posture because of its primary concern to advance the cause of Black liberation. All of this becomes clear, if we analyze Helga's protest, cited earlier, as a miniature theology of liberation from a Black humanist perspective.

In ridiculing the doctrine of God and eschatology, Helga is voicing a common protest of Black humanists as well as more recent theologians and philosophers of liberation. The oppressed are oppressed, in fundamental part, because of the beliefs they hold. They adopt or are indoctrinated to accept a belief system that stifles their motivation to attack the institutions and groups that oppress them.

This understanding of oppression is not restricted to humanism; leading Black theists have advanced the identical conclusion. The basic argument of Benjamin Mays's *The Negro's God*, claims that Blacks conform or rebel against their oppressive situation by virtue of the concept of God they endorse. Certain beliefs about ultimate reality helps Blacks to survive, "to endure hardship, suffer pain and withstand maladjustment, but . . . do not necessarily motivate them to strive to eliminate the source of the ills they suffer."[22]

Mays's autobiographical account is instructive here, particularly in light of the fact that he denounces, in the same work, the stereotyped view of the Black religion as an opiate and otherworldly.

Long before I knew what it was all about, and since I learned to know, I heard the Pastor of the church of my youth plead with the members of his congregation not to try to avenge the wrongs they suffered, but to take their burdens to the Lord in prayer. Especially did he do this when the racial situation was tense or when Negroes went to him for advice concerning some wrong inflicted upon them by their oppressors. During these troublesome days, the drowning of Pharaoh and his host in the Red Sea, the deliverance of Daniel from the Lion's Den, and the protection given the Hebrew children in the Fiery Furnace were all pictured in dramatic fashion to show that God in due time would take things in hand. Almost invariably after assuring them that God would fix things up, he ended his sermon by assuring them that God would reward them in Heaven for their patience and long-suffering on the earth. Members of the congregation screamed, shouted, and thanked God. The pent up emotions denied normal expression in every day life found an outlet. They felt relieved and uplifted. They had been baptized with the "Holy Ghost." They had their faith in God renewed and they could stand it until the second Sunday in the next month when the experience of the previous Sunday was duplicated. Being socially proscribed, economically impotent, and politically brow-beaten, they sang, prayed, and shouted their troubles away. This idea of God had telling effects upon the Negroes in my home community. It kept them submissive, humble, and obedient. It enabled them to keep on keeping on. And it is still effective in 1937.[23]

In addition to examining the concept of God, the Black humanist would also painstakingly inspect the understanding of human suffering, especially as this relates to the oppressed's beliefs about ultimate reality. That is, the theological method of Black humanism elevates the theodicy question to first rank, and this is the consequence of the nature of oppression and the inner logic of a liberation theology.

A phenomenological analysis will reveal that oppression is reducible to a form of negative suffering, a suffering that is regarded as detrimental or irrelevant to one's highest good. Moreover, given that the purpose of a theology of liberation is the annihilation of oppression, the theologian of liberation must provide a sturdy rationale that establishes the negativity of the suffering that is the core of oppression. For instance, it must be shown that the suffering that is oppression is not sanctioned by God's will nor the unfolding of some fundamental laws of nature. In short, the suffering in question must be desanctified, or else the oppressed will not define their suffering as oppressive, nor will they be motivated to attack it.

Liberation Theology and Theological Method

With this understanding as background, the primary purpose and initial step of the liberation theologian is unobscured: to free the mind of the oppressed from the enslaving ideas and submissive attitudes that sabotage any movement toward authentic freedom. This means several things for theological method. First, an exorcist or castration method is dictated. The ideas and concepts that undergird oppression must be clearly identified and systematically replaced with more humanizing and liberating beliefs. In this connection a clear differentiation must be made between those theological constructs that enhance *survival* in contrast to those which promote *liberation*.

In addition, the examination must be total and comprehensive. At the outset each and every theological category in Christian faith and the Black church must be provisionally regarded as suspect, as an unwitting prop for oppression or a fatal residue of the slave master's worldview. This means that God must also be ruthlessly cross-examined to determine her/his responsibility, if any, for the crimes of human history. In sum, Black humanism concludes that a liberation theology must self-consciously adopt a *de novo* approach to the Christian faith and its theological tributaries.

In advancing this theological method, the Black humanist is well aware that he is challenging the fundamental premise of Black theism and Christian faith; the intrinsic benevolence and justice of God. Since this challenge often serves as the grounds for questioning Black humanism's status as an authentic expression of Black consciousness, it is important to understand the rationale for this root-and-branch method.

The primary point to be made is that this approach follows from the concern of the Black humanist to correct Black oppression by formulating a viable theology of liberation. We have already seen that the primary goal of a liberation theology, to eliminate oppression, requires a theological method which isolates and excommunicates those enslaving beliefs, such as quietism, which smother the oppressed's motivation to replace the unjust social institutions. Until these manipulative and inauthentic elements of the tradition have been successfully identified and quarantined, the liberation theologian cannot recommend conformity to the tradition. Otherwise, s/he runs the risk of unwittingly endorsing ideas and concepts that support oppression, thus contradicting the explicit purpose of the liberation theology.

The Black humanist also advocates a total root-and-branch analysis because the character of Christian faith as a vehicle for liberation is unsettled and, further, the boundary between authentic Black theism and the counterfeit position of Whitianity is obscure.

As a representative of Black humanism I have often raised suspicions about Christian faith as a potent means for liberation. Though I am persuaded of its excellence as a survival religion, its quality as a religion of liberation is, for me, still unresolved. This issue was posed more pointedly for me as a result of a fortuitous comparison of the Jewish and Christian liturgical calendars. I was struck by the way in which the Jewish calendar revolved around the celebration of events of ESP (economic-social-political) liberation: passover, purim, hanukkah, and so on. In contrast, an examination of the general Christian calendar failed to reveal a single celebration of ESP liberation.

This absence is not accidental. Though Christianity began as the religion of an oppressed community, it appears that its liturgical calendar reflects an entirely different political and economic context.

I also inspected the calendar of the Black church. It had not modified the Christian calendar in a manner that reflected its own context as an oppressed people; nor had it significantly included its own Black saints in a way that other ethnic communities have done.

I did not conclude from this discovery that Christianity is not a liberation religion or that the Black church is still captive to Whitianity. Rather, it suggested to me the necessity of a certain theological method. Each and every aspect of the tradition must be examined to determine its liberation quotient, and on this basis, accepted or rejected.

The necessity of a *de novo* approach can also be substantiated through a logical analysis of the concept of intrinsic benevolence itself as well as its actual function in Black theism for some worshippers.

> To believe that the universe is in the hands of God is to believe that there is a purpose in the world and that God will guarantee the successful working out of affairs in the universe. In this sense the idea is compensatory. One can rest secure and feel satisfied because he knows that nothing can go wrong in the world since God governs it.[24]

Black humanism insists that the root-and-branch approach must be applied to the theology of the Black church as well as the more general Christian tradition. In this regard, the Black humanist is actually raising the question: How Black is Black Christian theism? Is it an authentic expression of the Black religious consciousness or is it Whitianity in Black mask? Because the *de novo* approach advanced here has not been adequately executed, Black humanism is uncertain where Whitianity ends and authentic Black theism and Christian faith begin. Is the affirmation of God's intrinsic goodness and justice for instance an appropriation of the slave master's religion that creates a theology of survival rather than a theology of liberation?

John Mbiti's research on the African concept of time strongly suggests to the Black humanist that the particular eschatological emphasis of much of Black religion, past and present, is an area where the religion of the slave master may have usurped the more liberating worldview of our African foremothers and forefathers. At least this radical shift in outlook supports the necessity of a total examination of the Black tradition to determine the liberation quotient of each of its parts.

> For the Akamba, Time is ... simply a composition of events that have occurred, those which are taking place now and those which will *immediately* occur. What has not taken place, or what is unlikely to occur in the immediate future, has no temporal meaning—it belongs to the reality of "no-Time ..." From the basic attitude to Time, other important points emerge. The most significant factor is that Time is considered as a two-dimensional phenomenon; with a long "past," and a dynamic "present." The "future" as we know it in the linear conception of Time is virtually non-existent. ... The future is virtually absent because events which lie in the future have not been realized and cannot, therefore, constitute

time which otherwise must be experienced. . . . It is, therefore, what has taken place or will occur shortly that matters much more than what is yet to be.[25]

There is also the growing acknowledgment that Black theistic belief was formulated as a self-conscious theology of liberation.[26] That is, its specific theological emphasis was not constructed with the requirements of a self-consistent theology of liberation in mind. From this admission the Black humanist again concludes that it is necessary to examine every jot and tittle of the thought and practice of the Black church to assess its liberation quotient.

In all of this, the Black humanist concludes that s/he is executing the actual operational methodology of current Black theologians, though in a more consistent manner. It is easy to show that Black theistic theologians do not simply read off their theologies from the testimonies of our foreparents. Black theology has not been simply the recording of a "latent, unwritten Black theology."[27] Instead a clear process of selection and rejection informs their approach to the tradition. Certain features of Black religion, for example, a pie-in-the-sky eschatology, have been Black balled because of their quietist entailments. Indeed, the following theological method advanced by the leading Black theologian, James Cone, is the precise point of view the Black humanist wants to endorse.

> We cannot solve ethical questions of the twentieth century by looking at what Jesus did in the first. Our choices are not the same as his. Being Christian does not mean following "in his footsteps . . ." His steps are not ours; and thus we are placed in an existential situation which we are forced to decide without knowing what Jesus would do. . . . Each situation has its own problematic circumstances which force the believer to think through each act of obedience without an absolute ethical guide from Jesus. To look for such a guide is to deny the freedom of the Christian man.[28]

Having granted us this latitude of authority relative to Jesus, how can the Black church theologian withdraw the same authority to those assessing the Black church? Surely, there is a clear inconsistency in denying absolute merit to Jesus but assigning it to the past of Black theism.

Notes

1 In this chapter I have not attempted to describe the theological *Weltanschaaung* of religious humanism, having outlined this elsewhere ("Theism and Religious Humanism: The Chasm Narrows," *The Christian Century*, 92:18, May 21, 1975). My focus here is narrowed to an analysis of religious humanism as expressed in the Afro-American experience.
2 The following pairs will be used synonymously: Black humanism and Black religious humanism; Black theism and Black Christian theism; humanism and nontheism; Afro-American and Black; humanism and religious humanism.

3 "Document: Bishop Daniel Alexander Payne's Protestation of American Slavery," *Journal of Negro History* 52 (1967): 63. (Emphasis in the original.)
4 Sterling Brown, "Negro Folk Expression: Spirituals, Seculars, Ballads and Work Songs." in *The Making of Black America*, ed. August Meier and Elliott Rudwick (New York: Atheneum, 1969).
5 John Lovell, "The Social Implications of the Negro Spiritual," in *The Social Implications of Early Negro Music in the United States*, ed. Bernard Katz (New York, Arno Press, 1969).
6 Preface, *Slave Songs of the United States:* Francis Allen, Charles Pickard Ware, and Lucy McKim Garrison, in B. Katz, *The Social Implications of Early Negro Music in the United States*, p. xxxii.
7 Ibid., p. xxxiii.
8 B. Katz, "Introduction," *The Social Implications of Early Negro Music in the United States*, p. xii.
9 The problem of ascertaining the actual latitude of Black religious humanism parallels the determination of the true dimensions of insurrectionary activity among the slaves. Recent research leads one to conclude that the number of slave revolts was considerably more numerous than the actual records indicate.
10 Charles C. Jones, *The Religious Instruction of Negroes in the United States* (Savannah: T. Purse Co., 1842), 127.
11 Gayraud S. Wilmore, *Black Religion and Black Radicalism* (New York: Doubleday & Co., 1972), 161.
12 Cf. the similar claim of Benjamin Mays. "The other-worldly idea of God . . . finds fertile soil among the people who fare worst in this world; and it grows dimmer and dimmer as the social and economic conditions improve." *The Negro's God as Reflected in His Literature* (New York: Atheneum, 1969), 28.
13 This is not to affirm an abandonment of theism per se but a movement toward those forms of theism which are closest to the anthropological position of humanism.
14 James Cone, *The Spiritual & the Blues* (New York: Seabury Press, 1972), 112.
15 "Message to the Churches from Oakland," the National Committee of Black Churchmen, 1969.
16 J. Deotis Roberts, *Liberation and Reconciliation: A Black Theology* (Philadelphia: The Westminster Press, 1971), 82–3.
17 Cecil Cone, *The Identity Crisis in Black Theology* (Nashville: African Methodist Episcopal Church, 1975), 143–4.
18 Mays, *The Negro's God as Reflected in His Literature*, 281–9. Mays correctly identifies the cultural matrix of Black religious humanism, but future research, no doubt, will challenge his claim about the historical location of Black humanism. "Prior to 1914, God is neither doubted nor is His existence denied. Doubt, lack of faith, and denial are definitely post-War developments. In other words, from 1760 to 1914 God's existence is not denied." *The Negro's God as Reflected in His Literature*, 252. The presence of the slave seculars and Payne's account of the God-defying slaves both suggest that the last word has not yet been said about the presence of humanism in ante-bellum Black thought.
19 Nella Larsen, *Quicksand* (New York: Alfred A. Knopf, 1928), 292. Though I contend that the fact of Black suffering forces the question: Is God a white racist? I do not conclude that the mere fact of Black suffering—no matter how severe—permits us to answer the question. In this sense, Helga's self-confident assertion of a logical contradiction is inaccurate.

20 Ibid., 297. This accent on the seeming disharmony between traditional categories of Black Christian theism and the existential situation of Black oppression is a characteristic feature of the Black humanist theology. It is still true today that the Black humanist fails to perceive the inner consistency between the claim that God is the God of the oppressed and the continued oppression of Blacks and other minorities. The more "The God of the Oppressed" theme is pressed, the more inexplicable becomes the point of departure for a black theology of liberation: the designation of the Black situation as oppressive. From the humanist perspective, the crucial issue for Black Christian theology is not that of original *sin,* but the original *oppression* that triggers the necessity of Black liberation. To be extricated from this dilemma, the Black Christian theologian will have to move toward more radical eschatological doctrine or adopt a view of human reality that will relieve God of the responsibility for the crimes of human history. The former will push the Black Christian theologian perilously close to a "pie-in-the-sky eschatology," a point of view that has been denounced. The latter cannot be accomplished without endorsing the radical view of human freedom/autonomy that is the acknowledged core of the humanist anthropology.
21 William R. Jones, "Toward a Humanist Framework for Black Theology," included in *Black Theology II*, ed. William R. Jones and Calvin E. Bruce (Lewisburg: Bucknell Press, 1977).
22 Mays, *The Negro's God as Reflected in His Literature*, principle. 23–4.
23 Ibid., 26.
24 Ibid., 149.
25 John Mbiti, *New Testament Eschatology in an African Background* (London: Oxford University Press, 1971), 24. Emphasis supplied.
26 "Black folk theology, despite its record of highly liberating activity, cannot be labeled exclusively a theology of liberation. Black masses unanimously intuit such a goal, but do not self-consciously characterize their beliefs as a body primarily designed for liberation. It is more likely a theology of existence or survival" Henry Mitchell, *Black Belief* (New York: Harper & Row, Publishers, 1975), 120.
27 Roberts, *Liberation and Reconciliation*, 16.
28 James Cone, *Black Theology and Black Power* (New York; Seabury, 1969), 139–40.

Chapter 5

OPPRESSION, RACE, AND HUMANISM

> The 1992 Humanist Pioneer asks the painful question: is humanism inadvertently supporting the oppression of people of color?
>
> —William R. Jones

I didn't know, at first, what to say in appreciation for this award.[1] Should I talk about how I became a humanist? Or should I speak about what the plaque says here-my "efforts to be a champion for the rights of the oppressed" . . . because that has been my primary research, my conviction, my career: to expose oppression, to try to eradicate it. And then I began to recognize that the "why" and "how" I became a humanist and my concern about oppression actually intersected.

Those of you who were at my Raymond B. Bragg Symposium lecture some years ago will recall that, as a teenager, I went around preaching biblical prophecy. Billy Graham was my idol—and yet, I stand here now a humanist. What led me here? What experiences undermined that religious faith which had been drummed into me by my parents and by my grandfather, the minister of the church in which I was raised? The answer is this: I came to realize that the religion I had been taught was a fundamental prop for oppression. And this insight led to another: there are only two kinds of religion—those that undergird oppression and those that *undermine* it.

At that point, I began to develop a grid of oppression that unerringly pinpoints neo-racism, the mutant form of racism that is prevalent today. I must warn you this evening that we are deluded about racism. We mistake the disguise of racism for its decline and fail to recognize that racism has mutated. Thus, we prematurely affirm its demise. Or we fail to heed the warning of each new Los Angeles that neo-racism is immune to the vaccines and "magic bullets" that earlier gave us security.

So what I've been trying to do recently is to apply this grid. I'll be returning to South Africa in a couple of weeks to look again at the situation there in light of this grid. Two years ago, we literally predicted every basic policy that the South African government advanced. To illustrate: when F. W. de Klerk came to Washington, DC, he praised two presidents—George Washington and Abraham Lincoln—and, as our grid had predicted, Martin Luther King Jr. As early as 1976 we forecast that white America would use and abuse King to perpetuate neo-racism. I was in New Haven, Connecticut, at the time and invariably I was asked to speak at the annual celebration held each year for King. It struck me that no other Black heroine or hero was commemorated—for example, Harriet Tubman or Malcolm X. Why always and only King? They were praising King-using King-not as a Black messiah but as a *white guardian.*

I have since begun to turn this light, this grid of oppression, onto humanism—and I have to confess that what I am finding is similar to what I found when I looked at the fundamentalism of my youth. Unitarians, Universalists, and humanists have not audited their philosophy, their life-stance, from the standpoint of whether or not it inadvertently supports oppression. So I look around me at the audience here this evening, and I see almost no people of color. I want you to tell me: Why is that? Why?

A woman in the audience has just offered me a possible answer. She identified a member of her church in Sacramento, California, as a person with a background similar to mine—a fundamentalist background. She suggested that for Black people to leave that background and identify themselves as humanists is to admit that some white person has messed up their minds. Such an admission is a very difficult thing to make. But I want you to focus on something here. I'm not being bitter; I'm not trying to put anybody on the spot. But please examine that explanation in terms of its implicit causality which, as our grid predicts, will blame the victim. The causality for the Black absence is traced back to the Black persons. To account for the absence of people of color in humanism, we heard a diagnosis that immediately shifted the causality and blame where? To *those* people, not to *yourselves.*

And that's exactly the way oppression operates. Oppression starts by highlighting a difference—either real or imagined. There are a lot of differences: this woman here has on a red dress, that one there has on a black dress. That's a difference. But what oppression always does is to arrange this difference in a hierarchy with a superior and an inferior. You don't have to respond to differences that way, but that's what oppression does. Then oppression will always justify that hicrarchy. Wherever you find oppression, you have one group—the alleged superior group—with an overwhelming surplus of power, and another group—the alleged inferior group—with a clear-cut deficit. The alleged superior group will also have the most of the best and the least of the worst, which dispenses the most of the worst and the least of the best to the alleged inferior group. And, invariably, the oppressors will always justify this unequal distribution of resources as moral and good.

Most often they do so by identifying a causality. I've found only three in thirty years of research. They'll drag in God as the cause for the inequality. Note the implication: if God made it, if God set up the inequality, then by definition it is good. You can't change it, so you have to conform to it. A second pattern is to shift the explanation for the inequality to nature. More recently, a third mechanism has surfaced, which to me is the prominent mechanism by which liberals justify the inequality that is among us. We blame the victim by shifting the responsibility for the inequality onto the very people who suffer from it.

I want to show you why that cannot be done. Let's take the United States, for instance. I want you to help me develop a portrait of the causality for the inequality in our nation. Who is responsible? First, I want you to list all the institutions in America that Black Americans created and controlled for 200 years. List number two: all the institutions in America that white Americans created and controlled for 300 years. List number three: all the institutions that Black Americans created and controlled for 25 years, adding this clincher: *under which white Americans have had to live*. And then list number four: all the institutions in America that white Americans created and controlled for 300 years under which Black Americans have had to live. Now tell me what you came up with. [Silence.] List number one: almost *nothing*. List number two: almost *everything*. List number three: almost nothing. List number four: almost everything.

Please understand the implications of your silence. If Black Americans have neither created nor controlled any of the basic institutions in this country, how can they be blamed for the consequences of those institutions? It does not matter what they are—tell me how? Yet that is the inner logic of our policies. In a number of subtle and indirect ways, responsibility is removed from the oppressor and transferred to the victim. Let me review those three ways for you again quickly: blaming God, nature, and the victim. Please note that all three have one thing in common: they remove the responsibility from the group with the surplus of power. Frederick Douglass once wrote:

> Where justice is denied, where poverty is enforced, where ignorance prevails, and where any one group believes that society is an organized conspiracy to oppress it, neither persons nor property will ever be safe.

Note what he is saying. He is describing a situation—the very reality in which we are living now, where persons and property are not safe—and he is identifying that as an effect. And he gives you the cause of that effect: oppression. That is the message I leave with you. Where oppression prevails, neither persons nor property will ever be safe.

Let me share with you a very unsettling experience that engulfed me when I returned from South Africa two years ago. I revisited Harriet Tubman. If I were to pick a Black heroine or hero as a mentor, it would be her, never Martin Luther King.

Harriet Tubman, as you know, was a slave. And after she had gained her freedom, she told about an agonizing experience she had as she was relishing her freedom. She talked about the sky as suddenly so blue and brilliant and bright she could hardly stand to look at it. And then she began to reflect upon the fact that she was free, while there were so many others who were still enslaved. And Harriet found it necessary to justify her being here and they being there. And she said, "Every time I tried to justify it, I found myself drawing upon one of the arguments that the slave masters had used to justify my own slavery. I knew then, I had to go back and give back."

Now, I dare any of you to do what she did. Look around you. You're going to find somebody who's "lower" than you—and, when you do, I want you to justify it.

I want you to give sound, moral, rational, scientific reasons for why you are up here and they are down there. And I'll bet that you're going to have to use an oppressor argument. I'll put $1,000 down on it right here and now. And that's what I leave you with here tonight—that dilemma. I want you to justify your being here with almost no people of color.

Question: So what can we do, then? What should we do?
Jones: You know, I was asked that very question on a panel Thursday evening. We were looking at the situation in Los Angeles and around the country. The first question asked of me was: "Are you shocked, are you surprised about what is happening?" I said, "No, no, no! We predicted this years ago."

And that's my point. Why were we able to predict this? Because we are operating on an accurate diagnosis of the problem. One of the fundamental principles by which I operate is this: the therapy is inherent in the diagnosis. How you diagnose the problem dictates how you're going to respond.

Case in point: I have a headache, so I go to the doctor. What does the doctor do? Diagnoses the cause of my headache. That diagnosis is always based upon what? A causality, right? In the diagnosis, the doctor is pointing to a cause. Okay, so his diagnosis is constipation. That's the causality, right? What is my therapy going to be? You know immediately what therapy I'm going to get based upon the causality. But I still have headaches, so I go back and get a second opinion. This time the doctor says, "I'm sorry, you've got a brain tumor." That's a different diagnosis, based upon a different causality, so it should yield a different therapy. If the doctor tells me to take a laxative again, I've got a case for malpractice, right? The therapy is inherent in the diagnosis, and the diagnosis always points back to a causality. That is the first principle to understand if you want to know what to do. You must have an accurate understanding about the causality of the problem.

Now today, we're operating with an inaccurate diagnosis of the racial problems in America. We do not understand what oppression is or how it operates. We have a distorted, outdated view that informs our response. Case in point: if I define the problem as prejudice, my response will try to eradicate prejudice. But oppression is a quite different thing from prejudice. What is prejudice? It's a prejudgment, a belief, a value. Note the difference between that and oppression. To cure prejudice, I aim to enlighten the person, to change his or her conscience or rationale or reasoning. Oppression is quite different. We have oppression whenever one group accumulates a surplus of power and is able to use that power as the basis for institutionalizing whatever their prejudices or their biases are. So if I want to eradicate oppression, what must I do? Reduce that power imbalance.

Now note how we humanists tend to define the race problem in America: we define it primarily in terms of prejudice. And that diverts attention away from the very factor that has to be corrected in order to solve the problem. If it's simply prejudice, you as a white person and I as a Black person could be prejudiced to the same degree. But if we're talking about power as the problem, it's a whole different thing—that surplus of power held by the white authority has to be corrected. And that's what

I'm saying. We must begin to understand how oppression operates—and it's a very predictable operation, it really is. It took me some fifty years to understand it, but we've got a handle on that sucker now, I'm telling you—it's absolutely predictable.

And that understanding is the basis for a number of initiatives we've started in Florida that are proving to be absolutely spectacular. I'll give you two examples. Our university—Florida State University—is the only one in the Florida State University system that has changed its whole core curriculum to include a multicultural component. Every person who graduates from FSU now has to take two courses from a multicultural component. We were able to get that initiative through without raising the issues of "political correctness" or "Afrocentrism" or whatever—all we did was internal criticism. And that initiative is now in place.

There is also a program in Tampa called the McKnight Black Doctoral Fellowship. It was inaugurated by a white Episcopalian minister by the name of Russell Ewald. You're familiar with the 3M Company; the president of 3M was William McKnight. The company's operations were located in Minneapolis, Minnesota, but the McKnight family spent some time in Florida every winter. Prior to his death, McKnight set up a philanthropic foundation—the McKnight Foundation—which gives out about $30 million a year, almost all of it in the Minneapolis area. But McKnight left this nondescript statement in his will: he wanted to do something for the state of Florida. Russell Ewald was the minister to the McKnight family, and he became the first director of that foundation. He came to Florida and said that he wanted to do something for minority graduate education there. He had read the Chronicle of Higher Education, which had indicated that, by the year 2000, one-third of all the professors presently in the United States would retire. There was going to be a one-third turnover. And Russell said, if we have minorities in place with a terminal degree, we can make a substantial impact in this area. So he came to Florida and met with the cabinet and said he wanted to do something for minority education. Let me tell you what the cabinet told him and then relate that to diagnosis and therapy. The Florida cabinet said, "Give us some computers." Now if computers are the therapy, you tell me what the diagnosis is. Russell said no; he said, "I'll give you $10 million, but you'll have to match it with $5 million and you have to set up some programs." One was the Black doctoral fellowship, which gives out twenty-five fellowships a year. The student can live anywhere in the United States but must attend one of the state universities in Florida. Each student gets $11,000 per year as a stipend, plus a tuition waiver. The foundation pays for three years, and then the university picks it up at the same level for the fourth year. There's also a junior faculty fellowship program for minorities and majority females. After you've been in the state system for two years, you can receive a year off at full pay to start, continue, or complete a doctorate. If you already have a PhD, you can use it for tenure purposes; in two cases, we've given majority females fellowships with tenure and terminal degree because they were in departments which had never given full professorial status to any female.

Well, I want to tell you some of the results of these initiatives. We have an 83 percent retention rate—show me any other unit in the United States with a similar record. I'll tell you now, there is none. In 1985, there was only one Black student in the whole United States to get a PhD in computer science—just one. Right now, in this one single program in Florida, there are seven Black students in computer science. In June 1991, we had the first two PhDs in computer science graduate from this program. This one program is almost matching the national output for Black PhDs in computer science. Last year there were only four Black PhDs in pharmacology nationwide—only four, check it out. Of those four, two were in this program. In 1985, there was not a single Black student in the United States—outside of Florida—to get a PhD in criminology. Not one. In a similar program, which our office directs, we have graduated eight Black PhDs in criminology in the past eight years.

Now note what this is: a public, private arrangement. I'm trying to show you what's necessary, and that is a public-private arrangement. And once again we are operating on the diagnosis that the problem is neo-racism—not on the notion that the problem is somehow with the victim. We have dedicated resources for this program in perpetuum, and I'm telling you this: every single thing they said couldn't be done we've done. They said that there weren't sufficient Black students out there; we found them. They said that the learning deficits were too great; we showed them that wasn't the case. In fact, we didn't have any department lower its standards at all, not a single department. And we got almost all of them through; we got 83 percent of them through. It can be done, but you have to diagnose the situation correctly.

> **Question:** You're talking about a half, dozen people here, but in Los Angeles we're talking about thousands of people, many of them unemployed. Would you speak to what your feeling is about the many people who need socially acceptable jobs, earning socially acceptable wages?
>
> **Jones:** My analysis would be the same: the problem is neo-racism. Let me give you an example of what I mean. What we find in neo-racism is this overwhelming power to define, to label things, to name things, which determines how you approach the problem. Case in point: you tell me the difference between welfare and a subsidy. Both start off as taxpayers' money, right? Ain't no difference there. And then we send the money to a governmental unit, right? Still no difference. And then what does the government do? Passes it back. Any difference? No. Wherein does the difference lie? In who gets that money. If it goes into certain people's pockets, we call it subsidies; in somebody else's pocket, we call it welfare. Now, when we call it welfare, whose pockets is it going into? Poor people, Black people, and the like. If it goes into rich people's corporations, we call it what? Subsidies. Note: we say you cannot stay on welfare too long, right? It makes you dependent. Do we say the same thing about subsidies? No. Go back and listen to George Bush's State of the Union Address, especially his analysis of welfare. He says that welfare was never meant to be permanent, but he doesn't say anything about that other form of welfare—that is, subsidies. So what we have set up in the United States, due to this power to

name things, is a situation in which it is acceptable to have welfare only for rich people. See, I'm renaming subsidies as welfare for rich people, right?

Another case in point: taxes. If you have enough money to buy a home, make a down payment, you can deduct the interest you pay on your mortgage, right? Isn't that a handout? Poor people don't have that option. If I have to pay rent, do I get a handout? Note what happened after the Second World War: taxpayers' money was sent to Western Europe—white Western Europe—under the Marshall Plan. Was that welfare? Of course it was—welfare that enabled them to get back on their feet and become productive once again. When Joseph Jacobs asked Bush to develop a similar kind of Marshall Plan for the inner cities, based on the peace divided that was supposed to be forthcoming, Bush's response was that we don't have the money because it's already gone into paying for the savings-and-loan bailout but welfare for the rich? You have all been mugged for more than $2,000—each one of you. But you don't hear politicians attacking the saving-and-loan bailout anywhere near as much as you hear them attacking welfare.

I don't talk about raising taxes anymore; I talk about reducing welfare. Welfare for whom?—for rich people. And when we begin to talk in these terms, when we begin to order our priorities like that, to me we will have a real start on solving the problem. But note how that will affect *you* now. How many of you are going to want to institutionalize policies that reduce your subsidies? How many of you are going to want to do that?

I just want to make a distinction here between *espoused* theory and *theory in use*. Here's what I mean: a Roman Catholic priest was doing a catechism on heaven and asked his listeners, "How many of you believe in heaven?" Everyone's hand went up. "How many of you want to go to heaven? How many of you think heaven's the best place?" Once again everybody's hands were raised. Then the priest asked, "How many of you are willing to die tomorrow to go to heaven?" Now please note: they said they believed in heaven, that it was the best place, and that they all wanted to go there. How should they have answered the priest? They should have said, "No, I don't want to wait for tomorrow—I want to *go right now!*" But they didn't.

So I want it to be clear now: when you raise your hand, be sure you're telling me your theory in use, because that's what you really believe. Your espoused theory can be a much different thing—that's what you tell me and you believe in order to legitimize what you're doing. But I determine your theory in use from how you actually act.

One further example of how this labeling operates: using crime statistics from throughout the United States, the FBI develops an index of different categories of crime: "Black crime," "white crime," "male crime," "female crime," and so forth. Now focus on the actual crime before it becomes a statistic for the index. When the police are trying to apprehend suspects, they will send out an all-points bulletin in which they identify a suspect's race, gender, and so forth. But they will also create descriptions on the basis of what? Height, weight, distinguishing features—for example, a bald head—and so forth. Now tell me why it is that they will set up a category based on race—that is, Black crime—but there's no category for bald-headed crime? Tell me why. Note the implication of that labeling, that naming. If you set up a system in which you focus on the *color* of a person, you're making some generalization about the connection between that person's race and criminality. And I'll bet you that, if they did the same thing with bald-headedness, you'd be looking at me *doubly* differently, right? [Audience laughter.] So I'm trying to show you how this naming is crucial.

My final point is one that bothers me all the time: the concept of *cause*. Causality is a funny concept, a real funny concept. I want to show you the distinction between what I call *initiating* cause and *consequent* cause. Imagine a row of dominos up here. If I push the first domino, it's going to hit the second one, which in turn will hit the third, which will hit the fourth, and so forth. My first domino is my cause—my *initiating* cause—and when it hits the second domino and that domino moves, that's an effect, right? Okay, I now want to start with domino two. Domino two relative to domino three is what—cause or effect? It's cause, but relative to domino one, it's the *consequent* cause. Please note that the same domino—the same event—can be *both* cause and effect, depending upon the context.

Now, I want you to go back to Daniel Moynihan, for instance, when he was trying to describe the problems of the Black family. What he said was that nearly every deterioration in the Black community was due to the deterioration of the Black family. So what is he saying here? The deterioration of the Black community is the *effect*, and the deterioration of the Black family is the *cause*. That locates the problem where? Within the Black family. Okay, so now go one step further: he also says in the same text that it is essentially the legacy of slavery and 300 years of white exploitation that is responsible for the problems of the African American family. If I make slavery the cause, then the deterioration of the Black family becomes what? An effect. Note what has happened by that change in context: I have shifted the responsibility, the culpability, for the problems of the Black family and the Black community where? To *you*, right? And that's what I'm trying to illustrate, that's how oppression operates: by blaming the victim, by labeling the victim, by locating the causality for the victim's plight with the victims themselves. By these means, the alleged superior group—white America—maintains its surplus of power, and the consequences are virtually the same as when people were excluded directly on the basis of race.

Note

1 On May 2, 1992, in Portland, Oregon, William Jones accepted the American Humanist Association's Humanist Pioneer Award. What follows is an edited transcript of his remarks and the question-and-answer session that followed.

Chapter 6

IS FAITH IN GOD NECESSARY FOR A JUST SOCIETY?

INSIGHTS FROM LIBERATION THEOLOGY

William R. Jones

I have selected liberation theology as the perspective from which to discuss whether faith in God is necessary for a just society. To avoid repetition, I shall refer to this as the *question*. There are several compelling reasons to seat liberation theology as a participant in this debate. It is one of the major movements today where the *question* is addressed not only theoretically but existentially in the daily life and death choices of millions. Moreover, because the goal of a just society is explicit in its announced purpose to eradicate economic, social, and political oppression (hereafter ESP),[1] we can examine how it links ESP goals and theological norms as one of the concrete answers to the *question*. Equally important is the fact that liberation theology has conducted a broad, though not exhaustive, audit of theological systems to assess which concepts of God are foundations for oppression, as well as which must be affirmed to correct the unjust community. In all of this, we find a wealth of case studies that help us to confirm or disconfirm various answers to the *question*.

However, certain preliminary matters must be treated. Any response to a question, especially the type we are considering here, should be approached as a response to two distinct but related questions. First, there is the logically prior issue: What is the meaning or sense of the stated question: or, for our purpose, the *question*? The issue commands our attention because a question is seldom, if ever, self-interpreting; nor is its meaning self-evident. We invariably imprison the question in a specific context as well as a particular universe of discourse. Additionally, unstated and question-begging presuppositions, even a hidden agenda, may be camouflaged and packed into the question. Thus, if we bypass this initial determination of the "real" question, not only are we apt to respond to a question that was not asked, but we are also likely to give certain answers a validity they have not yet earned. For these reasons, it is doubly important to isolate the multiple senses of the question. Given this understanding of what is at stake, let me identify the questions that I detect within the *question*.

Questions within the Question

The *question* can be reduced to the following questions or issues, although they are, obviously, not exhaustive.

(1) *What are the prerequisites for a moral system?* More precisely, what are the necessary and/or sufficient conditions for a viable moral code? If we accent this dimension of the *question*, the focus of the debate is whether theism is necessary and/or sufficient for morality. If the answer is affirmative, several other questions must be addressed: Which *variety* of theism? And the related issue, which *features* of theism? Is it the transcendent dimension, an ontological ground, a supra-human absolute, and so forth?

An analysis of the commonly established connection between immortality and immorality identifies the drift that the argument would take if this sense of the *question* is honored. Luther and, more recently, Francis Schaeffer,[2] among others, argued that immorality increases as belief in immortality decreases. Humans, it is concluded, adopt an "eat, drink, and be merry" morality if they think that there is nothing beyond the grave, especially no eternal punishment for ungodly acts committed in this life. The heart of this understanding is some belief about God as judge and punisher of the evildoer as a prerequisite for a moral code. In sum, the *question* forces us to identify the specific roles or attributes of God that the just society requires.

(2) Focusing the debate on the issue of prerequisites also forces us to consider a *logically prior* issue that the *question* appears to ignore: the *refutation* of moral nihilism. Since moral nihilism claims that morality is an illusion, that there are no moral facts or truths, in short, that morality is impossible, it constitutes the unavoidable threshold issue for any moral system. Given these claims, no code of morality is justifiable *a priori*. If we want to ground our just society on a foundation that is not question-begging, we must rebut the claims of moral nihilism. The *question*, unfortunately, states the issue as if moral nihilism had been disproved. In launching the debate at this point, where it is allowed that a moral system and a just society are both possible, the only unresolved issue is the content of the moral system. In this, there are unmistakable signs of begging the question.

What is at stake is the logical and theological maneuverability available to construct a moral code. Also at stake is whether the initial "taking a position" that the threshold issue of nihilism compels, establishes some of the parameters within which we must respond to the *question*. If we, for instance, are forced to invoke a subjective principle to rebut nihilism, internal consistency and coherence command us to construct our moral system within these restraints.

My only concern here is to highlight three things; that a refutation is necessary, that we identify the norms used in the refutation and that these norms must be part of the formula for constructing the moral system.

Otherwise, the refutation of nihilism is a sham, and we are back at square one, the original threshold issue.

(3) Another dimension of the question which requires illumination is the connection between faith in God and legitimating the blueprint for a just society. Given that the just society must be legitimated if it is to survive, the *question* yields the following meanings: Is (a) a *theistic*[3] legitimation or (b) a *specific*[4] form of theism necessary? A third meaning requires a more detailed discussion: (c) Is *God* or *faith* in God the foundation for a just society? It is important to decide whether God (i.e., a transcendent being) or whether belief in God, transcendent or not, is the minimal requirement. As in the case of Santa Claus, whether there is an objective reality corresponding to the content of our belief is not important. Or, as in the case of the Wizard of Oz, belief in the Wizard's power was efficacious though the Wizard actually lacked the powers ascribed to him.

(4) The final unpacking of the *question* must tease out the meaning of the just society since we lack a consensus about its essentials. One need only examine Hitler's model of the just society, or South Africa, or the slave period in America to recognize that gross inequalities are characteristically basic structures of the just society. Indeed, one is hard-pressed to isolate some form of dehumanization that has not been religiously sanctioned as part of the just or good society. Moreover, when one considers that the authority and name of God are commonly borrowed to support both the just and unjust society, it becomes clear that our reply to the *question* must accommodate a response to this query: Is faith in God necessary for the *unjust* society? Indeed, if we extract from liberation theology's method, we would have to conclude that we cannot adequately answer the *question* until the connection between God and the unjust society has been explored.

With the foregoing analysis as a background, let me indicate the focus of this chapter. My response to (1) is that theism or faith in God is neither sufficient nor necessary for the just society. This is discussed only tangentially. With regard to (2), I find Pascal's and Camus's[5] refutation of nihilism persuasive. Nihilism, they demonstrate, is ultimately inconsistent, affirming some value that cannot be defended by the nihilist's own claims. Moreover, because the inner logic of nihilism is self-negating, it leads, if consistently practiced, to its advocate's demise.

This way of rebutting nihilism requires that we adopt at least two norms: a method of internal criticism and the common distinction between what is practiced and what is preached. If the negation of nihilism is to stick, I suggest that these norms must become part of one's own theological apparatus. This is not consistently practiced by most thinkers, thus raising the issue of a question-begging element in their system.

The focus of this chapter will be questions (3) and (4).

ESP Oppression: A Preliminary Analysis

Liberation theology addresses the *question* from several angles, two of which are germane to our discussion: those concepts of the divine that must be rejected because faith in them maintains the unjust society, and those that must be affirmed if the unjust society is to be reformed. It is important to appreciate the radical difference between these pictures of the divine. This demands, however, that we grasp liberation theology's view of the nature and operation of oppression, for it is through this that liberation theology defines the just society and determines which concepts of God are compatible or antithetical.

It is also important to note that liberation theology approaches the *question* from a specific context that establishes the framework for its method. It is a context in which oppression is firmly entrenched and undergirded by a specific belief and value system. This means that liberation theology approaches the *question* from the perspective of theological *deconstruction*, isolating and exorcizing the ideological roots of oppression. Consequently, liberation theology approves those images of the divine that must serve as the anti-toxin for the conceptual toxin of oppression. For this reason it is more accurate to speak of those theological categories that support the unjust society and those that counteract that support. The latter is not necessarily the preferred picture of the divine that would emerge if one approached the *question* from a context in which oppression is not present.

Oppression, for liberation theology, is a defining element of the unjust society, and its advocates assert that any authentic definition of sin in the Judeo-Christian tradition must include ESP oppression as a necessary ingredient. Speaking in general terms, oppression structures the society to maintain a specific human group at the top of the ESP ladder, while chaining another to the bottom. The oppressor accordingly manufactures fundamental ESP inequalities that endure from generation to generation.

These transgenerational inequalities[6]—and this is the crucial feature for our discussion—are justified on the grounds that they have an ontological foundation. This point must be highlighted if we want to avoid the common misunderstanding that liberation theology is radically egalitarian, condemning all hierarchical arrangements. Speaking more accurately, liberation theology mistrusts hierarchical inequalities that are transgenerational and ontologically legitimated, because these two features conspire to maintain the unjust society. Inequalities that result from human exploitation—that are not the product of nature or the supernatural—are easily misinterpreted as ontologically based if the transgenerational factor is prominent. A creature from Mars would be hard-pressed to determine if the lower Graduate Record Examinations (GRE) scores of Blacks, for instance, indicate genetic inferiority or transgenerational oppression.

If we move from a general to a more detailed description of oppression, the following should be accented:

(1) Oppression can be analyzed from two different perspectives, both of which are critical for assessing the connection between God and the unjust society.

On the one hand, oppression can be reduced to *institutional structures:* this is its ESP or *objective* dimension. On the other hand, we can condense oppression to the *belief* and *value* system that is its anchoring principle. This, for our purposes, comprises its *subjective* factor.

If this point is understood, it should not be surprising that the most cursory historical analysis will show that gross inequalities, indeed identical ones, are characteristic of both the unjust and the just society. God has and can be invoked to support and attack the same inequalities. Liberation theology draws several critical conclusions from this. It is on this basis that a distinction is drawn between the pre- and post-enlightened oppressed. The latter interprets the objective inequalities as negative, as hostile to her/his highest good; whereas the pre-enlightened do not. Wherein lies the difference? Not, as many believe, in a marked difference in the *objective* situation of each, but in the dissimilar theological grids used to assess these inequalities.

(2) The inner logic of oppression divides the human family into at least two distinct groups, hierarchically arranged along lines of superiority and inferiority. In-group, out-group; human, sub-human; male, female; black, white; rich, poor; Christian, Jew; Aryan, non-Aryan; master, slave are familiar examples.

(3) The hierarchical division is correlated with a gross imbalance of *power*, as well as unequal access to life-sustaining and life-enhancing *resources* and *privileges*. The alleged superior group will possess the unobscured *surplus* and the alleged inferior group, a grossly disproportionate *deficit*. To make the same point in different terms, the alleged superior groups will have the *most* of whatever the society defines as the *best* and the *least* of the *worst*. In stark contrast, the alleged inferior group will have the *least* of the *best* and the *most* of the *worst*.

(4) The hierarchical division may be a necessary condition for oppression, but it is never sufficient. For oppression (i.e., the unjust society) to be born, the hierarchical division must be coupled with a gross imbalance of power enabling the alleged superior group—and here we come to the next controlling feature of oppression—to institutionalize its ESP rank order.

To avoid a fatal misunderstanding, it is necessary to explore in more detail the importance of the institutional factor. Examining the distinction between racism and racialism provides the nuances needed for an accurate interpretation. Racialism is a belief system that affirms both the reality of superior and inferior groups, and that ontological factors, natural or supernatural, are the ultimate foundations for this hierarchical division.

Racism, however, is not the inevitable product of racialism. Though racialism may be prominent in a group, racism does not always develop. And though reprehensible, its consequences are not as deadly. For racialism to blossom into racism, the racialist must amass power that places the organization and control of society in her/his hands. The Nation of Islam (the so-called Black Muslims), under the leadership of Elijah Muhammad, is a case in point. Tracing the genesis of whites to the machinations of a Frankenstein-type scientist, Elijah Muhammad affirmed the superiority of Blacks and the inferiority of whites; hence, the explicit racialism. But the Nation of Islam never accumulated the power to institutionalize its racialism as the ESP environment where white America had to live.

Given this understanding, a critical factor differentiating the unjust from the just society is the distribution of ESP power. Accordingly, liberation theology concludes that an adequate response to the *question* must address the connection between faith in God and the ESP institutionalization of power.

ESP Oppression: A Preliminary Analysis

This controlling feature of oppression brings us to the heart of our discussion. The hierarchical division, with the accompanying inequalities of power and resources, institutionally installed, all of this is alleged to be grounded in ultimate reality, God or nature.

This feature pinpoints the mechanism that oppression uses to maintain itself. To perpetuate the unjust society, the oppressor must persuade the oppressed to accept their lot at the bottom of the ESP totem pole and to embrace these inequalities as good and/or inevitable. It is here, as Benjamin Mays instructs us, that the linkage between one's concept of God and the unjust society is most evident.

> The Negro's social philosophy and his idea of God go hand in hand. Certain theological ideas enable Negros to endure hardship, suffer pain, and withstand maladjustment, but . . . do not necessarily motivate them to strive to eliminate the source of the evils they suffer. . . . The idea has persisted that hard times are indicative of the fact that the Negro is God's chosen vessel and that God is disciplining him for the express purpose of bringing him out victoriously and triumphantly in the end. The idea has also persisted that "the harder the cross, the brighter the crown." Believing this about God, the Negro . . . has stood back and suffered much without trying aggressively to realize to the full his needs in the world.[7]

What Mays is calling attention to here is the connection between quietism and our understanding of God's nature and operation in history. Whether the wretched of the earth embrace or take any means necessary to eradicate their maldistributed suffering depends upon the kind of God in which their faith resides. A review of a classic novel, written more than a century ago, reveals the same insight.

> Altogether *Jane Eyre* . . . is preeminently an anti-Christian proposition. There is throughout it a murmuring against the comforts of the rich and against the privations of the poor, which as far as each individual is concerned is a murmuring against God's appointment.[8]

To make clearer the connection that liberation theology sees between our God concept and the unjust society, it is necessary to look briefly at the inner logic of quietism and its kith and kin relations to oppression. Quietism, in the lexicon of liberation theology, is a refusal to reform the status quo, especially where traditional institutions and values are involved. Concession, accommodation, and acquiescence are its distinguishing marks.

Quietism becomes our operating principle if we believe that ESP correction is (a) *unnecessary*, (b) *impossible*, or (c) *inappropriate*. Corrective action is unnecessary, for instance, if we believe that some agent other than ourselves will handle it. Another quietist tendency is found in the familiar adage: "If it ain't broke, don't fix it." This bespeaks the attitude that correction is gratuitous if the ideal is already present, in the process of being realized, or if changing things will make them worse. We are also pushed to quietism if remedial action is impossible. We reach this conclusion when we encounter an invincible force or when the item to be corrected is a structure of ultimate reality.

With this analysis as background, we can now describe the mechanism of opportunity more adequately. The unjust society maintains itself by claiming that its fundamental institutions and its hierarchy of roles and status are the product of or in conformity with reality itself. By invoking the supernatural/divine order—one could just as well appeal to nature, the created order—as its foundation, we accomplish several things that the maintenance of oppression requires. On the one hand, we establish a supra-human foundation that, by virtue of its superior power, compels our conformity and obedience. Human power can never win against divine omnipotence; "Our arms are too short to box with God." On the other hand, we guarantee the goodness and moral superiority of the existing social order.

As the review of *Jane Eyre* shows us, rearranging the social hierarchy is unthinkable if the ESP order expresses the will of God. Whatever status we have is just: it is the station that God intends for us; what is, and what ought to be. Given this understanding, ESP remodeling would be sinful rebellion against God. Even if we had the necessary power to readjust things, ESP remodeling would be blasphemous and therefore inappropriate. A similar conclusion would follow if we interpret ESP suffering and inequalities as divine punishment.

The aforementioned mechanisms of oppression should be examined from another perspective: its strategy to remove human choice, power, and authority as casually involved in society's superstructures. To use Peter Berger's distinction,[9] oppression locates traditional norms and institutions in *objective reality*—that which is external to the human mind and not created by our hands—not *objectivated reality*, that is, that which is external to the human mind that we did create. Oppression, thus, reduces the conflict between the haves and have-nots to a cosmic skirmish between the human and the supra-human. The theological paradigm in liberation theology, as we will see, relocates the fray, making it a struggle between human combatants.

Theocentric Theism and the Logic of Injustice

Selecting a viable foundation for the just society is no simple matter. If the point of departure is the reality of an unjust society, as it is for liberation theology, a functional concept of God must serve two masters. It must counteract the extant God-consciousness already enlisted by the oppressor to guard her/his "sacred order," and it must also provide a sturdy foundation for the "new sacred order." These dual concerns must be executed in a manner compatible with the inner logic of each. Further, it must accommodate a legitimating authority that does not replicate the original theology of injustice. At the same time, however, it must provide the minimal sanctity that any institution requires for its longevity. Getting a handle on this is simplified if we interpret it from the background of our discussion of oppression/quietism. Using this approach, we can grasp which pictures of the divine have merit and which are useless in light of the foregoing criteria.

To draw up liberation theology's "most eligible list" of God candidates requires that we treat two opposing images of the divine, which I term *theocentric theism* and *humanocentric theism*. The former identifies the God concept that is most commonly associated with the unjust society, the latter with the just community. The distinction between these competing pictures of the divine is clarified if we analyze how each specifies: (a) God's role and manner of operation in human history and (b) the status and value of human freedom relative to divine freedom.

Taken to its logical extremes, theocentric theism affirms God's controlling and overruling sovereignty in history; whether the same claim is advanced for the natural order is unimportant for our discussion. To borrow the metaphor of the theater: God is our playwright, director, producer, star, agent, and critic. The inner logic of this way of thinking, as the following citation shows, relegates the human to the role of spectator or cheerleader for the "perfect play."

> There is only one almighty being whom we call God. He is eternal, infinite, invisible, perfectly wise and just. He created all things.... Everything was made in accordance with his plan and is dictated by his will. Everything has a cause and a purpose, and nothing happens by chance or by luck. Man exists for God and not God for man, but men should pray to God who will consider their prayers in the enactment of his will.
>
> Cannot we believe that God so overrules man's actions that no matter how when or where he dies, he does not die a moment before God meant him to.... With the solitary exception of the act of sinful will, nothing is done in the world of which God is not the doer.... Suppose A willfully murders B. The act of sinful will on A's part is his free act and A alone is responsible. But he could not have murdered B unless God had willed it. He could have had no power at all against him except it had been given him from above.[10]

The import of this understanding of the divine for the unjust society is obvious: quietism is the outcome. Given this view of God's causal linkage to history, the eradication of oppression is aborted at the outset. The preconditions for ESP correction are the beliefs that what is, is not what ought to be; that what is could be otherwise—even the opposite—and that what is not yet is what ought to be.

The inner logic of theocentric theism affirms the opposite sentiment, and we are back where Jane Eyre's reviewer left us. Whatever our station, we are where we ought to be; and we cannot dare, nor should we hope, to tear down what God has carefully planned and constructed.

Humanocentric Theism: Antidote to Quietism

Given the inner logic of oppression, especially its maintenance code, its opponents must endorse theological constructs that are antithetical to theocentric theism. Room must be made for the exercise of human freedom and authority with regard to at least the substructures of history. Such is the inner logic of humanocentric theism. It affirms the radical freedom of the human, but within a *theistic* framework—hence its difference from humanism that assigns a similar freedom to the human.

Humanocentric theism, as the adjective suggests, elevates human freedom relative to the sphere of history; the human is given the status of co-determining power with God, at least up to the eschaton. It also affirms a view of divine sovereignty that extends human freedom to other areas that once were under the direct sway of the divine, thus refuting the hypothesis: "If God exists, man is nothing; if man exists. . ."[11] To avoid collapsing humanocentric theism into humanism, it is important to note that the human has the exalted status of co-determining power by virtue of God's gracious endowment. Moreover, the ground for this endowment is the self-limitation of God's overruling authority in human history.

One can easily cull examples of this picture of the divine from the liberation theologians. For my illustrations here, however, I prefer to draw upon theologians not identified as liberationists. In this way, I can correct some common misperceptions. One inaccurate interpretation restricts the scope and popularity of this position to those concerned only with a self-serving ESP agenda. A second misunderstanding collapses humanocentric theism into humanism because human freedom is accented in both. The following descriptions from William D. Cobb and Eliezer Berkovits correct both misconceptions.

Arguing for "man as moral creator," Cobb opts for a "moral universe in the making." For Cobb, the Judeo-Christian affirmation of man as created "in the image of God" means:

> Man was not intended to be simply another natural being but to be an active participant in and creator of the moral orders of the Universe. . . . If he allows [the external moral (and natural) orders] to rule him completely, then he is living "heteronomously" and . . . in direct contravention of the will of God for his creation. The will of God . . . does not consist of specific rules and goals for human beings to conform to and seek, but of an *intention* that men and women exercise their creative moral powers to construct a *human* universe of *moral* order confluent with yet transcendent of the *natural* universe of *physical* order. . . . Indeed we might say that God created man with the intention that

man should "make what *God* did not make" and what is more, that man should "make what God did not *think* to make" as a consequence of God's gracious self-limitation of his own power in the act of creating man . . . [God has limited his own power] for the sake of giving man "space" in which to be more than a "robot" or a "puppet" in a "stage play."[12]

Eliezer Berkovits advances a similar view as a central motif of Judeo-biblical faith.

> Man alone can create value; God is value. But if man alone is the creator of values . . . then we must have freedom of choice and freedom of decision. And his freedom must be respected by God himself. God cannot as a rule intervene whenever man's use of freedom displeases him. . . . If there is to be man, he must be allowed to make his choices in freedom.[13]

With these descriptions as background we can now summarize the value of humanocentric theism as an antidote for quietism and oppression. (1) It cuts off the theological and moral escape route commonly used by the oppressor. The oppressor can no longer point to anything but the human being as the sustaining force behind the unjust society. (2) Central to humanocentric theism is the belief that "God has no hands but our hands," that "all is in our hands." Until the oppressed accept this belief and, accordingly, see themselves as centers of power and their communities as collective sources of transforming power, it is doubtful that they will become active agents for their own liberation. Nor are they likely to assume responsibility for eradicating their oppression as long as they believe that God will miraculously intervene and release them from the oppressor's clutches. (3) Further, it effectively de-legitimates those unjust structures, already in place, that carry the "divine" stamp of approval. This de-sanctification, as we have noted, is a sine qua non for ESP change.

Humanocentric Theism: Problems and Implications

The concern of this chapter has been to show how a particular theological perspective would address the *question*. However, even if we grant absolute merit and accuracy to liberation theology's analysis, which I do not, a number of unresolved issues and nagging problems remain. I consider the following to be the most important for our discussion.

(1) If our purpose is to reform the unjust society *where nature and supernatural, i.e., ontological absolutes, have been its legitimating foundation*, we face an immediate dilemma that Peter Berger's[14] formula helps us define. Given that what humans have created, other humans can change, societies are loath to ground morality on human authority. The need to protect the moral code from whim and caprice recommends the strategy of the divine logo. However, as we have seen, this carries within it the germ of quietism and its potential

for oppression. Thus, the ESP reformer must deabsolutize the extant ESP order to make place for the new, the just social system. This de-sanctification of the divine bulwarks is almost always advanced in the name of the divine. The result of this is pregnant with implications for the *question*.

(2) The clash of absolute and counter-absolute, of God's commandment to conform and to transform, diminishes the authority of absolutes per se. Absolutes are seen as devices of legitimation and not solely as divine revelation. This relocates the issue so that the issue becomes the *authority* by which to legitimate the legitimating apparatus. The legitimator must be legitimated, and here we appear to be plunged into an infinite regress where ultimately the human being, as the measure, must function as moral creator; in sum, the position of humanocentric theism.

But this is not without its improbable consequences for the just society. Does the "God has no hands but our hands" philosophy, or the elevation of the human to co-determining power, mean that everything is permitted? The problem of nihilism confronts us here again. (I would add in passing that my analysis of the most dehumanizing instances in human history have as their explicit legitimation the logo of the absolute—nature or supernatural—not the principle of human freedom and authority that informs humanocentric theism.)

(3) Given the insights of humanocentric theism, we are also pushed to ask what it means to advance God, the transcendent, as the grounds for the just society? Does it mean more than the claim that the transcendent is both the ground for human freedom/autonomy to operate as moral creator and foundation of the world in which this freedom is exercised? Or does it mean that ultimate reality sponsors, and thus guarantees, the ultimate triumph of specific activities in human history? That is, once humanity is given the status of moral creator, does *ontological priority*—that is, the transcendent—still establish *moral priority*? It seems clear that the species of human freedom endorsed by humanocentric theism precludes, at the very least, any immediate movement from ontology to ethics, from the "is" to the "ought," without the intermediate operation of human evaluation.

(4) Humanocentric theism is not without its quietist dimension. This potential becomes visible when we note that history here becomes open-ended and multi-valued, capable of supporting either the just or the unjust society. Does not the inner logic of humanocentric theism remove God from anyone's side? If this is so, then an oppressed group, that is both powerless and a numerical minority, is susceptible to defeatism. David is reluctant to challenge Goliath unless he or she believes that God will tip the scales in her or his favor.

(5) The previous comment points to an unsettled question in humanocentric theism that bears upon its attractiveness as a counterstrategy to oppression. It also raises a larger issue, also unsettled, that bears upon its value as the foundation for the just society. Having argued for the self-limitation of the divine freedom to counter the unjust society, are we forced to the conclusion

that marked an early stage of Howard Burkle's theological evolution? "God," he argued, "cannot guarantee the ultimate triumph of the good.... The good may be forever blocked.... The creature retains a veto even though he had nothing to do with the determination that gave him birth."[15]

If this is so, does the just society have an *ontological* base or warrant that is superior to its rival? Are both equally "right" as far as reality is structured? If not, how is the rank order to be determined? If so, why make the supreme sacrifice to usher in the just society if its day in the sun is in doubt?

Notes

1. This is the shorthand expression for economic, social, and political.
2. *The Christian Manifesto* and *Whatever Happened to the Human Race?* Both works are in *The Complete Works of Francis A. Schaeffer: A Christian Worldview,* Vol. 5 (Westchester, IL: Crossway Books, 1982).
3. Humanism, for instance, would be excluded if this is answered affirmatively.
4. Cf. Schaeffer's analysis, for instance in *Whatever Happened to the Human Race?*, that only specific form of theism, i.e., his interpretation of Reformation Christianity, can be the foundation for the just society.
5. *Pensées* and *The Myth of Sisyphus*.
6. The transgenerational feature differentiates oppression from catastrophe which can also be enormous. Since, however, the catastrophic event does not visit the same group generation after generation, the factor of maldistribution is less acute.
7. *The Negro's God* (New York: Atheneum, 1969), 155.
8. M. A. Stoddard, *Quarterly Review*, No. 84 (December 1848): 173-4.
9. *The Sacred Canopy* (New York: Doubleday, 1969), 11-12.
10. Robert P. Green, *The Problem of Evil, Being an Attempt to Show that the Existence of Sin and Pain in the World is not Inconsistent with the Goodness and Power of God* (New York: MW Books, 1920).
11. *The Devil and the Good Lord* (New York: Vintage, 1962), 141.
12. "Morality in the Making: A New Look at Some Old Foundations," *The Christian Century* (January 1-8, 1975).
13. *Faith After the Holocaust* (New York: KTAV Publishing House, 1973), 105.
14. "The historically crucial part of religion in the process of legitimation is explicable in terms of the unique capacity of religion to 'locate' human phenomena within a cosmic frame of reference…The efficacy of religious legitimation can be brought home by asking a recipe question…If one imagines oneself as a fully aware founder of a society…how can the future of the institutional order be best ensured…? Let the institutional order be so interpreted as to hide, as much as possible, its constructed character. Let the people forget that this order was established by men and continues to be dependent upon the consent of men. Let them believe that in acting out the institutional programs that have been imposed upon them, they are but realizing the deepest aspirations of their own being and putting themselves in harmony with the fundamental order of the universe." *The Sacred Canopy*, 33.
15. *The Non-Existence of God* (New York: Herder & Herder, 1969), 212.

Part II

PHILOSOPHICAL THEOLOGY

Chapter 7

RECONCILIATION AND LIBERATION IN BLACK THEOLOGY

SOME IMPLICATIONS FOR RELIGIOUS EDUCATION

William R. Jones

I

Many have advanced the doctrine of reconciliation as the very marrow of biblical thought and Christian dogmatics. Perhaps the most famous representative of this viewpoint in recent times, Karl Barth speaks of reconciliation as "the centre of all Christian knowledge." As the prototype of God's activity and the heart of the Christian message, reconciliation has naturally been established as the raison d'être of the church; it has instinctively become the standard for the purpose of the church in society as well as its moral imperative.

One of the most interesting features of Black theology has been its response to the doctrine of reconciliation. Today, Black theologians are challenging established and time-honored interpretations—if not the centrality—of this theological pillar. Why this attack upon the alleged hub of Christian faith? Because of the actual and potential misuse of reconciliation as an instrument of oppression. As we shall see, reconciliation has been defined as the alpha and omega of Christian faith in an exclusive manner that negates the centrality of liberation as a theological, social, and moral concern. Black theologians have found it necessary to apply [to reconciliation] what James Cone concludes about the doctrine of God. "Black people cannot adhere to a view of God that will weaken their drive for liberation."[1]

To make the same point in another way. Reconciliation admits to several interpretations. Thus, making it central for Christian faith is always to elevate selected interpretations of reconciliation and confine competing viewpoints to theological limbo. What concerns Black theologians is the character of this selective process, for the particular choices appear to coincide more closely with the interests of Whitianity than Christianity.

Thus the concern of Black theologians in this area is to force a comprehensive reappraisal of the nature, status, and function of reconciliation, especially its implications for the definition of the church's moral life and social activity. Looked at from another perspective, their concern is to expose those elements of racism and oppression which seek respectability by donning the cloak of key Christian motifs such as reconciliation. Obviously, this appraisal has the most far-reaching consequences for religious education.

Our purpose in this short chapter is to outline some of the important corrections that Black theologians advocate for the doctrine of reconciliation. In this way, we hope to stimulate debate on a crucial issue and provide some tentative guidelines for the religious educator as he examines his responsibility for this sector of the Christian message.

II

The first tactic of Black theologians has been to challenge the centrality of reconciliation, at least as previously interpreted. A quick survey of the card catalog at any seminary will spotlight the nature and extent of the problem that their protest attacks. One finds numerous titles where "reconciliation" appears prominently, especially when the essence of Christian faith is discussed. By contrast, "liberation" is almost invisible. Indeed, the recent works by Black theologians comprise the bulk of the entries where the heading "liberation" is a focal term.

It is not difficult to understand why Black theologians are concerned about the relative visibility of reconciliation and liberation. If reconciliation occupies and dominates the center stage, liberation is treated only as a faint voice unneeded off-stage—unless liberation is seen as part and parcel of reconciliation itself. But it is precisely this emphasis that Black theologians have not found. Is it accidental, for instance, that though Barth devotes several volumes to the topic, doctrine of reconciliation, one does not find corresponding volumes for the doctrine of liberation in his monumental corpus?

Faced with the problem of the exclusive centrality of reconciliation and the pointed omission of liberation, Black theologians have advocated two different corrections. On the one hand, the rank of reconciliation is adjusted downward by promoting the theme of liberation to co-equal status. J. Deotis Roberts, for instance, argues that two concepts, reconciliation and liberation, are required to capture the essence of authentic Christian faith and action. Both are "proper goals for the Christian church in general and the black church in particular."[2]

This "both-and" approach stands over against the more radical remedy of Cone. If we have read him correctly, he seeks to assign exclusive centrality to liberation. "Christian theology," he contends, "is a theology of liberation."[3] Based on this equation, one is not surprised to find the term, reconciliation, conspicuously absent from his various definitions of theology. The same emphasis upon liberation informs his analysis of revelation. "Revelation is God's self-disclosure to man in a *situation* of liberation ... God's revelation means liberation, an emancipation from the political, economic, and social structures of the society. This is the essence of the biblical revelation."[4]

However, Roberts finds Cone's peremptory model of liberation to be one-sided and unbalanced, hence his purpose of correcting Cone's alleged narrow interpretation. Simply juxtaposing the title of Roberts's work, *Liberation and*

Reconciliation: A Black Theology, and Cone's second volume, *A Black Theology of Liberation*, pinpoints his amendment of Cone's credo. But if Roberts believes that Cone has displayed only one side of the Christian coin, the liberation face, others, he concludes, have erred by negating the liberation side. "The liberating Christ," he argues, "is also the reconciling Christ; the one who liberates reconciles, and the one who reconciles liberates."[5] When this aspect of Roberts's position is illuminated, it is clear that he, like Cone, voices the same criticism: recent theology has given only niggardly attention to the doctrine of liberation and thus has distorted the biblical message itself. Indeed, every Black theologian expresses the identical protest.

We have suggested that Roberts's approach gives co-equal status to reconciliation and liberation. From another perspective, however, he appears to assign a certain priority to the theme of liberation. This point becomes obvious when we consider this position in the context of other views of reconciliation.

It is not hard to uncover spokesmen who allow that reconciliation does not necessarily demand a radical change in social, economic, and political structures, for example, Eph. 6:5-9, Col. 3:21-4, I Cor. 7:20-24, 12:13. It is allowed that reconciliation can occur even in the framework of oppression and slavery. In this framework, liberation from oppression and slavery is seen, if at all, as a *post-reconciliation event* or as an eschatological occurrence.

Roberts, however, reverses this arrangement by making reconciliation a *post-liberation event*. "Reconciliation in the church must be beyond liberation from all types of bondage, and most important, it must be a reconciliation among equals."[6] Special attention must be given to the latter condition: the creation of a situation of co-equality of freedom and power among the parties to be reconciled. What Roberts is, in fact, doing here is to make liberation a *necessary condition* for the occurrence of reconciliation. The consequence of this shift for the life of the church is substantial. It clearly suggests that as long as there is a gross imbalance of power between Blacks and whites, rich and poor, and so on, authentic reconciliation is not possible. Moreover, before the church can legitimately be about the task of reconciliation, it must first effect the liberation of those to be reconciled. If not this, then at least its strategy of reconciliation must be capable of effecting liberation and vice versa.

Another corollary flows from the post-liberation status of reconciliation. The Black quest for *liberation* must be seen as integral to its role of reconciliation. In so far as Blacks aim at liberation, their actions help to produce the co-equality of freedom which is the necessary condition for reconciliation. Unless we relate liberation and reconciliation in this manner, liberation will be regarded as less than reconciliation. And this step is certain to follow: the accusation that the Black drive for liberation is sub-Christian.

For the sake of accuracy, one final observation must be made to explain the full scope of the Black theologians' correction. The observant reader, no doubt, will say that the concept of liberation is, in fact, present in many more doctrines of reconciliation than our analysis seems to allow. Donald G. Miller's article, "God Reconciles and Makes Free,"[7] is a concrete case in point. There is no question that reconciliation and liberation are correlative in Miller's interpretation. Yet there is a singular difference between his analysis and that of the Black theologians. Liberation for him does not necessarily entail socio-political and economic emancipation. Emphasizing that political liberation is *not* what is meant by Christian freedom in the New Testament, he proceeds to give the following account:

> At the time of Jesus' birth, the righteous remnant were "looking for the liberation of Jerusalem" (Luke 2:38). At the time of his death, his disciples had been hoping that he was the man to liberate Israel. But neither Jerusalem nor Israel was "liberated" from Rome, they were destroyed by her.[8]

The crucial implication Miller draws is this: release from bondage and oppression means something quite different from being set free from the chains of poverty, racism, and so on. Rather,

> the bondage from which Israel was to be released is variously referred to as "the commands of sin" (Rom. 6:22): "the law of sin and death" (Rom. 8:2). . . . It is unnecessary to present evidence that sin is the prideful human disobedience to the will of God, which sets the human will at the center of reality. It is this from which man must be delivered.

We will criticize this interpretation later. Our only purpose here is to accent the concern of Black theologians to make social, political, and economic liberation correlative with reconciliation. And this way of relating the two does appear to be a new slant in American theology.

In sum, from the perspective of Black theology, reconciliation can be central for Christian dogmatics—and by implication of religious education—only if liberation is implicit in it, and only if liberation means the deliverance from the bondage of racism and its attendant evils.

III

Up to this point, we have been discussing the effort of Black theologians to make liberation normative for the message and the work of the church. Our concern now is to identify some of the special issues which arise as a consequence of this new arrangement of the theological furniture. In particular we will focus upon those interpretations of reconciliation and cognate categories, for example, sin, which become questionable in light of this revision.

The first general consequence is to force a discussion of reconciliation in a quite different theological context.[9] Johann Baptist Metz has argued for "the development of theology as eschatology." Eschatology, he contends, must be "the determining factor in all theological statements,"[10] with each dogmatic position and category being evaluated in terms of its eschatological quotient.

For a theology of liberation and liberation-reconciliation, we would insist, however, upon the development of theology as *theodicy*. Theodicy must assume the rank that Metz assigns to eschatology. By making oppression and its elimination the point of departure for theological reflection, we are in the debate that Moltmann describes in the following passage:

> Since we experience reality as history and no longer as cosmos, the fundamental theodicy question is still with us and is more pressing than before. For us, it has no longer only its old naturalistic form, as in the earthquake of Lisbon in 1755. It appears today in a political form, as in the question of Auschwitz. . . . We ask the question . . . Whether God is? on grounds of history and its crimes.[11]

Albert Camus has put the issue even more pointedly when he questions if the initial intent of the cross-resurrection was, in fact, reconciliation.

> For as long as the Western world has been Christian, the Gospels have been the interpreter between heaven and earth. Each time a solitary cry of rebellion against human suffering was uttered, the answer came in the form of even more terrible suffering. In that Christ had suffered, and had suffered voluntarily, suffering was no longer unjust. . . . From this point of view, the New Testament can be considered as an attempt to answer in advance every (rebel) by painting the figure of God in softer colors. . . . Christ came to solve two major problems, evil and death. . . . His solution consisted, first, in experiencing them. The man-God suffers, too—with patience. Evil and death can no longer be entirely imputed to Him since he too suffers and dies.[12]

To speak of the cross, in the Christian tradition, has been to speak of man's redemption, salvation, and deliverance. But the fact of oppression after the occurrence of the normative event of reconciliation raises special questions. Camus is asking if liberation was, in fact, its original intent? An allied question also surfaces here about the determined universality of reconciliation.

Camus's analysis points to another crucial context within which reconciliation must be analyzed. Camus concludes that the cross-resurrection intended to foster a spirit of quietism in the breast of man. Its purpose is to make man embrace his suffering without rebellion and rancor because God himself has also suffered.

However, a theology of liberation must eschew the prevalent forms of quietism and the theological positions, for example, specific interpretations of reconciliation, which are its ground. To explain this point, however, requires an initial discussion of the meaning of quietism.

The equation of quietism and "doing nothing" is obviously unacceptable, for doing nothing is always reducible to doing something, a concrete activity. We come closer to the nucleus of quietism if we see it as a choice and/or execution of a certain type of action. It is to choose and act in a manner that conserves and preserves what is: ultimately, it is a form of conformity. One can regard it as well as the refusal to engage in corrective activity, particularly as regards basic institutional structures and cultural practices. Thus the fundamental distinction between quietism and its opposite is not between activity and doing nothing, but rather conformity as opposed to rebellion relative to the status quo.

To continue our analysis, we would also urge that quietism appears to be the consequence of a particular set of conclusions about the nature of man and his situation relative to ultimate reality. Quietism results, for instance, when corrective actions are deemed unnecessary. We reach this conclusion when we believe that the ideal is already present or in the process of being realized. Action is also unnecessary if we believe that those corrections that will produce the ideal have already begun or will be undertaken by some other agent, for example, God.

One is also pushed toward quietism if he believes that corrective action is impossible because it will not be successful. One does not knowingly defy the law of gravity unless suicide is his aim. Accordingly, specific measures are labeled impossible because apparently invincible forces confront man, and correction involves modifying some ultimate structure of reality or human nature. Finally, quietism is the usual response to believing that corrective action is inappropriate. If I think that the intended remedy will produce even more undesirable consequences, I am disinclined to execute it.

IV

With the foregoing background we can now identify some specific interpretations of reconciliation which seem to involve one or more of the aforementioned forms of quietism.

The first interpretation is a summary of our discussion in Section II. Any view of reconciliation which omits liberation or reduces social, economic, and political liberation to the second rank will collapse into some form of quietism relative to the latter.

We would also detect the specter of quietism in those views that emphasize reconciliation as God's exclusive work. We have in mind, for instance, the view of James Denney where reconciliation is "a finished work of Christ . . . which has been achieved independently of us." Hence, reconciliation is an act of God "the effects of which men may receive but in which historic man did not participate and to which he contributed nothing."[13]

The implications of this view for a theology of liberation become clear in Miller's analysis. Since social and economic liberation was not central in the definitive event of reconciliation, "the finished work of Christ"—in fact, according to Miller, it was absent—the betterment of the oppressed is a secondary concern of the church.

> The world's call to the Church to join in its emancipation may, in the form in which it now comes, be the call Jesus refused in his temptation and the call of the reviling thief on the cross, whose demand that Jesus solve his problem at the superficial level of release from political bondage was answered with silence. The Church may also have to resist those within her fellowship who seem to deal with the problems of freedom in terms that do not plumb the depths of the New Testament faith.[14]

To make the same point from another perspective, an extreme objectivist or theocentric interpretation of reconciliation is vulnerable to quietism in another place. To stress the finished character of reconciliation in the death and resurrection of Jesus tends to confine the locus of God's reconciling-liberating activity to that specific point. The consequence, it appears, is to exclude the cooperative activity of God and man that figures most prominently in a theology of the politics of God. In fact, the politics of God is an essential feature of each contemporary theology of liberation, determining where God is at work in human history and adding our human efforts to his. Obviously, an emphasis on the finished character of reconciliation leaves little room or fertile soil for the emergence of the politics of God approach. Accordingly, an essential core of a theology of liberation is snipped away.

When we recognize that every doctrine of reconciliation also presupposes a specific interpretation of sin, it is useful to analyze the letter for its possible quietistic elements. Is it not the case that identifying X as sin dictates that the church and God should be actively engaged in eliminating it? And to identify the quintessential sin is to designate where the supreme energies of the church must be focused. Accordingly, any position which does not make socio-political and economic oppression central to the definition of sin will ultimately fall back into a position of "benign neglect." To attack such oppression is to approach the problem, as Miller argues, "at the superficial level." And thus, the church is persuaded to channel its primary energies and resources to attack the real human problem.

Given Miller's framework, we are not surprised to hear him argue that the elimination of oppression will in no way diminish the problem of sin. "To take power from some . . . so that others may have it but to leave those others outside the sphere of Christ's master of the demonic in all power, is a reshuffling which may exchange the personnel of ruler and ruled but will only perpetuate a corrupt situation in other hands." Corrective action in this context is inappropriate because it will in no way rectify the nuclear sin. Indeed, his claim that "men are bound by an enslavement they can never conquer" strongly suggests the futility of human amelioration of oppression. Nor should we overlook that his analysis of sin places both oppressor and oppressed on the same level; both are equally guilty. Where in this analysis do we find any theological or moral leverage for the oppressor to renounce his oppression?

We must single out another interpretation for special treatment though it could easily be analyzed under the previous rubric of quietism. The crucial issue here is the means of reconciliation. It is unnecessary to repeat here the well-known argument that certain techniques commonly connected with liberation—confrontation, conflict, violence—are somehow incompatible with the nature and method of reconciliation. Thus the activism, if not perhaps the success, of the church's social ministry is blunted by accentuating a single model of reconciliation, a model which negates formulae some regard as not only appropriate but necessary for liberation.

Dieter Hessel has correctly attacked this strategy; we will do well to reflect upon some of the primary insights of his work *Reconciliation and Conflict*. "We cannot assume," he concludes, "that we already know what reconciliation is and what it requires behaviourly." The crucial consequence of this principle, in our view, is to press for a contextual analysis of the means of reconciliation in a manner parallel to the way we define self-defense.

Moreover, he rightly points to the different and contrasting types of reconciling activity of Jesus himself, noting that Jesus's "complete obedience led him into conflict with his own people." That is to say, God's act of reconciliation in Christ was, itself, a source of conflict. In sum, conflict in the church and the society is not to be avoided on the presupposition of a single model of reconciliation. Rather, we must conclude that "reconciliation embraces conflict. It leads to and through conflict."[15]

A special warning must also be directed against a particular Pauline passage which is often invoked as a model for the character and aim of reconciliation. In Galatians 3:28, we hear that there is neither Jew nor Greek, neither male nor female, neither bond nor free, but all are one in Christ. This passage is often interpreted in a manner that is tantamount to cultural genocide for Blacks. This deeper unity in Christ invariably has the coloration and lifestyle of the white church. John Leith rightly warns us that "the text does not say that racial, sexual, or class differences are erased." The oneness we affirm in Christ cannot legitimately require the annihilation of Blackness in the process of reconciliation. Reconciliation should not collapse into assimilation.

V

One final issue falls outside the scope of our chapter, but because of its importance for religious education, we will simply mention it here. Paulo Freire, rightly we think, enunciates the principle; the method is the message. Arguing that no educational process—and this applies as well to religious education—is economically, politically, and socially neutral, he isolates certain pedagogical approaches which are constitutionally oppressive. What he terms the "banking" concept of education is the prototype that the oppressor normalizes to guarantee the continued oppression of the oppressed. Their liberation, consequently, requires a new pedagogical model.

It appears to us that too much of religious education can be classified as "banking education," with the obvious disastrous consequences for a theology of liberation. Hence our conclusion: religious education must reappraise its content, for example, vis-à-vis reconciliation, and its method, if it desires to be part of the solution rather than the cause of oppression.

Notes

1 James H. Cone, *A Black Theology of Liberation* (Philadelphia: Lippincott, 1970), 136.
2 J. Deotis Roberts, *Liberation and Reconciliation: A Black Theology* (Louisville: Westminster, 1971), 70.

3 Cone, *A Black Theology of Liberation*, 17.
4 Ibid., 91.
5 Roberts, *Liberation and Reconciliation*, 48.
6 Ibid., 69–70.
7 *Reconciliation in Today's World*, ed. Allen O. Miller (Grand Rapids: Eerdmans, 1969).
8 Ibid., 25.
9 There is insufficient space to present the complex of conclusions which lie behind this claim. The issue is treated in detail in a forthcoming work, *Is God a White Racist* (New York: Doubleday, 1973).
10 *New Theology No. 5*, eds. M. Marty and D. Peerman (New York: Macmillan, 1968), 135.
11 Jurgen Moltmann, *Religion, Revolution and the Future* (New York: Charles Scribner, 1969), 205.
12 Albert Camus, *The Rebel* (New York: Vintage, 1956), 32–3.
13 Miller, *Reconciliation in Today's World*, 17.
14 Ibid., 22.
15 Hessel, *Reconciliation and Conflict* (Louisville: Westminster, 1969), 23.

Chapter 8

Theodicy

The Controlling Category for Black Theology

William R. Jones

Johann Baptist Metz has argued that "the demands of Christian faith require the development of theology as eschatology . . . Christians," he concludes, "must therefore develop eschatology in all parts of their understanding of faith. It must not be reduced to a part Christian theology but must be understood radically: as the determining factor in all theological statements."[1] Major Jones articulates a similar view when he approvingly cites Harvey Cox's assertion that "the only future that theology has . . . is to become the theology of the future."[2]

I contend, however, that Black theology requires an altogether different arrangement of the theological furniture. For it, theology must assume the first rank that Metz emphatically assigns to eschatology. Christology and eschatology must be appraised with the theodicy issue always in the background; Black theology, in short, must be an extended theodicy.

This brings us to the statement of the major thesis I wish to defend today: Theodicy is the controlling category for Black theology. I will utilize two arguments to establish the theological prominence of theodicy. First, theodicy is pivotal because Black theology defines itself as a theology of liberation. Here I will argue that the peculiar requirements of a theology of liberation ordain theodicy's sovereign status. Specifically, I will establish that theodicy is the nucleus of quietism, and quietism, in turn, is the vital nerve of oppression. Thus, to escape the fatal clutches of quietism, the theologian of liberation cannot avoid the enterprise of theodicy.

The second plank of the argument for the centrality of theodicy focuses upon the special character of Black suffering, or what I prefer to term *ethnic suffering*. Black suffering is maldistributed, enormous, and non-catastrophic. Its unique quality forces us to ask: Is God a white racist? And to raise this question, in the final analysis, is to introduce the theodicy question.

A former colleague directed the following criticism against my proposed treatment of Black theology and theodicy. He challenged my concern to make theodicy central on the grounds that I am forcing the formal question of theodicy. That is to say, I am comprehending Black theology in the context of traditional Western religious philosophy and its conventional problems and categories. To put the challenge baldly, I do not sufficiently honor the integrity of the Black perspective.

This is an eminently fair challenge, and the bulk of my talk involves an implicit reply to it. I would argue that I am not elevating theodicy to a rank it does not already possess. As I will show in a moment, theodicy is already the dominant category for Black theology. It is dominant because the Black theologians themselves have adopted specific theological orientations, for example, a theology of liberation. In my view, consequently, I am not establishing the centrality of theodicy; instead, I simply call attention to the fact of its already established but unacknowledged preeminence.

The Theological Preeminence of Theodicy

In support of this claim, I would advance this observation. Each individual has a functional theodicy. Look closely, and you will uncover an aspect of his worldview which treats the issue of human suffering and relates it to his ontological and epistemological presuppositions. Examine his actions, and you will soon discover that he makes a fundamental judgment about the quality of, at least, particular instances of suffering. It is unmistakable that we either endure and embrace the suffering we encounter or seek to annihilate it or reduce its sway. Whatever stand we take relative to suffering presupposes an implicit conclusion about the positive, negative, or neutral structure of suffering. Our response to suffering—acceptance or rebellion—also reflects a prior conclusion about the ontological status of suffering: Is it eliminable or an inevitable feature of the human condition?

Additionally, it appears to be the case that each individual acts on the basis of an essential conclusion about the source or cause of suffering. Indeed, it would be strange if mankind as a whole did not reflect upon suffering and if theodicy were not an inescapable concern, precisely because suffering seems to be an inevitable part of the life of each of us.

If this analysis is correct, then the mystery to be explained is why the centrality of theodicy is not an accepted theological axiom. No doubt, the astute members of the audience have noticed that the necessity to demonstrate the centrality of theodicy seems to contradict my previous claim for its unfailing presence. Thus, I am forced to account for the unexplained obscurity of an alleged manifest reality.

We fail to discern the centrality of theodicy because we define the category too narrowly. The customary definition of theodicy places too much weight upon the etymology of the term. Theos—God and dike—justice, for too many, comprise the total meaning of theodicy. An exclusively etymological analysis, unfortunately, collapses theodicy into apologetics and thus illuminates only one aspect of the theodicy enterprise. Theodicy is more than the attempt to exonerate and justify God's ways and works in the light of apparently contrary evidence. There is, for instance, another basic dimension to theodicy, the explanatory. In point of fact, it can easily be argued that the apologetic is at the same time an implicit analysis of the cause or origin of suffering.

Theodicy is also defined too narrowly if we regard it as an abstract and theoretical exercise executed only by professional theologians and philosophers and of interest only to them. Leszek Kolakowski states the point well when he observes that "theodicy belongs to the field of popular philosophy of everyday life. Although it sometimes takes the form of historiosophical abstractions, its acceptance or rejection is expressed in common attitudes, in that semiconscious practical philosophy that influences human behavior."[3]

To put the point rhetorically: What is the suffering-servant theme but a miniature theodicy? Are you willing to say that just because our Black forefathers did not discuss the hypostatic union, they did not advance a Christological position? Is not Du Bois raising the essential theodicy question when he asks: "O God? How long shall the mounting flood of innocent blood roar in thine ears . . . ? We raise our shackled hands and charge Thee, God, by the bones of our stolen fathers, by the tears of our dead mothers, by the very blood of Thy crucified Christ: What meaneth this? Tell us the plan; give us the sign!"[4]

Indeed, it does not do violence to the total salvation history of Christian faith to see it as a pattern of theodicy as well as soteriology. There is insufficient time to establish this point, fully, but I think it can be argued that soteriology is actually grounded in theodicy. More precisely, theodicy is logically prior to soteriology. To talk about the *saving* work of God is to presuppose a conclusion about his *benevolence*. It is to affirm that God is good and not demonic; it is to assert that the divine activity is actually for the well-being and not the detriment of man. But it must be noted that this alleged benevolence is asserted in light or spite of the prior "evil" which necessitates God's saving work in the first place. The prior "evil" which is the precondition for soteriology constitutes possible counter-evidence against God's benevolence. Accordingly, its counter-evidential quality must be defused before one can affirm God's soteriological, that is, benevolent, activity. Salvation, in short, is meaningless without the prior affirmation of God's essential benevolence.

The supremacy of theodicy and its inescapability for the Black theologian also follow from a far quality of suffering. Suffering is multi-evidential; it harmonizes equally well with opposing interpretations. The biblical account makes it clear that suffering can be an aspect of God's grace (the suffering servant) or God's curse (suffering as deserved punishment), or neither divine favor nor disfavor. But once we acknowledge that suffering is multi-evidential, we are faced with this crucial and difficult question: How do we determine in which class a given instance of suffering belongs? How do we differentiate between that suffering which is an expression of God's grace and that which indicates his judgment? How do we know if the sufferer is an agent of God's salvation or a sinner receiving his deserved punishment? In short, given the multi-evidentiality of suffering, one must formulate a criteriology for separating negative and positive suffering, and this task, obviously, is at the center of the enterprise of theodicy.

Oppression, Quietism, and Theodicy

If the position I am advancing is to be secure from the challenge of not honoring the Black perspective, it is still necessary to establish the centrality of theodicy for

Black theology without importing categories alien to a Black perspective and Black needs. The surest way to accomplish this is by way of internal criticism: to begin with Black theology's own statement of purpose and show that it presupposes the centrality of theodicy. This analysis, however, must be preceded by some general observations about oppression, suffering, and theodicy.

Oppression, I contend, is reducible to a form of suffering. If one dichotomizes between negative and positive suffering, oppression is a sub-class of negative suffering. It comprises a suffering that is detrimental or irrelevant to one's highest good.

To assign a positive quality to suffering, for instance, in vicarious suffering, dictates that we endure or embrace it; to define it as negative motivates us to crush it. By definition, the theologian of liberation is committed to exterminating oppression, and this commitment obliges him to eliminate that suffering that is the core of oppression. But to accomplish this, he must provide a conceptual framework that defines that suffering as negative, which desanctifies it, and demonstrates that it is not God's will and has no merit for one's salvation. In sum, he must engage in the task of theodicy if he is to accomplish his task.

We can reach the same conclusion from another side. The worldview of oppression presupposes specific theodicies that legitimate and justify the suffering that is at the heart of oppression. The *Weltanschauung* of oppression advances a theodicy that sponsors quietism, such as a theodicy based on a "pie-in-the-sky" eschatology. Thus, the theologian of liberation, whether he wants to or not, must engage in theodicy if only to subvert those treatments of suffering which are conceptual props for oppression.

Perhaps a closer examination of quietism will clarify the point. We misunderstand the nature of quietism if we define it as "doing nothing." Is it not true that doing nothing is always reducible to doing something, that is, a concrete activity? We come closer to the heart of quietism if we perceive it as the choice to act in a way that conserves or preserves what is. The quietist refuses to engage in corrective activity, particularly where basic institutional structures and cultural practices are involved. Quietism, ultimately, is a form of conformity. Thus, the fundamental distinction between quietism and its opposite is not that between activity and doing nothing, but conformity as opposed to rebellion relative to the status quo. Quietism also appears to be the consequence of a particular set of conclusions about the nature of man and his situation relative to ultimate reality. Quietism results, for instance, when corrective actions are deemed unnecessary. We reach this conclusion when we believe that the ideal is already present or in the process of being realized. Ameliorative action is also unnecessary if we believe that those corrections which will produce the ideal will be undertaken by some other agent, such as God.

One is also pushed toward quietism if he believes that corrective action is impossible in the sense that it will not be successful. Specific actions are labeled impossible because man confronts apparently invincible forces or because correction involves modifying some ultimate structure of reality or human nature. Note the quietist implications in the maxim: You can't change human nature! Finally, quietism is the usual response to the belief that corrective activity is inappropriate. If I think that the intended remedy will produce even more undesirable consequences, I am disinclined to execute it.

Given this understanding of quietism, the theologian of liberation must show, for instance, that the oppression-suffering he seeks to eliminate can, in fact, be exterminated or lessened. He must demonstrate that it is not sanctioned by God, supported by nature, or the consequence of human nature; nor is it vital for one's *summum bonum*. Further, he must persuade us that it is appropriate to initiate its extermination. In all these ways, he must reach specific conclusions about the value and ontological status of suffering, and these inevitably carry us into the province of theodicy.

Let us consider the issue of theodicy and quietism from another side, and here I wish to draw upon an intriguing question that Albert Camus raises in The Plague. He asks: "Is it illogical for a priest to call a doctor?" This question expresses the agonizing dilemma faced by each Christian when he tries to justify ameliorating his own suffering or that of his neighbor. The dilemma is heightened when we comprehend the following argument that lies between the lines of Camus's novel.

On the basis of the biblical record, it is established that man sometimes suffers because he has sinned; suffering in some instances is divine punishment for prior sins. Accordingly, for any given suffering, we must grant the possibility that it is deserved punishment. But if it is divine punishment and deserved, then we must accept and endure it without a dodge. Otherwise, the initial sin which originated the punishment is compounded; one would now be guilty of the additional offense of disobedience, of imposing one's own will for God's. But if it is divine punishment, then it is inappropriate to attack it, hence the consequences of quietism.

In the light of this analysis, the theologian of liberation must show that the "oppression" he criticizes and seeks to eliminate is not deserved punishment; he must necessarily refute the theodicy of divine punishment. A similar case can easily be made for other traditional theodicies with a high quietist component.

Theodicy and Divine Racism

Thus far, I have argued that the essence of a theology of liberation makes theodicy the controlling category for Black theology. I now wish to demonstrate that the Black theologian cannot avoid the issue of divine racism, and this too establishes the theological preeminence of theodicy—at least for Black theology. Because of the nature of suffering in general and Black suffering in particular, the Black theologian must address the question: Is God a white racist?

It has already been stated that suffering is multi-evidential; it can express a relation of favor or disfavor between man and ultimate reality. Consequently, in the face of suffering, whatever its character may be, we must grant the possibility that the relation of divine disfavor obtains, and divine disfavor, in the context of Black theology, is tantamount to divine racism.

The peculiar quality of Black suffering points to the same possibility. Black or ethnic suffering is characterized by three essential features: it is maldistributed, enormous, and non-catastrophic. By accenting the ethnic factor, I wish to call attention to a suffering that is maldistributed; it is not spread more or less randomly and equally over the total human race. Rather, a double portion of suffering is concentrated in a particular ethnic group.

A second feature of Black suffering is its enormity, and here I refer to several things. There is the factor of numbers, that is the number of suffering Blacks in relation to the total number of Blacks. Enormity also designates suffering unto death or that oppression which reduces life expectancy and frustrates self-realization. The importance of this factor is that it effectively eliminates specific theodicies with a long ancestry in the Christian tradition and thereby narrows the possible options for the Black theologian. Suffering unto death, for instance, negates any pedagogical interpretation of suffering, for example, we learn from a burn to avoid fire. This explanation of suffering, obviously, makes little sense if the learning process destroys the learner.

The final feature is the non-catastrophic aspect of Black suffering. Ethnic suffering does not strike quickly and then leave after a short and terrible siege. Rather, it strikes not only the father but the son and the grandson; it is, in fine, transgenerational.

When one connects these features of ethnic suffering, one is not tempted to account for their presence on the grounds of indifferent laws of nature. Instead, one is more inclined to explain their causal nexus in terms of purpose and, consequently, person. One is tempted to ask: Is God a white racist?

I am commanded to pose this question, in part, as a consequence of trying to relate some central biblical themes to the issue of ethnic suffering. The principle that God is the sum of his acts is, for me, a central biblical motif. We know who God is by what he has done and is doing. When we unpack the essentials of this principle, several illuminating points emerge. First, one's character is the sum of one's acts. To speak of God as loving or honest is always to refer to a complex of loving, honest acts. The principle thus places what amounts to exclusive weight upon the individual's activity with a corresponding devaluation of one's motive. In fact, in the context of this principle, a motive is actually an inference from the real acts of the individual. To assign a motive, for example, God's desire to liberate the oppressed commits one to substantiate it by reference to God's actual practice. This principle negates any effort to confirm a person's character which is contrary to or discontinuous with the veritable acts of the person at issue.

The principle that X is the sum of his acts also places a premium upon the present and past acts of an individual. An appeal cannot be made to anticipated or future acts as determinative for one's present character. Whatever motive or character is assigned to God relative to Blacks must be based on his past and/or present acts. Further, one is not permitted to speak of a motive or character which is different from God's actual performance relative to Blacks.

An eschatologically grounded theodicy is obviously problematical in this context. This becomes clear when we consider the following theological formula. The principle that God is the sum of his acts decrees that we must move from

(a) the actual acts of God in the past and/or present to (b) conclusions about his character and mode of activity. But in the context of this principle, (b) is equivalent to (a), and (a) is thus the primary basis for speaking of (c) God's future activity. Consequently, (a) is determinative for (c). What is ruled out—and this is the crucial point for the argument—is to make (c) determinative for either (a) or (b). This conclusion seems inevitable unless one argues for God's radical conversion.

This principle also entails a crucial methodological consequence for Black theology. The Black theologian must draw conclusions about who God is on the basis of what he has done and/or is doing for Black people. The exodus from Egypt may refute the charge of divine anti-Semitism, but it is irrelevant to the charge of divine racism. If we accent what is central to the Black past—slavery and oppression—the Black theologian cannot presuppose God's intrinsic benevolence for all mankind. Black theology cannot proceed as if the goodness of God for all mankind were a theological axiom. God's benevolence for Blacks can be affirmed, if at all, only on the grounds of his actual benevolent acts for Blacks.

It is my contention that the peculiarities of Black suffering make the question of divine racism imperative; I do not conclude that an inspection of Black suffering provides the answer.

Not all has been said on the matter of eschatology and theodicy. It appears that Black religionists beg the question in their appeal to the future. Believing that the plight of Blacks is unjust, and that God is benevolent and just, they must necessarily look forward to the future for the actualization of Black liberation and the manifestation of God's justice and might. But does not the special character of Black suffering call into question the very presupposition that makes the eschatological orientation theologically feasible: God's goodness relative to Blacks? The assertion of God's benevolence, at least for the Black theologian, must be a conclusion to be substantiated rather than a prejudgment that he brings to his analysis.

It is interesting to note John Mbiti's description of the African concept of time, which also denies normative and controlling status to the future. Indeed, when I reflect upon this account, I am forced to conclude that Black religion would be better served if it returned to the worldview of its African ancestors and denounced that of the slaveholder.

> Time is . . . simply a composition of events that has occurred, those which are taking place now, and those which will immediately occur. What has not taken place, or what is unlikely to occur in the immediate future, has no temporal meaning—it belongs to the reality of "no-time."
>
> From this basic attitude to time . . . the most significant factor is that time is considered a two-dimensional phenomenon: with a long past and a dynamic present. The "future" as we know it in the linear concept of time is virtually non-existent. The future is virtually absent because events that lie in the future have not been realized and cannot, therefore, constitute time that otherwise must be experienced. It is, therefore, what has taken place or will shortly occur that matters much more than what is yet to be.[5]

This concept of time must inform the Black theologian's analysis of the divine activity; otherwise, he fails to honor the priority of the Black perspective that he acknowledges.

Theodicy: Some Biblical Insights

The biblical account of suffering throws considerable light on the issue of Black suffering and theodicy. It goes without saying that the biblical perspective supports the conclusion that suffering is multi-evidential. But do the biblical writers provide a criteriology for differentiating between that suffering which is divine favor and that which is divine disfavor? Obviously, the fact of suffering itself is not sufficient to decide the case. Both the recipient of divine grace and divine punishment can suffer. Nor does it appear that the character of the suffering, such as its severity, permits us to remove one alternative in favor of the other.

The biblical treatment of suffering, ESP the suffering-servant theme, provides this possible hint: a radical shift in the status of the sufferer is evidence that his suffering is not divine punishment. This shift comprises something akin to the principle, "from last to first," and in this sense can be designated as the *exaltation* event. In the context of oppression, the exaltation event would be labeled the liberation event, for example, the exodus.

Thus, to index Blacks as the suffering servant, to affirm that they are the object of God's favor, to demonstrate that their suffering is not deserved punishment, it is necessary in each instance to identify the definitive exaltation-liberation event(s) for Blacks. The point must also be underscored that the suffering servant is claimed to be innocent; his suffering is not deserved punishment. But it is the exaltation event which substantiates the sufferer's innocence. Prior to the exaltation event it is not possible to differentiate between the suffering servant and the sinner encountering deserved punishment.

This emphasis upon the exaltation event is not confined to the suffering-servant model. The cross (humiliation) is followed by the resurrection (exaltation). The suffering of Job demands restitution; he must be vindicated if the interpretation of the prologue—he is being tested by God—is to be distinguished from deserved punishment. Or consider Jeremiah's heart-rending question: "Why is my pain perpetual, and my wound incurable?"[6] Because the suffering is not replaced by its opposite, that the suffering is unrelieved triggers the thought of the loss of God's favor. And does not this same view lie behind Jesus's own plaintive cry from the cross, "My God, my God, why hast though forsaken me?"

Toward a Black Theodicy

I hope it is now clear that Black theology cannot develop and thrive without giving its concerted and focused attention to the theodicy question. I trust that this limited effort will help to initiate that necessary debate and hasten the formulation of a viable theodicy for Black theology—something which, in my view, is yet to come.

But this leaves the crucial question unresolved: is there a normative theodicy for Black theology or a theology of liberation. The exposition of this question lies outside the scope of this analysis, though I have discussed it elsewhere. I suggest there that the traditional theodicies, as well as the more recent formulations of John Hick and the theologians of hope, are not especially serviceable.

It is my conviction that the problem of Black suffering and divine racism, when correlated with the needs of a theology of liberation, will push Black theology toward the functional ultimacy of man as its prescriptive principle. This principle, I conclude, informs the positions of secular humanism and what I term *humanocentric theism*. Accordingly, these positions are the most promising for a viable and consistent Black theodicy.

Notes

1 *New Theology No. 5*, eds. M. Marty and D. Peerman (New York: Macmillan, 1968), 135.
2 Major Jones, *Black Awareness: A Theology of Hope* (Nashville: Abingdon, 1971), 12.
3 Leszek Kolakowski, *Toward a Marxist Humanism* (New York: Grove, 1969), 13.
4 W. E. B. Du Bois, *Dark Water* (New York: Harcourt, Brace & Howe, 1920), 25.
5 John Mbiti, *New Testament Eschatology in an African Background* (New York: Oxford University Press, 1971), 24.
6 Jeremiah 15:18.

Chapter 9

THE RELIGIOUS LEGITIMATION OF COUNTERVIOLENCE

INSIGHTS FROM LATIN AMERICAN LIBERATION THEOLOGY

William R. Jones

Liberation Theology: Saint or Satan?

Unquestionably both the content of liberation theology and the approach it proposes . . . [namely] its insistence on a total economic and political structuring through violence (if necessary) . . . create a difficult if not dangerous atmosphere . . . [and] complicate the ability of the United States to conduct business in the Western Hemisphere.[1]

This citation from a recent participant in the Strategic Studies Program at the National War College summarizes what the current administration and its apologists calculate to be the intrinsic morality and geopolitical impact of liberation theology. The core of this calculation is a condemnation of liberation theology in general and Latin American liberation theology (LALT)[2] in particular on the grounds that they provide "the license and possibly the inspiration for violence in the underclass' struggle for economic social and political equality."[3] Critics of liberation theology also seize upon its alleged commitment to revolutionary violence to link it with Marxism and further excommunicate it from the circle of legitimacy. It goes without saying that crucial geopolitical decisions have and will continue to flow from this understanding of liberation theology.

Proponents of liberation theology have endorsed what for many is a dubious even nihilistic right: the right to violence. Detractors of LALT find it particularly ironic that liberation theologians legitimate this right on moral and religious grounds. Some twenty years later, the image of the Columbian priest Camilo Torres—calling his people to rise up and revolt, taking up arms himself and being killed by government troops—is still vivid. This and similar images continue to fuel a caricature of liberation theology as a "bible and bazooka" Christianity where ultimate homage is rendered to the cannon instead of the crucifix.

The purpose of this chapter is to challenge this portrait of liberation theology. I want to show that its perspective on violence is grossly misinterpreted and misunderstood. In what follows, I want to provide a more accurate and adequate picture of how LALT views the role, value, and morality of violence in social change, a view which, if accurate, dictates a radically different rationale for opposition to liberation theology.

It should be clear to all that if policy makers are responding to an inaccurate picture of liberation theology's theory of violence, their game plan can not be trusted. What is at stake here extends beyond a faulty strategy based on background information that is inaccurate or incomplete. I want to suggest that the enormity of the logical and moral inadequacy of this criticism of liberation theology forces one to search for a hidden agenda and ask what appears to be a loaded question: Is this criticism part of a calculated strategy to demolish liberation theology's moral legitimacy and thereby defuse a major threat to the economic, social, and political status quo that the current administration wants to maintain in the southern hemisphere? However, the question is entirely appropriate if one illuminates the maintenance needs of oppression, in particular the concepts and values it needs to perpetuate itself. It will become clear that the attack on LALT's theology of social change incorporates the basic operation of oppression itself.

The importance of isolating the inner logic of LALT and its theology of social change should be clear for public policy makers. The geopolitical implications of LALT's ultimate resolution of this issue are especially acute for the United States because of the obvious proximity of our borders. There is also the factor of numbers. Latin America is part of the so-called Third World where it is estimated that the majority of Christians will be located by the year 2000.[4] Liberation theology's popularity must also be taken into account. Richard C. Brown contends that an estimated "20 to 30 percent of bishops (including archbishops and cardinals) are probably dedicated proponents" and "40 to 50 percent among the rank-and-file clergy could be classified as enthusiastic advocates." In addition, he allows that "possibly over 60 percent of the hierarchy" is also sympathetic, eschewing, however, its advocacy of "revolutionary violence."[5]

The impact of liberation theology's theology of social change also looms in importance once we consider what its popularity reveals: large numbers of the underclass, with lifelong commitments to the church and Christianity, no longer swallow this food of non-violence as the only or even the best fare. And it must not be forgotten that these are individuals claimed to be the church's most loyal and dedicated followers. A similar movement beyond non-violence is clearly documented in the civil rights struggle in North America. Nor can we be blind to a similar demystification in South Africa at this very hour. What I draw from these connected events is this fact: policy makers can no longer praise non-violent methods as the ideal and condemn revolutionary violence as a strategy for keeping the underclass in their place at the bottom of the economic, social, and political ladder. This strategy is exposed daily as a hypocritical policy with an inner design to maintain the status quo with its massive inequalities. This, in essence, is the case that I will make in this chapter.

Method, Scope, and Semantic Clarifications

Because of a possible misunderstanding, it is important to identify precisely my approach. To the extent that I challenge certain criticisms directed against liberation theology and seek to establish the presence of ideological taint in the critics' arguments, my general approach can be regarded as apologetic. Technically, however, I am advancing an interim assessment of selected criticisms of liberation theology. An interim assessment is, in essence, a corrective enterprise, a criticism of criticism. Like Janus, it looks both backward and forward. It peers backward toward an earlier criticism—here the attack on liberation theology's theory of revolutionary change—that is seen as deficient and invalid. Given its forward bearing, an interim assessment becomes a proposal for a new method and a more adequate critical apparatus that seeks to avoid the errors of the earlier analyses. In this sense, my concern is not to establish the validity of LALT's theology of social change. Rather, it is to show that specific attacks upon LALT are neither accurate nor successful, thus leaving the door open for LALT's critics to reestablish their charges on other grounds.

Let me outline the basic strategy of liberation theology's apologetic that we will explore in this chapter—a strategy that boldly removes the moral onus from itself and places it on the shoulders of its critics! For our purposes, the heart of liberation theology's apology is the refocusing of the issue as the moral and religious legitimacy of *counter*violence—rather than violence. This means apologetically that the violence of the oppressed, the group for which liberation theology speaks, is a response to a *prior*, "original" violence that created and maintains the oppression that liberation theology attacks. Hence the moral rationale of counterviolence, of *self*-defense, and of the *just* war. Any criticism of liberation theology that fails to engage this moral position as the fundamental issue is attacking a straw man.

Liberation theology's moral rationale for counterviolence, we will argue, is also misinterpreted if we fail to see it as the outcome of a specific understanding of the nature and operation of *economic, social, and political* oppression. This understanding must be also regarded as foundational to avoid the unsound policy that accompanies a faulty decoding. For instance, to establish the legitimacy of counterviolence, liberation theology is obliged to show that the group for which it speaks is *oppressed*. Obviously, this makes the category of oppression normative for the debate. The category of oppression is preeminent as well at another level; it serves to back LALT's critics into a corner, forcing them to respond to the charge that their criticism, almost without exception, is hypocritical, self-serving, and part of the ongoing operation of oppression itself. In this way liberation theology reduces the "legitimate" critics of counterviolence to that of the strict, absolute, and consistent pacifist—a creature as rare as the statistical non-entities in the Kinsey Report who don't masturbate.

Two comments about the scope of the materials in this chapter. My purpose here is not to give a general survey of the literature on these issues, but to anticipate as it were the religious justification for revolutionary violence that public policy makers in the future are almost certain to encounter in Latin America and the Third World.

This means that our purpose here is not simply to focus on the general argument that LALT has already advanced but also to anticipate the further evolution of its defense of counterviolence. To facilitate this, LALT will not be my exclusive focus. Illustrative materials will be drawn as well from other representatives of liberation theology, in particular the Black theology of the United States. Materials from the latter are valuable for several reasons. Drawn from our own recent national history, they provide an earlier, but parallel, evolution of this issue that is more familiar to us. In addition, the response of the establishment class in America to these contrasting models of social change, associated with Malcolm X and Martin Luther King, is part of the history that informs liberation theology's own theology of social change.

Finally by way of introduction, let me outline the major sections of our chapter and discuss some semantic stipulations. "LALT and Violence: The Critics' Case" summarizes the basic argument that we want to critique. "Towards a Phenomenology of Oppression" articulates the particular understanding of oppression that informs liberation theology's moral rationale for counterviolence. "Quietism, Anti-Powerism and Violence: The Mechanism of Oppression" illustrates the ideological manipulation of values to maintain oppression.

It is also important to unpack the meaning of *ideology* for this chapter, since a specific negative connotation of ideology controls an essential part of the liberation theology argument. Ideology, on the one hand, can be used in a neutral sense, "as a person's basic systems of goals and values, plus the means to achieve them—"[6] in sum, one's belief or faith system. On the other hand, we can speak of ideology in a pejorative sense, "as a mental mechanism that serves certain class, race or other interests by concealing or sacralizing a given situation."[7] The latter definition's stress on conceptual manipulation and deception is usually coupled with a call for critical demystification and exposure. Certain methodological consequences follow from this second understanding of ideology, one of which is crucial for our argument. The presence of ideological taint can only be established by identifying a basic inconsistency between what one preaches and what one practices.

The term "violence" also presents critical problems that demand special attention. I will argue later that the very definition of violence includes a subjective component that is characteristically question-begging. Moreover, the counterviolence advocated in the liberation theology apologetic is not simply a negative mirror image of violence. For that reason, I will speak initially of LALT's theology of social change rather than of its "revolutionary violence" until we can explore the kind of "violence" contained in liberation theology's defense of counterviolence.

LALT and Violence: The Critics' Case

Richard C. Brown's article noted earlier is representative of the typical strategy and argumentation of the critics of liberation theology. Their argumentative strategy, which can best be described as a "Saint and Satan" approach, is intended to destroy the theological basis for LALT's theory and practice of counterviolence. The logical scenario proceeds as follows: first, the "saint" of the Christian, biblical, or Catholic tradition embodies the definitive norm for Christian moral theory and public policy; second, liberation theology's theory and practice of social change contradicts this saintly prerequisite for economic, social, and political holiness; therefore, liberation theology's moral imperatives and revolutionary policies must come from some "satanic" source that is unwholesome and unprincipled. Most often, this satanic influence is identified with Marxism.

It is important to show how the specific category of violence links up with the "Saint and Satan" strategy. The argument begins by establishing that violence is antithetical to the Christian's moral strategy. Here, papal citations, some of which were directed specifically to LALT and others from an earlier context, are cited. The following are representative:

> We are obliged to state and reaffirm that violence is neither Christian nor evangelical, and that brusque, violent structural changes will be false, ineffective in themselves, and certainly inconsistent with the dignity of the people.[8]

> The sort of liberation we are talking about knows how to use evangelical means, which have their own distinctive efficacy. It does not resort to violence of any sort, or to the dialectics of class struggle. Instead, it relies on the vigorous energy and activity of Christians, who are moved by the Spirit to respond to the cries of countless millions of their brothers and sisters.[9]

Next, the Marxist insistence on the necessity and legitimacy of violent revolution is stressed and compared to liberation theology's alleged commitment to revolutionary violence. Thus, LALT's moral imperative for radical social change is undercut in two ways. Its Christian legitimation is denied and its alleged Marxist inspiration is exposed.

Further consideration of Brown's refinement of the "Saint–Satan" strategy provides additional background for understanding liberation theology's apologetic position. The "bottom line" of this strategy is the charge that liberation theology's vital concerns are basically political and sociological, not spiritual or theological. Moreover, Brown insists that liberation theology's theological warrants for radical social change are only "secondarily" biblical. They are actually derived from the Roman Catholic social doctrine of the 1960s, particularly the papal encyclicals—*Mater et Magistra, Pacem in Terris, Populorum Progressio*—the conclusions of Vatican II and the Conference of Latin American Bishops held in Medellin, Colombia, 1968.

These papal encyclicals contained a number of revolutionary economic and political ideals. They affirmed that "the absolute right to private property and the virtues of individualism over collective action" must be challenged, that "wealthier nations [have] a responsibility to provide aid to underdeveloped nations in such a way as to avoid creating a new form of colonialism," that the "fulfilling of people's social as well as their spiritual needs is central to the definition of the Church's mission," that "the Church must take a more verbal stand on social, political and economic issues," that "the rigid anti-communism of Pius XII is deemed no longer adequate. [Accordingly] capitalism, imperialism and underdevelopment [are] all subject to review and criticism."

Catholic leaders in Latin America, Brown concludes, translated these papal promptings pronouncements into the agenda and norms of liberation theology. This translation is especially evident in the controlling affirmations of the Medellin conference that are worthy of note. The Bishops declared that Latin America was living in "dependency" on foreign powers and suffering from "economic colonialism." Within this interpretive framework, the causal nexus of poverty is redefined. "The poor are poor because the rich are rich, and the rich are rich because they exploit the poor, and the rich want to stay rich badly enough to keep on exploiting the poor."[10] In sum, poverty did not come about because of the poor's failures and shortcomings, but it was the result of a defect in the structure of the prevailing economic and political systems. From the recognition that Latin America was the victim of systemic oppression followed in lock step with the recognition that it was also the victim of institutional violence.

Brown's analysis of LALT's explicit ties to Roman Catholic teaching would seem to provide a "saintly" foundation for its theory of social change. But even this foundation is judged "satanic." The church's social teachings that emerged during the 1960s are tainted, Brown claims, because "they were tailored to meet several underlying realities confronting the Church in Latin America," particularly the "conviction that if the Church did not radically change its policies, it would simply not survive as a relevant institution."[11] Thus we see the critics "satanize" and contaminate the liberation motifs that LALT stresses by tying them to a particular pope at a specific historical juncture, motivated by self-interest and controlled by self-preservation, with all the desperation that such defensiveness involves.

In all of this we see several things that are significant for our analysis: The first matter of import follows from the fact that though Brown correctly traces the foundational elements of LALT to movements internal to the Roman Catholic tradition itself, he invalidates these elements by virtue of his normative conclusions about the essence of the faith and practice of Roman Catholicism. Brown's acknowledgment is, however, grist for liberation theology's mill, for it shows us that the Saint and Satan criticism revolves around a specific interpretation of the church's tradition. Accordingly, for this strategy to be valid and, particularly, to avoid a questioning-begging foundation, its advocates must substantiate that their particular reading is the only acceptable reading of the tradition.

What this shows us apologetically is that Marxism need not be the source for the tenets of liberation theology and that LALT and its critics are endorsing rival interpretations of Roman Catholic faith. Thus the crucial and yet unanswered question here is: "What is the essence of Roman Catholicism, and by extension, Christian and biblical faith?" This leads to the question of questions: "Who is to define this?" or as Humpty Dumpty, in *Alice in Wonderland*, poses the issue: "Who is to be the master?"[12]

Finally, in the next section, we will call attention to the central role that economic, social, and political oppression plays in the LALT apologetic. It should now be obvious why LALT must document such oppression in a manner that moves beyond idiosyncratic and arbitrary judgments. By demonstrating that it is responding to an established oppression, it documents part of the moral base that an apologia for counterviolence requires.

Toward a Phenomenology of Economic, Social, and Political Oppression: LALT's Apologetic Norm

Liberation theology is "a theological reflection born . . . of shared efforts to abolish the current unjust situation and to build a different society, freer and more humane."[13]

Liberation theology claims that counterviolence is a permissible Christian means for radical social change *in the context of historic economic, social, and political oppression*. This crucial qualification establishes a normative grid that critics of liberation theology tend to overlook, namely its understanding of oppression. Fleshing out this category is the purpose of this section.

Deciphering liberation theology's rationale for counterviolence begins with its claim that economic social and political liberation is a necessary dimension of Christian and biblical faith. It is on this principle and its corollary—the definition of ESP oppression as sin and its eradication as fundamental for any understanding of salvation—that liberation theology constructs its methodology, rank orders its moral imperatives, establishes its policy norms, and assesses its moral and theological rivals. Speaking politically then, the first purpose of liberation theology is to eradicate economic, social, and political oppression. Speaking religiously, its purpose is to establish the orthodoxy and orthopraxy of this mission as a Christian, biblical, moral, and spiritual imperative.

Liberation theology links its program of economic, social, and political liberation to biblical and Christian faith. This account, however, falls outside the scope of this chapter. For the validity of our argument here it is sufficient to note that, drawing upon a wide range of theological and biblical resources, including mainstream elements of the church tradition, liberation theology affirms and impressively documents this connection as its explicit point of departure. Given this documentation, critics can no longer blithely point to Marx as liberation theology's unquestioned parent: Mark is an equally probable womb.[14] This documentation also relocates the nature of the debate as one between different Christian factions, thus forcing the question of whether liberation theology or its critics present the more accurate interpretation of biblical and Christian faith.

A further preliminary observation: liberation theology's description of oppression should be interpreted as a phenomenological analysis that aims to move beyond idiosyncratic and arbitrary judgments—indeed, a picture can be drawn with biblical as well as Marxist strokes. For this reason the accuracy of its description should be approached as an unsettled empirical question that can and must be negotiated independently of its rationale for counterviolence. The apologetic importance of this approach should not be overlooked. It means that to establish a sound criticism, the critics must first show that liberation theology's description of oppression is an inaccurate and inadequate account of its existential and historical situation.

One final observation is needed to introduce liberation theology's concept of oppression. Liberation theology approaches its task from the context and the vantage point of those labeled variously as the oppressed, the wretched of the earth. These are the people who view the parade of history from that place where the "trickle down," theoretically, but not actually, reaches its final destination. This is the population whose economic, social, and political situation constricts it to a "worm's eye view" of reality.

With these preliminary observations as background, we can obtain an overview of liberation theology's understanding of oppression if we do two things: reflect on why the *worm* has often been chosen to symbolize the oppression and unpack some of the important nuances in the contrasting images of a worm's eye and bird's eye view. There is a singular reason why the worm is the preferred symbol for the oppressed, rather than the snake or some other creature that has to see things from the ground up instead of from the sky down. The worm expresses the essence of defenselessness against a more powerful, wide-ranging, and far-seeing predator. Translating the issue into economic, social, and political categories, the enormous armaments of the bird—its superior size and speed, its menacing beak—represent the immense surplus of death-dealing power and spacious access to life-enhancing resources of the elite in the society that equip them for their role as exploiters of the oppressed. From the vantage point of the worm and its gross deficit of power and resources, it appears that not only the early bird gets the worm, but the late bird as well. Only in death, when the body returns to the earth from whence it came, does the worm have its day in the sun. The oppressed are also aware of the time-honored justification for the gross inequalities of power and privileges that mark the respective roles of the elites and the masses; these inequalities are legitimated by appealing to the heavens, the abode of the creator and ruler of the ultimacy, and, not accidentally, as the worm sees it, the playground of the bird.

The Binary Logic of Oppression

With this understanding before us, let us now take a "creature from Mars" perspective and indicate how we would explain oppression to our visitor.

1. Speaking in the most general terms, oppression can be seen as a form of economic, social, and political exploitation, as a pervasive institutional system that is designed to maintain an alleged superior group at the top of the ladder, with the superior accouterments of power, privileges, and access to society's resources.

2. If we move from a general to a more detailed description of oppression, the following should be accented. Oppression can be analyzed from two different perspectives: objective and subjective. The objective elements can be reduced to pervasive economic, social, and political inequalities. But inequalities, per se, are neutral. There is nothing that forces one automatically or as a matter of course, to appraise any inequality as negative or instinctively to seek its eradication. Both the negative and positive features lie outside the mere identification and description of the inequality. The most exhaustive, detailed, and factual description of the inequality will not uncover its unjust or negative quality; the same applies for the positive label. Both the negative and positive tags are generated by a particular worldview, a specific value system, a discrete theology, or identifiable picture of ultimate reality—in short, something that is not part of the facts in question. This, for our purposes, comprises its *subjective* component, the *belief and value system* that anchors oppression.

This feature of oppression—and this is the crucial point for our analysis—tells us that the oppressed, in fundamental part, because of the beliefs, values, and theology they adopt or, more accurately, are socialized to accept. Benjamin Mays's criticism of "compensatory ideas" in Afro-American Christianity is a classic statement of this insight.

> The Negro's social philosophy and his idea of God go hand in hand. . . . Certain theological ideas enable Negroes to endure hardship, suffer pain and withstand maladjustment, but . . . do not necessarily motivate them to strive to eliminate the source of the ills they suffer. . . . The idea has also persisted that "the harder the cross, the brighter the crown. Believing this about God, the Negro . . . has stood back and suffered much without bitterness, without striking back, and without trying aggressively to realize to the full his needs in the world."[15]

This leads, in the vocabulary of liberation theology to quietism, the stifling of any desire to attack or eradicate the economic, social, and political inequalities that characterize oppression. Whether the wretched of the earth embrace non-violence or take any means necessary to eradicate their maldistributed suffering depends upon the kind of God in which their faith resides and what one thinks that God demands. The implications of this for valuing or disvaluing violence are obvious.

Since liberation theology's apologetic connects violence and quietism, it is helpful to look briefly at the inner logic of the latter and its close relation to oppression. Quietism, in the lexicon of liberation theology, is a refusal to reform the status quo, especially where traditional institutions and values are involved. Conformity, accommodation, and acquiescence are its distinguishing marks.

Quietism becomes our operating principle if we believe that economic, social, and political correction is unnecessary, impossible, or inappropriate. Corrective action is unnecessary, for instance, if we believe that some agent, other than ourselves, will handle it. Another quietist tendency is found in the familiar adage,

"If it ain't broke, don't fix it." This bespeaks the attitude that correction is gratuitous if the good, the ideal, is already present or in the process of being realized. We are also pushed to quietism if remedial action is thought to be impossible. We apparently reach this conclusion when we encounter an invincible force or when the item to be corrected is a structure of ultimate reality. Finally, change is rejected if changing things will make things worse or involve us in actions deemed inappropriate, for example, violent. (This will be discussed in more detail later.)

3. The inner logic of oppression affirms a two-category system. It divides the human family into at least two distinct groups, hierarchically arranged into alleged superior and inferior classes: in-group, out-group; male, female; rich, poor; Greek, barbarian; Aryan, non-Aryan; master, slave are familiar examples.
4. This hierarchical arrangement is correlated with a gross imbalance of life-extending and life-enhancing power, resources, and privileges. The alleged superior group will possess a grossly conspicuous surplus and the alleged inferior group a grossly disproportionate deficit. To make the same point in different terms: the alleged superior group will have the most of whatever the society defines as the best, and the least of the worst. In stark contrast, the alleged inferior group will have the least of the best and the most of the worst.
5. This hierarchical division and the economic, social, and political inequalities it expresses are *institutionalized*. The primary institutions are constructed to maintain an unequal distribution of power, resources, and privileges. This is their inner design and the actual product of their operation.

Religious Legitimation and the Mechanism of Oppression

6. The next component of oppression demands special attention, for it brings us to the heart of the topic: the religious legitimation of economic, social, and political oppression which introduces the possibility of ideological taint. The hierarchical division, with the accompanying inequalities of power, resources, and privileges institutionally installed—all of this is alleged to be grounded in ultimate reality—God or nature or blame is shifted to the oppressed themselves for their status at the bottom of the ladder.

This maneuver is in line with the maintenance of oppression. To perpetuate inequalities, the oppressor must persuade the oppressed to accept their lot at the bottom of the economic, social, and political totem pole and to embrace these inequalities as good, deserved, and inevitable. In all of this, responsibility is conveniently lifted from the shoulders of the oppressor. To accomplish this, the inner logic of oppression claims that basic inequalities are the product of and in conformity with reality itself. By invoking the supernatural/divine order—one could just as well appeal to nature—oppressors accomplish several things that the maintenance of oppression requires. On the one hand, they establish a superhuman foundation that by virtue of its superior power compels conformity and obedience. On the other hand, they guarantee the goodness and moral superiority of the existing social order. Rearranging social inequalities is unthinkable if the economic, social, and political order expresses the will of God. Even if we had the power to reform things, such remodeling would still be inappropriate and blasphemous. Whatever status we have is just; it is the station that God intends for us; what is, is what ought to be. A similar conclusion would also follow if we interpret economic, social, and political suffering and inequality as divine punishment.

We have identified the central role that religion plays to legitimate both the objective and subjective elements of oppression. At this juncture it is important to identify the implications that liberation theology draws from this use of religion, recognizing, of course, the checkered history of religion as both goad to the oppressed and guardian of the oppressor.

For liberation theology, this means that moral and theological authenticity can no longer be determined solely or primarily by certifying that it is part of the tradition of the church. Religion's checkered history, where the church usually has sided with the powerful and the wealthy, tells us that the tradition itself is suspect; even the core tenets of the faith can be part of the scaffolding of oppression. Accordingly, a new test is necessary. For liberation theology, that test comes down to whether or not religion supports or subverts oppression.

Liberation theology also concludes that a total and comprehensive audit of the faith must be executed. Like the discovery of the single med-fly, nothing at the outset can be regarded as uncontaminated. Rather, each theological and moral imperative must be provisionally regarded as suspect and, accordingly, must be quarantined until it has been certified to be free of contamination.

To illustrate this method, it is helpful to recall the critical challenge of Black theologians in North America to theological formulations, like those of Martin Luther King, which reduce Christianization and biblical faith to agape, self-sacrificing love for the other. These reductions were attacked as ideological tools to maintain oppression.

> By emphasizing the complete self-giving of God in Christ . . . the oppressor can then request the oppressed to do the same for the oppressors. If God gives himself without obligation, then in order to be Christian, men must give themselves to the neighbor in like manner. Since God has loved us in spite of our revolt against him, to be like God we must too love those who . . . enslave us. . . . In fact, they are permitted to do whatever they will against black people assured that God loves them as well as the people they oppress.[16]

7. Historically speaking, oppression is initiated through the violence of the oppressor. The pattern that history reveals is this: there is an original violence that initiates and establishes the economic, social, and political inequalities that comprise oppression. "With the establishment of a relation of oppression, violence has *already* begun."[17] However, the oppressor

invariably suffers historical amnesia regarding this original violence, or that violence is transmuted into a more "benign" action through the oppressors' power to legitimate. Stressing original violence as part of the very definition of the problem is central to liberation theology's apologetic, as is implied in its accent on counterviolence.

Allied with this understanding is a particular conclusion about how power is transferred in human history, namely that force is required to effect a more equitable distribution of economic, social, and political power, resources, and privileges. "No upper class," Gunnar Myrdal concludes, "has ever stepped down voluntarily to equality with the lower class or as a simple consequence of moral conviction, given up their privileges and broken up their monopolies. To be induced to do so, the rich and privileged must sense that demands are raised and forcefully pressed by a powerful group assembled behind them."[18]

Oppression and Anti-Powerism

To explain the final dimension of oppression to be treated here, it is necessary, first, to differentiate between two antithetical philosophies: *anti-powerism* and *powerism*. Anti-powerism regards power as essentially negative or evil. The essence of this position is best expressed by Jacob Burckhardt: "Now power, in its very nature, is evil, no matter who wields it. It is not stability but lust and, ipso facto, insatiable. Therefore, it is unhappy in itself and doomed to make others unhappy."[19]

Powerism expresses a quite different understanding about the role, status, and value of power in human affairs. Power, from this perspective, is neutral, neither evil nor good; rather its quality depends upon who wields it and for what purpose. Advocates of this position advance power as a preeminent interpretive category for all aspects of human affairs as well as the natural and supernatural world.

Disciples of powerism would consider the following an appropriate description. "In any encounter of man with man, power is active, every encounter, whether friendly or hostile, whether benevolent or indifferent, is in some way, a struggle of power with power."[20] Or the equally comprehensive scope of power that is affirmed by Romano Guardini. "Every act, every condition, indeed, even the simple fact of existing is directly or indirectly linked to the conscious exercise of power."[21]

Part of the mechanism of oppression is to socialize the oppressed to adopt a philosophy of anti-powerism, though the oppressor lives by the opposite philosophy of powerism, both to create and maintain oppression. The consequence of this maneuver is to keep intact the oppressor's massive surplus of power. The underclass can be kept "in its place" to the degree that it adopts the inner logic of anti-powerism. Based on anti-powerism's characterization of power as evil, the oppressed are indeed in the *best* place by virtue of their deficit of power. Below, we will show how the advocacy of anti-powerism and non-violence meets one of the maintenance needs of oppression.

Violence and Moral Legitimacy: The Not-So-Odd Couple

It is not difficult to understand liberation theology's rationale for counterviolence if we begin with this conclusion: individuals and groups regard their actions—no matter how heinous they may appear to others—as moral and right. In the case where actions are defined as morally reprehensible, what we find is exactly what we discover for morally approved actions; both are advanced as a legitimate and moral means to an end that is also regarded as morally correct. If this is the case—and slavery, the Holocaust, and terrorism warrant this conclusion, as well as the checkered history of religion as moral exemplar—we will always misinterpret those actions we deem immoral if we fail to ferret out the "moral" rationale that underlie these alleged "reprehensible" acts.

Powerism and Anti-Powerism

This methodological axiom is peculiarly crucial when we are analyzing a category like violence which is used in a highly partisan fashion. However, most liberation theology's critics ignore this approach. They apparently start with the questionable conclusion that certain actions, such as violence, cannot be legitimated morally or religiously. But any action can be wrapped in a moral or religious justification, depending upon what a given moral or religious perspective allows. There is hardly any action—I have yet to uncover one—that has not been morally and religiously sanctioned.

If this is an accurate view of what is at stake, it is important to consider liberation theology's moral base for counterviolence. Other features of liberation theology's social ethics must also be treated here: (a) the actual status and value of the violence that it affirms, (b) the distinction it makes between types of violence, (c) the critical qualifications that hedge the sanction of counterviolence and show that there is no absolute endorsement even of counterviolence, (d) its identification of an inevitable subjective component in the very definition and classification of violence, (e) a contextual approach that excludes the *a priori* classification of any act as violence, (f) a logical grid that convicts its critics of hypocrisy and inconsistency, and (g) establishing counterviolence as a form of self-defense. Obviously the soundness of this argument depends upon liberation theology's success in showing that its clients are the oppressed and this, in turn is contingent upon the accuracy and adequacy of its account of economic, social, and political oppression. Nothing more needs to be said about this point except to alert future critics of liberation theology that attention should be riveted on this issue.

At the outset, let us note that critics of liberation theology label it a theology of violence. As part of the Saint and Satan strategy, liberation theology's critics reduce its theology of social change to one that glorifies violence. But liberation theology's actual position says something quite different. Liberation theology does not glorify violence or counterviolence; nor does it make counterviolence the preferred or even the necessary response to oppression. Neither should we reach the erroneous conclusion that all liberation theologians endorse counterviolence. As the debate among Black theologians in North America reveals, this issue splits liberationists into opposing camps though I sense that the larger group in the future will be the advocates of counterviolence.

An Anatomy of Violence

A fuller sense of liberation theology's theory of social change requires us to identify some of the different types of violence that inform its analysis. A helpful starting point is Dom Hélder Câmara's phenomenology of violence, now more than a decade old. Câmara labels the first appearance of violence as violence number 1^{22} or what might be termed: "original violence," or what has been categorized as "structural" or "institutionalized" violence.[23] This is the violence that lays the initial foundation for the oppression and maintains it. Violence number 1, in Câmara's analysis, calls forth the response of violence number 2, that is, counterviolence. And violence number 2 triggers violence no. 3, "repressive violence." To maintain their surplus of power and privilege, the established authorities invoke repressive actions to put down the usurpers, the practitioners of violence number 2. This, in turn, triggers further counterviolence, and the spiral continues—unless we move, as Câmara recommends, to the level of active non-violence.

Several features of Câmara's analysis require further analysis. First, given this typology, one can say that liberation theology legitimates only violence number 2 and even this, as we will see later, is not endorsed absolutely but only in highly selective and rigidly defined contexts. Next, the meaning of violence in violence number 1 has been enlarged beyond conventional definitions which reduce violence to an overt physical act of injury or destruction. "Violence is physical force resulting in injury or destruction of property of persons in violation of more general moral belief or civil law."[24] We will critique this definition later as question-begging. Câmara and liberation theology extend the meaning of violence to include institutionalized covert actions or injustices such as "the violence of hunger, helplessness, and underdevelopment . . . of persecution, oppression and neglect . . . of organized prostitution, of illegal but flourishing slavery, and of social, economic, and intellectual discrimination."[25]

Understanding the rationale for counterviolence also requires that we recall the composite character of violence, its objective and subjective elements. Reducing violence to its essentials, we find objective force or power. But we also find that this power/force is labeled or classified. There is always a labeling, generated from the subjective side, that is added to the objective power and force; a labeling that the most minute description of the force itself will not reveal. Thus the same force or power in the hands of different persons yields different labels. Deadly force for the soldier or policeman would escape the label of violence; the same force used by the mugger would not. The difference is not in the amount of force but in the context; who uses it and for what purpose. This feature of violence, liberation theology contends, entails the conclusion that violence is a political category which can only be defined contextually. Whether the destruction associated with violence goes "too far" can only be determined with reference to a concrete situation. Any *a priori* labeling is problematic.

Given this understanding, liberation theology challenges all definitions of violence in terms of "the violation of civil law," as question-begging. Is not the final logic of this stipulation that the state can never be convicted of violence until it is overthrown? Does it not give the government the right and power to legitimate its use of force, no matter what its character, as "legal" and therefore not violent? Moreover, this political and contextual nature of violence means that the definition of violence itself is always an exercise in power. This means in turn, that any discussion of the legitimacy of violence, counterviolence, or the new pariah, terrorism, ultimately rests on the logically prior question, "Who will define?"

At this juncture, the imbalance of power that defines oppression comes to the fore in liberation theology's apologetic. The oppressed's deficit of economic, social, and political power means that they do not participate in the labeling that determines whether a given instance of force is violence. Their lack of co-equal power to define and authorize violence is seen by liberation theology as simply another mode of oppression. Given this sense, any definition of violence by the establishment is provisionally suspect and question-begging.

A Moral Defense of Counterviolence

Liberation theology's rationale for counterviolence, as Alfredo Fierro correctly indicates, is ethical. "Its talk centers around the conditions that make violence licit. What is more, and also somewhat surprising, this discussion tends to remain within the context formulated by classic moral theology."[26] In the final analysis, the case for counterviolence rests on the legitimacy of self-protection or self-defense.

> To be specific, it tends to adopt as its basic criterion the age-old moral principle of legitimate defense and its proper proportions. Thus the new current theology of violence tends to be no more than a new application of an old principle; it takes the classic principle of the individual's right to defend himself by violence against an unjust aggressor and then applies it to revolutionary violence perpetrated by a group. Almost everything that has been written by Christians on this topic . . . remains within this relatively traditional framework.[27]

Gustavo Gutiérrez makes the same point.

> [Liberation] theology's position on violence is the same as the Church's traditional teaching on "just wars" that date to Thomas Aquinas that violence is possible as a lesser evil and last resort against greater violence. Of the crucial decisions in that choice is whether counterviolence is effective. If it is not, it should not be chosen.[28]

> LALT remains within the mainstream of traditional moral theology when it interprets unjust laws as a form of violence. "Laws not derived from eternal law," according to Aquinas, "lack the true nature of law [and are] rather a kind of violence."[29]

Two things stand out in liberation theology's rationale for counterviolence: its preeminent use of traditional arguments from moral theology and, on the other side, the failure of its critics to engage and accommodate this point in their condemnation. The critics construct a false picture of liberation theology's rationale which they then conveniently demolish. Their error is twofold: they omit liberation theology's essential and traditional moral defense for counterviolence, seeing instead a borrowing from Marxist ideology which is interpreted as basically nihilistic or amoral. In addition, they refuse to debate a major plank in liberation theology's rationale: that the group or class which is advancing counterviolence is oppressed. As shown earlier, the validity of liberation theology's case for counterviolence as self-defense depends upon the accuracy and adequacy of its analysis of economic, social, and political oppression, in particular the assertion of the latter's substantial presence. Accordingly, to rebut liberation theology's case requires the critics to demonstrate that the situations which have spawned liberation theology do not constitute oppression.[30]

Note the consequences if critics are allowed to skirt this part of liberation theology's argument. Violence number 1 becomes invisible, thus providing an illegitimate escape from the other part of liberation theology's argument: the charge of a hypocritical endorsement of non-violence only when it serves to protect the status quo. Richard Brown's inaccurate criticism of Gutiérrez's analysis of the just war theory points to precisely such a consequence. Brown contends that Gutiérrez "strays outside the [just war] theory confines," and moves the question of whether to commit violence beyond the matter of its "justness" to the "application of the amoral criterion of 'effectiveness' . . . This new standard admits to a high degree of pragmatism and neatly coincides with Marxist-Leninist dogma."[31]

Quietism, Anti-Powerism, and Violence: Ideological Perpetuation of Oppression

> It is evident that recommending nonviolence to blacks is an effort to retain the Christian vocabulary which has kept them imprisoned in passivity for so long.

Asking blacks to be nonviolent means that whites are demanding a Christian virtue which they themselves do not possess. That means that whites are once again trying to dupe the blacks.[32]

A conceptual and value system has been built up to destroy the ability of the oppressed to see the exploitation to which they are subjected and to understand its causes. The system we now want to consider involves the ideological manipulation of the maintenance concepts of oppression, in particular the establishment of anti-powerism and non-violence as ultimate moral imperatives. We also will examine liberation theology's response to this ploy: the charge that its critics are guilty of an unrighteous hypocrisy.

One aspect of the ideological use of religion to maintain oppression is the establishment of anti-powerism and its correlation with non-violence as preeminent moral ideals. To decipher this feature of oppression we should recall the gross imbalance of power that characterizes the unequal status of oppressor and oppressed. To the degree that the oppressed accept the logic of anti-powerism, that power is evil, they will regard their deficit of power as good, as necessary for their highest good. In this way their pursuit of co-equal economic, social, and political power, a necessary condition for their liberation, is aborted at the outset. In short, one of the maintenance formulae for oppression is anti-powerism = quietism. The formula, violence = evil, produces the same result.

This strategy of the oppressor, however, can be undercut in several ways, the most effective of which is the charge of hypocrisy against those who attack the violence of the oppressed against the system, but not the violence ingrained in the system itself. The charge is easy to document and difficult to escape, as this rhetorical question suggests: "Why, in a world of violence, should only the proletariat not have the right to use violence?"[33]

It also appears to be the case that any effort to invalidate LALT's use of the just war theory or self-defense has a boomerang effect. If the use of force by the oppressed against an unjust internal order is ruled invalid, is not the traditional justification of war against an external threat likewise invalidated?

Consider also that if one is not a rigid and consistent pacifist or practitioner of non-violent resistance, the logical and moral barriers for the legitimation of counterviolence have already been scuttled. Any movement away from pacifism, for example, as just war, self-defense, counteracting a greater evil, the American invasion of Grenada, means that violence has been sanctioned or legalized at some point. Add this to the actual historical situation where force was used to establish oppression, violence number 1 or, to continue oppression as in violence number 3. The norms used to justify these instances of force provide all the maneuverability that the moral rationale of counterviolence requires and more. Moreover, if violence number 2 is not granted to the oppressed, their critics are required to defend a superior-inferior arrangement where they assign to themselves rights and privileges that are denied to others. In short, the critics must show that their rejection of counterviolence is not the operation of oppression in a new guise.

Another strategy relocates and broadens the parameters of the moral issue in several significant ways. If violence is already part and parcel of the situation of oppression—and this is implied in the category, violence number 1—the moral issue is not simply the question of non-violence as the only permissible action. Nor can the issue of moral obligation be collapsed, as the critics of liberation theology do, to the oppressed's or the Christian's obligation not to negate the life and person of the oppressor. A context of oppression spawns other moral dilemmas. The fact of violence number 1 raises the question of one's moral responsibility to the oppressed, the object of violence number 1 as well as 3. The oppressor is not the only neighbor whose humanity must be considered; the oppressed, the object of the oppressor's violence are equally one's neighbor. Thus, one has to decide not simply between non-violence and violence toward the oppressor but between violence toward the oppressor or violence toward the oppressed. "I do not opt for violence, it is forced upon me. I have no other choice. If I opt for nonviolence, I am the accomplice of oppression. I take sides on behalf of the violence of the state."[34]

If this is the case, then responding to the oppressor in a manner that leaves violence number 1 essentially intact means that one is perpetuating violence against one's other neighbor, the oppressed. Given this dilemma, that one can choose only violence, liberation theology argues that one must simply take sides or, as Robert M. Brown has aptly put it, change sides.

Non-Violence and Its Ideological Manipulation

Some examples from our own recent history, the establishment response to Martin Luther King, Jr. and Malcolm X, also help to illustrate the ideological manipulation of non-violence to further oppression. King's philosophy of non-violence was incessantly pressed upon Blacks—when faced with the alternative of a Malcolm X—as the sole instrument for economic, social, and political change. Yet when King advanced the same policy for Americans in Vietnam, he was dropped like a hot potato. This refusal to acknowledge that what is good for the goose (the oppressed) is good for the gander (the oppressor) unwittingly documented for Blacks the establishment's ideological manipulation of non-violence.

A similar manipulation is also apparent in the gross caricature of Malcolm's philosophy of social change, particularly the attribution of a theory of violence that was in fact alien to his actual position.

Malcolm X never rejected the validity of non-violence. He only challenged its absolute validity, which is to say, its validity for all contexts. Malcolm opposed Mao's contention that the gun is necessary and violence inevitable, arguing instead for the "ballot or the bullet."[35] Violence is not advanced as the superior or the oppressed's *first* response to their plight. The ballot is to be the first strategy, and only if the oppressor rejects the ballot is the bullet permitted. Rather the oppressed's method of social change is dictated by the context, specifically by the severity of the oppression and the character of the oppressor's response to demands for social justice. Indeed, Malcolm even allowed that America could spawn a revolution "without violence and bloodshed"—if "the black man is given full use of the ballot in every one of the fifty states."[36]

Just as Malcolm's position on violence was grossly misinterpreted, so was his principle, "any means necessary." For Malcolm, this principle recognizes a plurality of moral and political strategies, for example, non-violence and counterviolence, in contrast to King's exclusive advocacy of the former.

> We're at a time in history now where we want freedom, and only two things bring you freedom—the ballot or the bullet . . . If you and I don't use the ballot and get it, we're going to be forced to use the bullet. And if you don't want to use the ballot, I know you don't want to use the bullet. So let us try the ballot. And if the ballot doesn't work, we'll try something else. But let us try the ballot.[37]

"Any means necessary," in Malcolm's view, is also a call for a contextual analysis of means-ends questions. But in deliberating means and ends, the right and necessity of self-defense must be safeguarded.

> Since self-preservation is the first law of nature, we assert the Afro-American's right to self-defense. . . . The history of unpunished violence against our people clearly indicates that we must be prepared to defend ourselves or we will continue to be a defenseless people at the mercy of a ruthless and violent racist mob. . . . We assert that in those areas where the government is either unable or unwilling to protect the lives and property of our people, that our people are within our rights to protect themselves by whatever means necessary.[38]

Finally, any means necessary also justifies counterviolence—which, in the context of oppression, is self-defense.

> You should never be non-violent unless you run into some non-violence. I am non-violent with those who are non-violent with me . . . But don't die alone. Let your dying be reciprocal. This is what is meant by equality. "What's good for the goose is good for the gander."[39]

It is important to identify the context in which counterviolence is legitimated. Malcolm argues from a context where there is "a history of unpunished violence" against Blacks and a demonstrated failure of the government to protect the lives and property of Blacks. Moreover, the society is grounded in an immoral system such as racism. "Tactics based solely on morality can only succeed when you are dealing with people who are moral or a system that is moral. A man or system that oppresses a man because of his color is not moral."[40] Further, we have a society that responds only to force or power. "The only real power that is respected in this society is political power and economic power. Nothing else. There's no such thing as a moral force that this society recognizes."[41] Finally, we have a society where violence is inconsistently sanctioned. Non-violence is not advanced as a matter of principle, as Gandhi and King did, but approved when it is advantageous to the oppressor and disapproved when it is not.

Implications for the Coming Debate

From the vantage point of its critics, liberation theology's advocacy of counterviolence is most threatening to geopolitical stability, especially where American interests are involved. For this reason, I would suggest that too much of the response of public policy makers to liberation theology reflects cold war rhetoric and logic. Approaching liberation theology as an ally of communism is to misread the intent of liberation theology and more important, to spin out national policy that the future will show to be inept and ineffective. A more accurate reading of liberation theology's lineage and future would tie it to the spirit and strategy of the American Revolution, the celebrated last great hope for humankind. In all of this, we must not forget that counterviolence was the foundation for the American Revolution. In the words of the Declaration of Independence,

> Whenever any form of government becomes destructive of these ends, it is the right of the people to alter or to abolish it, and to institute new government. . . . When a long train of abuses and usurpations, pursuing invariably the same object, evinces a design to reduce them under absolute despotism, it is their right, it is their duty, to throw off such government.

One final observation is in order that should be a central focus of future examination of liberation theology. When one inspects liberation theology's rationale for counterviolence, as well as its understanding of oppression, there will be little doubt that its theology of violence is not the most threatening feature to the status quo. Rather, its principle of authority—the affirmation of the individual as a co-equal center of freedom authority and value—is most unsettling.

I make this point for several reasons. To reach the point where the faithful give a moral rationale for counterviolence means first that their consciousness has been illuminated to see the ideological manipulations to which they have been subjected, in fundamental part through the exercise of religion. In addition, this means that they have already deabsolutized and desacralized the religious tradition and authority, making the latter the product of human power and authority which other humans can reform or eradicate. Looking at the same point from another perspective, the very fact of the existence of liberation theology, as well as its self-designation as Christian and biblical, automatically destabilizes the monopolistic authority of any Christian tradition that supports the status quo. This sets up a situation where rival interpretations of the faith not only vie with each other but force a decision as to which is authentic. This choice has already undermined the maintenance structures of oppression, even prior to developing a rationale for counterviolence. The very fact of a rival rationale, irrespective of its validity, means that the previous norms that informed America's geopolitical policies are already hopelessly outdated.

In a similar way, the oppressed's position at the bottom of the social heap is no longer connected with their salvation but is seen as an obstacle to their highest good. At this point, the mechanism of quietism that oppression requires to maintain itself has been short-circuited beyond salvage. In addition, the analysis of violence in terms of the power to define shows us that all that the oppressed need to establish the legitimacy of counterviolence is co-equal economic, social, and political power and authority, a status that they are daily assigning to themselves. All of this is the result of a new consciousness of their status as co-equal to those at the top of the social ladder. Daily events in Latin America, South Africa, the Philippines, and Afghanistan tell us that there appears no way to return them to an earlier stage of involuntary hierarchical servitude.

Notes

1. Liberation Theology and Latin American liberation theology will be used interchangeably. LALT is the shorthand for the latter.
2. *Mission Trends No. 3*, eds. Gerald H. Anderson and Thomas Stransky (New York: Paulist Press, 1976), 1.
3. Brown, LTLA, 21.
4. *Mission Trends No. 3*, ed. Gerald H. Anderson and Thomas Stransky (New York: Paulist Press, 1976), 1.
5. Brown, LTLA, 32.
6. Alfred Hennelly, *Theologies in Conflict: The Challenge of Juan Luis Segundo* (Maryknoll, New York: Orbis Books, 1979).
7. Ibid.
8. Paul VI, Homily of the Mass on Development Day, Bogota, August 23, 1968.
9. Latin American Bishops' Third General Conference Statement, Puebla, 1979.
10. Robert McAfee Brown, *Makers of Contemporary Theology: Gustavo Gutierrez* (Atlanta: John Knox Press, 1980), 9.
11. Brown, LTLA, 25.
12. "'When I use a word, it means just what I choose it to mean, neither more nor less.' 'But the question,' Alice Asked, 'is whether you can make words mean so many different things.' 'No,' said Humpty Dumpty, 'the question is: Who is to be the master.'" Lewis Carroll, *Through the Looking Glass*, in *The Complete Works of Lewis Carroll* (New York: Random House, 1949), 214.
13. Gustavo Gutierrez, *A Theology of Liberation* (Maryknoll, New York: Orbis Books, 1973), ix.
14. The following are among the increasing number of exegetical studies that provide a biblical ground for liberation theology's analysis of oppression.
Tela Tame, *The Bible of the Oppressed* (Maryknoll, New York: Orbis Books, 1982); Julio de Santa Ana, *Good News to the Poor: The Challenge of the Poor in the History of the Church* (New York: Maryknoll, 1979); Thomas D. Hanks, *God So Loved the Third World* (New York: Maryknoll, 1984).
15. Benjamin Mays, *The Negro's God* (New York: Atheneum, 1969), 155.
16. James Cone, *A Black Theology of Liberation* (New York: Lippincott, 1970), 133-4.
17. Denis Collins, *Paulo Freire: His Life, Words and Thought* (New York: Paulist Press, 1977), 41.

18 Gunnar Myrdal, *Beyond the Welfare State* (New Haven, CT: Yale University Press, 1960), 227.
19 Jacob Burkhardt, *Force and Freedom* (Boston: Beacon Press, 1943), 184.
20 Paul Tillich, *Love, Power and Justice* (New York: Oxford University Press, 1960), 87.
21 Helder Camara, *Spiral of Violence* (Denville, NJ: Dimension Books, 1971).
22 Romano Guardini, *Power and Responsibility: A Course of Action for a New Age.* (Washington, DC: Regnery, 1961).
23 Robert McAfee Brown, *Religion and Violence* (Philadelphia: Westminster Press, 1973), 35. "Violence can have structural forms built into an apparently peaceful operations of society as well as overt physical expressions." SODEPAX, *Peace: The Desperate Imperative* (Geneva: Committee on Society, Development and Peace, 1969), 13.
24 George Edwards, *Jesus and the Politics of Violence* (New York: Harper and Row, 1972), 2.
25 Peruvian Bishops' Commission for Social Action, *Between Honesty and Hope* (New York: Maryknoll, 1970), 81.
26 Alfredo Fierro, *The Militant Gospel* (Maryknoll, New York: Orbis Books, 1977), 202.
27 Ibid., 202–3. LALT could also profitably utilize the following principle to establish its claim of self-defense. No practical distinction can be made between the right of governments to use force to maintain order and the right of armed revolution to overthrow those governments when the order they maintain is anti-human." J. Andrew Kirk, *Liberation Theology: An Evangelical View from the Third World* (Atlanta: John Knox Press, 1979), 31.
28 Penny Lernoux, *Cry of the People* (Garden City, NY: Doubleday & Co., 1982), 432.
29 Aquinas, *Summa Theologica*, Ia, IIae, question 96.4.
30 What Richard Brown incorrectly identifies as "pragmatism" and "Marxist Leninist dogma" is, in fact, the principle of the just war theory that asserts that the undertaking must have a reasonable chance of success.
31 Brown LTLA, 28.
32 Jean Genet, *Ramparts*, June 1970, 31.
33 Cited in Jacques Ellul, *Violence* (New York: Seabury Press, 1969), 33.
34 Jalles Costa, *IDOC International* (North American Edition), May 1969, 64.
35 "It is only by the power of the gun that the working class . . . can defeat the armed bourgeoisie and landlords; in this sense we must say that only with guns can the whole world be transformed." Mao Tse-tung, *Quotations from Chairman Mao Tsetung* (Peking: Foreign Languages Press, 1972), 61–2.
36 *Malcolm X Speaks: Selected Speeches and Statements*, ed. George Breitman (New York: Grove Press, 1966), 57.
37 *Malcolm X, By Any Means Necessary: Speeches, Interviews, and a Letter* by Malcolm X, ed. George Breitman (New York: Pathfinders Press, Inc., 1970), 89.
38 *Interviews*, 41.
39 *Speaks*, 34.
40 *Interviews*, 23.
41 *Interviews*, 88.

Chapter 10

PURPOSE AND METHOD IN LIBERATION THEOLOGY

IMPLICATIONS FOR AN INTERIM ASSESSMENT

William R. Jones

Our Purpose and Scope

This chapter treats two concerns that are central for our coming together. One is to enlarge and enhance our understanding of liberation theology, especially its core concepts. The other purpose is to test the cogency of some of the common criticisms advanced against liberation theology. A systematic understanding of liberation theology's purpose and method, I suggest, is germane to both goals.

The hypothesis I want to test is this: any accurate exposition of liberation theology must begin with its claim that economic, social, and political (ESP) liberation is a necessary dimension of Christian and biblical faith. It is on this principle and its corollary, the eradication of ESP oppression, that liberation theology constructs its methodology, rank orders its ethical imperatives, establishes its epistemological norms, and assesses rival theological and moral perspectives. These twin purposes, to eradicate ESP oppression and to show that this purpose is central to the good news of the Bible, control its entire theological enterprise and content.

Both its critics and its advocates see liberation theology as the new kid on the theological block. Its unforeseen birth has triggered a theological earthquake, rattling the very foundations of Christian faith. To the dismay of many, the tremors and shock waves show no signs of subsiding. Indeed, the revolutionary impact that Frederick Herzog foresaw for Black theology aptly describes the after-effects of liberation theology as well. "Black theology," he concluded, "forces us to raise questions about the very foundations of Christian faith. By the time we have understood what it is all about, we will have realized that the whole structure of Christian theology will have to be rethought."[1]

Each new kid on the block faces a barrage of challenges, often bareknuckled, that oblige it to defend its newly acquired turf and to justify its reason for "moving in." That this is also true for spiritual and theological matters is confirmed by the stormy debate about the theological merit and moral legitimacy of liberation theology. Because of its radical and abrupt encounter with the elder guardians of the faith and canon, the transgressions attributed to liberation theology have a more insurrectionary character. Liberation theology has to respond not only to antagonistic questions about its unique arrangement of the theological furniture but also to searching questions about its prescriptions and its proscriptions, its parentage and its progeny, its policies and its practices. Liberation theology also faces the charge of idolatry, the quintessential challenge to "new comers" into the circle of Christian monotheism. Further, it is denounced for an alleged unholy alliance with "atheistic" Marxism, and it is discredited on the grounds that its sanction of counterviolence, in highly selective and rigidly defined contexts, blackballs it from the community of authentic disciples of Jesus.

Make no mistake, both the orthodoxy and orthopraxy of liberation theology are at stake in this debate. Liberation theology, in the eye of its critics, is not simply the new kid on the block, the waif from the other side of the tracks, but the "enfant terrible," the theological pyromaniac, hell-bent on desecrating the altar and breaking out the irreplaceable Tiffany windows.

My purpose in what follows is to test the cogency of these common criticisms. The critics of liberation theology are vulnerable, I contend, because they have engaged the debate at the wrong point, ignoring antecedent issues that are crucial for the validity of their criticism. I want to show that the critics have slighted the logically prior issue of appropriate assessment criteria, failing, in particular, to validate the norms they use to probe, assess, and indict liberation theology. Thus, the critics beg the question at the foundational level of their critique, and, accordingly, any criticism that rests on this unsturdy scaffolding is suspect and must be rebuilt on a different foundation.

The other focus of my argument is that the critics misinterpret the purpose and method of liberation theology, thus enlarging the question-begging dimension of their attack.

It is important to pinpoint the exact object of my critique and outline my basic argument. My challenge is directed against the critics' assessment criterion, their norms and methods, rather than their specific conclusions about liberation theology. The truth or falsity of the critics' claim remains open and undecided. My argument, if successful, will not establish that the critics' charges are false but that the criticisms are grounded on insufficient evidence. To be valid, the criticisms must be reestablished on different grounds. Our purpose, in sum, is to force the critics back to the drawing board to produce a new blueprint for their critique.

Perhaps an ongoing debate in philosophy of religion—the validity of arguments to provide God's existence—will clarify the exact purpose and object of our investigation. Much of this debate has centered on the potential of familiar arguments, for example, the cosmological, to demonstrate that God exists. But demonstrating the invalidity of the cosmological argument, or the invalidity of all extant arguments for God's existence, does not establish that the proposition, God exists, is false. The most that this logic can accomplish is force the demonstrator of God's existence to "try again," this time using a different logical maneuver.

10. Purpose and Method in Liberation Theology

Methodological Considerations: Interim Assessments, Logical Priority, and Internal Criticism

What are the appropriate criteria for an assessment is the first question to be treated in any assessment of liberation theology—or for that matter, any evaluation or criticism. For an interim assessment, this question converts into two related inquiries: (1) Was the criteriology used in the initial assessment adequate? (2) What guidelines should govern future appraisals?

It should be understood that our purpose is to formulate guidelines that exclude question-begging and self-serving criteria for both liberation theology and its critics; this is not a backdoor strategy to construct privileged and customized norms for liberation theology. The rationale for all of this becomes clear once we analyze the activity of assessing, unpack the inner logic of an interim assessment, and discuss the linkage between this genre of argumentation and the categories of logical priority and internal criticism.

An interim assessment or criticism—the terms in this context are the same—is, in essence, a corrective enterprise. Like Janus, it looks both backward and forward. It peers backward toward an earlier criticism that is seen as deficient and invalid, and it glances forward toward a future assessment that seeks to avoid these deficiencies. Given its backward orientation, an interim assessment reduces to a *criticism of criticism*, here a challenge to the widespread denunciations of liberation theology that are still in vogue. Given its forward bearing, an interim assessment becomes a proposal for a new method and approach that hopefully points the way to a more accurate and adequate criticism of the object under analysis.

It is important at this juncture to analyze the general activity or criticism/assessment as background for treating the inner logic or *interim assessment* and *logical priority*. This analysis also helps us to understand the preeminence of the internal criticism as a methodological norm.

First, logical priority x is logically prior to y if any claims made about y involve an antecedent claim about x. In sum, we cannot establish y without first confirming y. The methodological consequence of logical priority for our argument becomes clear when we accent an inevitable feature of any assessment/criticism. Is it not the case that each criticism draws upon some norm or standard? Let us call this *the omnipresent critical apparatus*—to measure whatever is being criticized? The apparatus is obvious to most when physical characteristics, such as size and weight, are measured.

But it should be no less obvious dealing with abstract features like beauty, truth, the morally correct or incorrect and, yes, the orthodoxy or orthopraxy of liberation theology. Nor should it be overlooked that arguments about the Christian or biblical character of the new kid on the block commonly drag in a normative definition of biblical and Christian faith as an unstated and unvalidated premise. It should also be clear that liberation theology also attacks its critics with a like norm.

What methodological conclusions can we draw from the logically prior aspects of assessing/criticism? The logically prior question for any criticism is the legitimacy and authority of its yardstick or measuring apparatus, its assessment criteria.

Given the fact that every critic has recourse to the omnipresent cosmological apparatus, that critic faces this logically prior question: How to guarantee that the critical apparatus is in fact the rightful authority for the analysis? Clearly, if this question is not answered and if this guarantee is not given, the critic has begged the question by assigning to her/his yardstick an authority it has not yet earned and may not deserve.

S. Paul Schilling's analysis of theological question-begging helps to identify what is methodologically at stake here.

> As a Christian theologian, I am constantly guided in my thinking and living by the biblical witness to God's creative and redemptive action in the world. However, it would be inappropriate to use a norm derived from my own faith commitment as a criterion for persons who do not share that commitment. . . . It would beg the question to turn for authoritative guidance to writings which proclaim the very truth we seek to examine.[2]

Three implications for the validity of a criticism can be drawn from this analysis: (1) The whole chain of any critic's argument is suspect if it can be shown that logically prior issues have been ignored. (2) The critic's position is especially vulnerable to the charge of begging the question if it was not consciously formulated with the logically prior questions in mind. (3) To avoid the question-begging fallacy, the critic must adopt the method of *internal criticism*.

Internal criticism obviously requires further elucidation. A practitioner of internal criticism constructs her/his critical apparatus from norms that one's opponent implicitly or explicitly acknowledges. If we adopt this strategy, it is not necessary to validate one's assessment criterion since my opponent has already established and acknowledged it as a norm.

That the failure to utilize internal criticism involves begging the question is obvious in certain contexts—for instance, when criticism norms are challenged and when the challenge is advanced as an internal criticism. This is the actual situation today where both liberation theology and its critics invoke the banner of Christian and biblical faith to legitimate their respective positions. That liberation theology is especially challenging the established societal and theological authorities is evident from Segundo's outline of its approach:

> Firstly, there is our way of experiencing reality, which leads us to ideological suspicion. Secondly, there is the application of our ideological suspicion to the whole ideological superstructure in general and to theology in particular. Thirdly, there comes a new way of experiencing theological reality that leads us to exegetical suspicion, that is, to the suspicion that the prevailing interpretation of the Bible has not taken important pieces of data into account. Fourthly, we have our new hermeneutic, that is, our new way of interpreting the fountainhead of our faith (i.e. Scripture) with the new elements at our disposal.[3]

Given this context, an external criticism by either party means that it brings the inherent superiority of its position to the assessment as a *self*-established, *self*-confirmed norm. Is this not tantamount to a self-serving norm that collapses into the question-begging fallacy?

Let us be clear about the case we are attempting to make here. We are not arguing that the critic's norm is inherently question-begging but *in this context* where it has not been validated to accommodate challenges made against it, the norm is *self-validated* and therefore question-begging. In sum, we are attempting to define question-begging contextually. What is asked for here as a condition for validity is not for the critic to jettison her/his norm, replace it with its opposite or even alter it, but to validate it in a manner that is not itself question-begging. Given the fact of rival exegesis, as well as divergent understandings about the essence of Christian and biblical faith, each critic of liberation theology, and its own apologists, are inevitably drawn into this validation process.

In this regard the significance of liberation theology's "birth" must not be overlooked nor shortchanged; to do so merely enlarges the question-begging factor. The actual effect of liberation theology's existence, as well as its purpose to validate itself as Christian theology, is to delegitimate, provisionally, the guaranteed authority of the established theologies and their norms. That is to say, the very entry of a rival perspective, temporally at least, destabilizes their prevailing authority. Accordingly, their norms cannot be drawn upon to critique the new kid on the block at this time. At best, the norms of the established theologies can only be regarded as co-equal in rank and authority to those of its rival, here liberation theology and, therefore, not yet established and not yet available as the authoritative norm.

Let us be clear in our minds what is at stake here. The heart of the matter, as every new kid on the block understands, is an issue of power and authority, the authority and power to define. We must never forget the conversation from *Alice in Wonderland* when Humpty Dumpty says to. Alice: "When I use a word, it means just what *I choose* it to mean, neither more nor less." "But the question," Alice asked, "is whether you can make words mean so many different things." "No," said Humpty Dumpty, "the question is: who is to be the master?"[4]

It should be understood that none of this is to argue for the truth of liberation theology's claims or the validity of the criticisms it makes against its critics and the established theologies. Rather it is to show that the existence of liberation theology, as a new kid on the block, triggers the question of theological authority, and this issue must be negotiated before the correctness of either position can be decided.

To clarify this point, it is important to consider the issue of question-begging and the norm of internal criticism from the viewpoint of the new kid on the block. The critic is doomed if the established gang is allowed to bypass the revalidation process, assume the ultimacy of its norms and, bully-like, force them on the new comers. An actual case of "moving" into a neighborhood may be fruitful here.

Before the era of open housing, certain groups were not allowed to move into certain neighborhoods. This exclusion was commonly justified by an appeal to the homeowner's "property rights" to do as wished. In the region where I was living, the popular slogan for this residential racism and classism was: "A man's home is his castle."

Advocates of open housing wisely recognized that the only successful attack was to challenge the validity of this specious theory of property rights through a strategy of internal criticism. They pointed out the inconsistency of using the principle of eminent domain, a denial of absolute property rights, to change the thoroughfares of the inner city to accommodate entry and exit routes for suburbanites but then arguing that those displaced can be excluded from neighborhoods that their displacement made possible.

The method of internal criticism should also be viewed as a logical and theological "equalizer" for the new kid on the block. Given her/his deficit of power to define and determine the norms, the new kid can best enhance and enlarge her/his turf by "exposing" the actual foundation of the established gang's authority. Lacking the power to obtain parity, the new kid must resort to exposure tactics, "the emperor has no clothes on" to neutralize the bully's superior power.

"Liberation theology rereads the history of Christian piety action and thought through the means of analysis adopted to unmask and expose the ideological misuse of Christianity as a tool of oppression."[5] Using selected logical principles, for example, logical priority, to establish the primacy of internal criticism and the necessity to validate the norms used in any criticism puts the new kid on an equal level. To establish this parity, the new kid must make the issue of question-begging norms the threshold issue. Forcing the issue of question-begging norms and its cognate questions also enables us to see the actual foundation for the theological authority of the original inhabitants of the neighborhood. Is it grounded on logical or evidentiary superiority, or is their authority a consequence of their surplus of power, a power that allows them to legitimate their authority through self-definition?

This confrontation, Segundo concludes, is necessary for the liberation of theology itself.

> Perhaps it is now time to go on the offensive.... Perhaps we should now challenge theological methodology as it is practiced in the great centers of learning... I am suggesting that we hurl down a challenge that is authentically and constructively theological in nature. Every Latin American knows from experience that any struggle or combat of this sort is a rematch of David against Goliath. Perhaps subsequent critiques and criticisms of Latin American theology, if they are sufficiently erudite, will be forced to begin by justifying themselves. And that in itself could mark the start of a dialogue.[6]

If the foregoing analysis is anywhere near the mark, then it should be clear that what is at stake here is the co-equality of the experience of the oppressed; the co-equality of their right to preach the good news of their encounter with the divine, the co-equality of their history in the recipe of Christian theology. Given the accuracy of this analysis, it also follows that an oppressed group announces its own inferiority if it does not force the established theologies to revalidate and reconstruct their normative apparatus in light of its experiences.

Critics of Liberation Theology and Theological Question-Begging

The purpose of this section is to isolate and analyze question-begging features of liberation theology's critics. We will begin by isolating the pattern of the critics' argument. Let us begin the analysis of question-begging norms by outlining the critics' argument. The pattern is unobscure. (1) In each case the critic embeds in her/his omnipresent critical apparatus a specific theological or moral norm. Some of the most prominent to emerge are descriptions of Christian and biblical faith, for example, justifications by faith, particular moral imperatives, for example non-violence, the core spirituality of the American republic, and the perspective of selected theologies of prominence. (2) Each of these descriptions becomes the norm by which liberation theology is probed for signs of ill health. (3) On the basis of this norm, a prescription and therapy are recommended. The therapy requires that liberation theology abandon those theological elements, alleged to be diseased, and incorporate the healthy ingredients that "accidentally" turn out to be the very norms used to diagnose liberation theology as needing therapy.

Having identified the structure of the critics' argument, the reader no doubt will say that the question-begging factor has not been isolated, and ask: "Wherein lies this feature?" The question-begging feature emerges in a number of places, several of which will be considered here. The remainder must await the background analysis of the purpose and method of liberation theology in the next section of this chapter.

The question-begging becomes apparent when we note that liberation theology has challenged each of these norms as an accurate, trustworthy, and definitive statement of Christian and biblical faith, in fact, citing several of these as part of the maintenance system of oppression itself. (This point is part of the discussion of quietism and oppression in the next section.) Cone, and others, for instance, question the centrality of agape, in part because of its maintenance utility for oppression.[7] Even where it may be granted that a particular norm, like agape, is the quintessential Christian imperative, liberation theology contends that the same imperative yields opposite moral duties.

> The ethical question of "What ought I to do?" needs to be divided and an answer to such an ethical question needs to be attempted from both the black and white ethical frames of reference. It may well be that the ethical problems in relation to black and white relations are centered in the fact that those who have traditionally written Christian ethics have heretofore attempted to be too general in their ethical formulations. The ex-slave master and the ex-slave are bound by the same imperative, but the implementations of the same ethical mandate may be different. . . . If he is black, the answer might be one thing; if he is white, it might be quite another . . . Ethical responsibility varies according to the freedom and power possessed by each of the individual participants in society as a whole. For the socially advantaged white person it means yielding old privileges, accepting new risks, and giving up traditional positions of economic advantage. For the socially disadvantaged black man, it means accepting social status, assuming

new positions of power and responsibility, and acquiring a new sense of justice for those whom he had displaced as oppressors.[8]

Similar rearrangements of the theological furniture can be cited for almost every single category and norm. Once liberation theologies rearrange the theological furniture this way, not simply as an alternative redecoration but as an authentic and more accurate statement of the faith, and once they affirm the theological hypothesis that the *content* of one's moral and theological commitments reflects one's economic, social, and political *context*, the locus of the debate is changed. This follows not because liberation theology is right, but because it makes this challenge to the critics' norms, a challenge that must be answered if the use of these norms is to avoid the question-begging error.

Linking violence and the theological/political ethics of liberation theology is another place where the critics' question-begging surfaces. First, to pose the issue in terms of the Christian legitimacy of violence rather than *counter*violence by-passes the customary way that liberation theology would define the problem and thereby insulates the critic from an internal criticism.[9] Arguing from the historical premise that oppression is in fact initiated and maintained by the violence of the oppressor, liberation theology would pose the issue in terms of the legitimacy of *counter*violence for the Christian. Making non-violence the context permits the introduction of certain questions that would not surface in the opposite context. Among these are the following: What force, if any, is morally and theologically available to the Christian when the object of "oppressive power?" Am I permitted to counter a force directed against me with an equivalent force? Can anyone other than the strict pacifist challenge the legitimacy of *counter*violence? The point of these questions is not to argue that liberation theology is right in any of its answers or that the critics are wrong but that their case has not addressed the issues as liberation theology has delineated them.

I also detect a theological equivocation among many of the critics, a shifting back and forth between their espoused theory and theory-in-use in a manner that has all the appearances of a self-serving strategy.[10] The "liberationist spirituality of the American republic," for instance, is a case in point.[11] The belief and value system symbolized by this concept is advanced as the authentic model for liberation movements today to emulate. But how is "the liberationist spirituality of the American republic" established as the moral and theological exemplar. From where or from whom does it obtain its credentials? Consider: All of the *potential*—that is, not yet actualized—dilemmas and defects in liberation theology that the spirituality of the American republic allegedly corrects; liberation theologies point to the same moral and theological deficiencies in the *actual practice* of this New World spirituality. Moreover, each meritorious feature of American liberationists' spirituality that its advocates point out to liberation theologies and counsel them to borrow and weave into their own, and theological tapestry can already be found in liberation theology's pattern. Given this state of affairs, one must ask to inspect the principle of rank order that makes the party with the potential for injustice, that may never be realized, the student and commands her/him to sit at the feet of the actual perpetrator of injustice and absorb the latter's ideals.

Context, Purpose, and Method in Liberation Theology

Though an assessment, especially a critical one, involves some preliminary conclusion about the nature of the object that is evaluated—here the essential character of liberation theology—it is questionable whether the critics have uncovered its essence prior to their critical examination. In what follows, I want to identify one of its core theological and methodological norms, its understanding of oppression. To identify this is to indicate where I feel critics have incorrectly deciphered liberation theology; to identify this is also to show how the purpose and method of liberation theology impact our previous discussion of logical priority, and internal criticism, as well as highlighting other question-begging parts of the critics' thesis.

Two major and interlocking purposes[12] control the theological enterprise for liberation theology, and these twin purposes reduce to a normative theological grid to critique rival perspective, in short, assessment criteria. The first purpose is to eradicate ESP oppression especially its theological and ecclesiological expressions. Gutiérrez specifies this purpose as "a theological reflection born . . . of shared efforts to abolish the current unjust situation and to build a different society, freer and more humane."[13] To establish the orthodoxy and orthopraxy of this activity is the second purpose that controls liberation theology.

James Cone's position is also representative of this understanding.

> The hermeneutical principle for an exegesis of the Scriptures is the revelation of God in Christ as the Liberator of the oppressed from social oppression and to political struggle, wherein the poor recognize that their fight against poverty and injustice is not only consistent with the gospel but is the gospel of Jesus Christ. Jesus Christ the Liberator . . . is the point of departure for valid exegesis of the Scriptures from a Christian perspective. Any starting point that ignores God in Christ as the Liberator of the oppressed or that makes salvation as liberation secondary is *ipso facto* invalid and thus heretical.[14]

In the inner logic of liberation theology, these twin criteria are designed as a first step toward the goal of a more adequate interim assessment. A particular understanding about the nature and operation of ESP oppression (criterion 1) is the normative grid for the first purpose, and the second purpose (criterion 2) expresses a specific viewpoint about the essence of Christian and biblical faith. Criterion 2 also operates as a method of internal criticism, forcing, as it were, an internal debate about the essence of Christian faith and practice. The presupposition here is that some consensus about theological authority, for example, the meaning of the biblical message and the person and work of Jesus is the first step toward the erasure of question-begging norms. Criterion 1 moves toward a phenomenology of oppression, attempting to reduce oppression to a set of empirical items and concepts. Using this operationally defined grid, we can determine if ESP oppression is present or absent in a manner that moves beyond idiosyncratic and arbitrary judgments. This also ties in with the effort to determine if this understanding and that of the Bible cohere.

To grasp the inner logic of liberation theology, it is also necessary to comprehend its context. Robert McAfee Brown has accurately pictured this context as a world where:

> Twenty percent of the people control eighty percent of the world's resources, where two-thirds of the human family goes to bed hungry every night, in which the economic disparities between the rich nations and the poor nations are mammoth, in which there is a clear and ugly equation that goes: rich = white; poor = non-white. . . . There is a further equation that goes: affluent white nations = northern hemisphere, poor non-white nations = southern hemisphere. . . . The context is a history in which the powerful rich minority has been increasing its power and riches . . . and a history in which, with very few exceptions, the church has been on the side of power and wealth.[15]

With this understanding of the context of liberation theology as background, the purpose and method of liberation theology can now be outlined. Speaking politically, its raison d'être, whatever its geographical location may be, is to correct the gross inequalities and imbalances just described; in sum, to eradicate ESP oppression. Its primary purpose, speaking religiously, is to demonstrate that putting an end to oppression is a moral, spiritual, Christian, and biblical imperative.

An Anatomy of ESP Oppression

Liberation theology approaches the theological task from the vantage point of those labeled variously as the oppressed, the wretched of the earth, the underclass. These are the groups that occupy the lowest rung of the ESP ladder; these are the people who view the parade of history from that place where the "trickle down" theoretically reaches its final destination; this is the population whose ESP situation restricts it to a "worm's eye view" of reality.

An overview of oppression can be obtained if we do two things: reflect on why the *worm* has often been chosen to symbolize the oppressed and unpack some of the important nuances in the contrasting images of worm's eye and bird's eye view.

There is a singular reason why the worm is the preferred symbol for the oppressed, rather than the snake or some other creature that has to see things from the ground up instead of from the sky down. The worm expresses the essence of defenselessness against a more powerful, wide-ranging and far-seeing predator. Translating the issue into ESP categories, the enormous armaments of the bird—its superior size and speed, its menacing beak—represent the immense surplus of death-dealing power and spacious access to life-enhancing resources of the elite of the society; all these express *objective* advantages that equip it for its role as exploiter of the oppressed. From the vantage point of the worm and its gross deficit of power and resources, it appears that not only the early bird gets the worm, but the late bird as well. Only in death when the body returns to the earth from whence it came, does the worm have its day in the sun. The oppressed are also aware of the time-honored justification for the gross inequalities of power and privileges that mark the respective roles of the elites and the masses; these inequalities are legitimated by appealing to the heavens, the abode or the creator and ruler of the universe, and, not accidentally, as the worm sees it, the playground of the bird.

With this understanding before us, let us now take a "creature from Mars" perspective and indicate how we would explain oppression to our visitor.

Speaking in the most general terms, oppression can be seen as a form of ESP exploitation, as a pervasive institutional system that is designed to maintain an alleged superior group at the top of the ESP ladder, with the accoutrements of power, privileges, and access to society's resources that this status provides.

If we move from a general to a more detailed description of oppression, the following should be accented. Oppression can be analyzed from two different perspectives that are germane to our discussion. On the one hand, oppression can be reduced to *institutional structures*; this is its ESP, its *objective* dimension. On the other hand, one can examine oppression in terms of the *belief and value system* that is its anchoring principle. This, for our purposes, comprises its *subjective* component.

It is important to examine the objective and subjective aspect in more detail. The objective elements can be reduced to pervasive ESP inequalities. But inequalities, per se, are neutral. There is nothing that forces one automatically or as a matter of course, to appraise any inequality as negative or instinctively to seek its eradication. Both the negative and positive features lie outside the mere identification and description of the inequality. The most exhaustive and detailed description of the inequality will not uncover its unjust or negative quality; the same applies for the positive label. Both the negative and positive tags are generated by a particular worldview, a specific value system, a discrete theology or identifiable picture of ultimate reality—in short, something that is not part of the object in question.

Precisely because of this ongoing possibility of opposed labels for inequalities of power and privilege, liberation theology differentiates between the *pre-* and *post-enlightened oppressed*. The latter interprets the objective situation of inequality as negative and hostile to her/his highest good; the pre-enlightened do not. Wherein lies the difference? Not, as many believe, in a marked difference in the *objective* conditions of each; it is not the case that the post-enlightened oppressed suffer the more severe inequalities. The difference lies rather at the subjective level, with the dissimilar belief and value grid used to assess these objective inequalities.

The inner logic of oppression affirms a two-category system. It divides the human family into at least two distinct groups, hierarchically arranged into alleged *superior* and *inferior classes*: in-group, out-group; male, female; rich, poor; Greek, barbarian; Aryan, non-Aryan; master, slave are all familiar examples.

This hierarchical arrangement is correlated with a *gross imbalance of power*, access to life-extending and life-enhancing *resources*, and *privileges*. The alleged superior group will possess the unobscure *surplus* and the alleged inferior group, a grossly disproportionate *deficit*. To make the same point in different terms: the alleged superior group will have the *most* of whatever the society defines as the best, and the *least* of the *worst*. In stark contrast, the alleged inferior group will have the *least* of the *best* and the *most* of the *worst*.

This feature of oppression helps us to understand the objective and subjective factors of oppression already discussed. Looked at in terms of its objective dimension, oppression exhibits a gross imbalance of power. This manifest inequality, however, need not be regarded as reprehensible. If, for instance, power is judged to be evil, as does the position of anti-powerism discussed below, persons with a deficit of power would conclude that they are already in the preferred ESP situation. This is the worldview of the pre-enlightened oppressed. The conviction that one is oppressed does not emerge in this context. To think that one's deficit of power constitutes oppression would require a radically different worldview and understanding of power. Likewise, if the ascetic life is elevated to ultimacy, those with a paucity of material goods and societal privileges would hardly interpret this lack as something that requires correction.

The hierarchical division and the ESP inequalities it expresses are *institutionalized*. The primary institutions are constructed to maintain an unequal distribution of power, resources, and privileges. This is their inner design and the actual product of their operation.

Oppression can also be interpreted as a form of *suffering*, and suffering, in turn, is reducible to a form of inequality of power or impotence. In addition, the suffering that comprises oppression is (a) maldistributed, (b) negative, (c) enormous, and (d) non-catastrophic. Let me denominate this type of suffering as *ethnic* suffering.

Speaking theologically, maldistribution of suffering raises the issue of the scandal of particularity. The suffering that characterizes oppression is not spread randomly and impartially over the total human race. Rather, it is concentrated in particular groups. This group bears a double dose of suffering; it must bear that suffering that we cannot escape because we are not omnipotent and thus subject to illness, and so on. Additionally, however, for the oppressed there is the suffering that results from their exploitation and from their deficit of power.

If we differentiate between *positive* and *negative* suffering, ethnic suffering would be a sub-class of the latter. It describes a suffering that is without essential value for one's well-being. It leads one away from, rather than toward, the highest good.

A third feature of ethnic suffering is its enormity, and here the reference is to several things. There is the factor of numbers, but numbers in relation to the total class. Where ethnic suffering is involved, the percentage of the group with the double portion of suffering is greater than for other groups. Enormity also refers to the character of the suffering—specifically that which reduces the life expectancy or increases what the society regards as things to be avoided.

The final feature of ethnic suffering to be discussed is its non-catastrophic dimension. Ethnic suffering does not strike quickly and then leave after a short and terrible siege. Instead it extends over long historical eras. It strikes not only the parents but the children and their children. It is, in short, *transgenerational.*

The transgenerational dimension differentiates oppression from catastrophe which also can be enormous. Since the catastrophic event does not visit the same group generation after generation, the factor of maldistribution of suffering is less acute.

The last two components of oppression to be discussed here demand special attention, for they bring us to the heart of the topic: criteria for an interim assessment of liberation theology that do not beg the question. *The two-category system, hierarchically arranged, the gross imbalance of power/privilege, and the institutional expression of these are all alleged to be grounded in ultimate reality— the world of nature or the supernatural (God).*

The point to be emphasized here is the controlling role of religion, theology, and the ecclesiastical structures to legitimate both the objective and subjective elements of oppression, especially its institutional expression. This means ultimately that the worldview of the established gang and its omnipresent critical apparatus may be props for oppression. The methodological consequences of these are obvious: a radical examination of the established theologies to determine which parts, if any, undergird ESP oppression.

All of this is also to say that the oppressed are oppressed, in fundamental part, because of the beliefs, values, and theology they adopt, or more accurately, are socialized to accept. Benjamin Mays's criticism of "compensatory ideas" in Afro-American Christianity is a classic statement of this insight.

> The Negro's social philosophy and his idea of God go hand in hand. . . . Certain theological ideas enable Negroes to endure hardship, suffer pain and withstand maladjustment but . . . do not necessarily motivate them to strive to eliminate the source of the ills they suffer.
>
> Since this world is considered a place of temporary abode, many of the Negro masses have been inclined to do little or nothing to improve their status here; they have been encouraged to rely on a just God to make amends in heaven for all the wrongs they have suffered on earth. In reality, the idea has persisted that hard times are indicative of the fact that the Negro is God's chosen vessel and that God is disciplining him for the express purpose of bringing him out victoriously and triumphantly in the end. The idea has also persisted that "the harder the cross, the brighter the crown." Believing this about God, the Negro . . . has stood back and suffered much without bitterness, without striking back, and without trying aggressively to realize to the full his needs in the world.[16]

This analysis pinpoints the mechanism that oppression uses to maintain itself; the oppressor must persuade the oppressed to accept their lot at the bottom of the

ESP totem pole and to embrace these inequalities as good and/or inevitable, thus stifling any desire to attack or eradicate these ESP inequalities.

Oppression and the Inner Logic of Quietism

How is this accomplished? A review of a classic novel, written centuries ago, gives us the formula. "Altogether *The Autobiography of Jane Eyre*," the reviewer tells us, "is preeminently an anti-Christian proposition. There is throughout it a murmuring against the comforts of the rich and against the privations of the poor, which as far as each individual is concerned, is a murmuring against God's appointment."[17]

This review reveals that the inner logic of oppression requires an attitude of *quietism*, which we will discuss now, and a philosophy of *anti-powerism*, which we will treat next. Oppression maintains itself by claiming that its fundamental institutions and its hierarchy of roles and statuses are the product of and in conformity with reality itself. By invoking the supernatural/divine order—one could just as well appeal to nature, the created order—as its foundation, we accomplish several things that the maintenance of oppression requires. On the one hand, we establish a superhuman foundation that, by virtue of its superior power, compels our conformity and obedience. Human power can never win against divine omnipotence; "Our arms too short to box with God." On the other hand, we guarantee the goodness and moral superiority of the existing social order.

To make clear this connection between religious legitimation and oppression, it is helpful to look briefly at the inner logic of quietism and its kith and kin relation to oppression. Quietism, in the lexicon of Black theology, is a refusal to reform the status quo, especially where traditional institutions and values are involved. Conformity, accommodation, and acquiescence are its distinguishing marks.

Quietism becomes our operating principle if we believe that ESP correction is *unnecessary, impossible, or inappropriate*. Corrective action is unnecessary, for instance, if we believe that some agents other than ourselves, will handle it. Another quietist tendency is found in the familiar adage, "If it ain't broke, don't fix it." This bespeaks the attitude that correction is gratuitous if the good, the ideal, is already present or in the process of being realized.

We are also pushed to quietism if remedial action is thought to be impossible. We reach this conclusion, it appears, when we encounter an invincible force or when the item to be corrected is a structure of ultimate reality. Finally, change is rejected if changing things will make it worse.

As the review of *Jane Eyre* shows us, rearranging the social inequalities is unthinkable if the ESP order expresses the will of God. Even if we had the power to reform things, ESP remodeling would still be inappropriate. Whatever status we have is just; it is the station that God intends for us; what is, is what ought to be.

This feature of liberation theology's understanding of oppression parallels Peter Berger's analysis of social legitimation.

The historically crucial part of religion in the process of legitimation is explicable in terms of the unique capacity of religion to locate human phenomenon within a cosmic frame of reference. . . . If one imagines oneself as a fully aware founder of a society . . . how can the future of the institutional order be best ensured . . . ? Let the institutional order be so interpreted as to hide, as much as possible, its constructed character. Let the people forget that this order was established by men and continues to be dependent upon the consent of men. . . . Let them believe that, in acting out the institutional programs that have been imposed upon them, they are but realizing the deepest aspirations of their own being and putting themselves in harmony with the fundamental order of the universe. In sum, set up religious legitimations.[18]

Oppression and Anti-Powerism

To explain the final dimension of oppression to be treated here, it is necessary, first, to differentiate between two antithetical philosophies: *anti-powerism* and *powerism*. Anti-powerism regards power as essentially negative or evil. The essence of this position is best expressed by Jacob Burckhardt: "Now power, in its very nature, is evil, no matter who wields it. It is not stability but lust and, ipso facto, insatiable. Therefore, it is unhappy in itself and doomed to make others unhappy."[19]

Powerism expresses a quite different understanding about the role, status, and value of power in human affairs. Power, from this perspective, is neutral, neither evil nor good; rather its quality depends upon who wields it and for what purpose. Advocates of this position advance power as a preeminent interpretive category for all aspects of human affairs as well as the natural and supernatural world.

Disciples of powerism would consider the following an appropriate description. "In any encounter of man with man, power is active, every encounter, whether friendly or hostile, whether benevolent or indifferent, is in some way, a struggle of power with power."[20] Or the equally comprehensive scope of power that is affirmed by Romano Guardini. "Every act, every condition, indeed, even the simple fact of existing is directly or indirectly linked to the conscious exercise of power."[21]

Part of the mechanism of oppression is to socialize the oppressed to adopt a philosophy of anti-powerism, though the oppressor lives by the opposite philosophy of powerism. The consequence of this maneuver is to keep intact the oppressor's massive surplus of power. The underclass can be kept "in its place" to the degree that it adopts the inner logic of anti-powerism. Based on anti-powerism's characterization of power as evil, the oppressed are indeed in the *best* place by virtue of their deficit of power.

Based on this understanding of inner logic of oppression, liberation theology inspects the theory and practice of other religious perspectives to see if anti-powerism dominates. If so, these theological designs are singled out for drastic remodeling.

Implications

With the foregoing as background, let us examine some of the major implications of our analysis for the method and content of liberation theology. This will serve as a backdrop for some final implications for our analysis for an interim assessment.

Liberation theology's self-conscious purpose to eradicate ESP oppression dictates a precise theological method, namely a method of *antithetical correlation*, in contrast to Tillich's model of "question-answer correlation." To borrow a medical metaphor, liberation theology is committed to a toxin/anti-toxin or virus/vaccine design.

Speaking methodologically, the toxin/anti-toxin design reduces to a two-phase model. In phase one, attention is focused on isolating the infectious agent and acquiring as much knowledge as one can about its biological composition and processes. The objective in phase two is to develop a specific anti-body or anti-toxin that can neutralize or destroy the noxious agent. Obviously, if the findings in phase one are inaccurate, phase two will be a hit-and-miss affair.

It is important to note that phase one controls the entire enterprise in the sense that the products of phase two are customized to fit, *antithetically*, the constitution of the toxin. A similar connection obtains between liberation theology and its understanding of ESP oppression; the subjective and objective components of oppression are the toxin for which liberation theology is formulated as the effective anti-toxin.

Liberation theology interprets this to mean that a total and comprehensive audit of the faith must be executed. Like the discovery of the single med-fly, nothing at the outset can be regarded as uncontaminated. Rather, each theological and moral imperative must be provisionally regarded as suspect and accordingly must be quarantined until it has been certified to be free of contamination. To translate this into the terminology of our discussion, the critics' omnipresent critical apparatus is a suspect authority until it responds to the questions posed by liberation theology's phenomenology of oppression.

To illustrate this theological method let us focus on two theological norms: the concept of sin and justification by faith. Liberation theology recognizes the linkage between our understanding of sin and ecclesiastical commitment. To define something as a sin tells us where the corrective actions of the church and synagogue are to be focused. And where we identify the quintessential sin dictates where the supreme energies of the church are to be directed. Accordingly from the perspective of liberation theology, any definition of sin that omits ESP oppression is suspect. The criticisms directed against liberation theology engender the spirit of quietism in the oppressed, thus leaving the ESP inequalities intact.

The criticism that liberation theology abandons a doctrine or justification by faith in favor of a works soteriology illustrates the point. Though it is debatable that liberation theology is more Pelagian than its critics, one could not find a more striking example of theological quietism than the critics' advocacy of justification by faith. What better rationale to do nothing to eradicate one's oppression than the belief that one's salvation comes only from God, an extrahuman source, that it is a gift that cannot be demanded or sought after, and that it is an unmerited gift, and so on. In all of this we see the effort of liberation theologians to focus attention on the critical apparatus of the theological combatant, in particular the unacknowledged and unidentified ESP presuppositions and judgments.

A similar strategy informs their theological treatment of theodicy. Here, time-honored theodicies, for example suffering as deserved punishment, have been systematically thrown on the theological dung heap. The rationale: this theodicy's poor antithetical fit with ESP oppression especially quietism. The theodicy of deserved punishment leads to quietism at several significant points. If God is the author of the suffering or if she permits it, then it would be inappropriate, indeed sinful, to try to make God's judgment null and void. In addition efforts to thwart or change the suffering would be futile since God's omnipotence is its foundation.

What I am suggesting in all of this is that liberation theology utilizes a specific understanding of oppression as a theological norm and as part of its omnipresent critical apparatus. Central to this apparatus is the quietist quotient of a theological category. If the theological or moral ideal generates a strong disposition to quietism, its merit is diminished. Accordingly, if the critics' case against liberation theology is to stand, they must address the logically prior question of the accuracy and adequacy of liberation theology's description of ESP oppression.

There is a "which comes first, the chicken or the egg" issue that merits discussion: Does the liberation theologian start with a preunderstanding of oppression which is then legitimated by marshaling the biblical and Christological authority? Or is it the other way around? Is it the encounter with the centrality of liberation in the biblical story that then instructs the liberationist to be about the business of eradicating ESP oppression?

As far as an interim assessment is concerned, it makes little difference which scenario is adopted. Both options challenge the received interpretations and trigger the internal debate that is central to the issue of theological question-begging.

This issue introduces another question of crucial significance to our topic: What is the source of liberation theology's understanding of oppression. Is the source more sociological than theological, more phenomenological than biblical, or to make plain what usually lurks behind questions of this type: more Marxist than Christian?

The question is still open. Recent developments in biblical studies such as Elsa Támez, *The Bible of the Oppressed*,[22] and Julio de Santa Ana, *Good News To The Poor: The Challenge of the Poor in the History of the Church*,[23] permit at least these tentative conclusions. The model of oppression derived sociologically or phenomenologically coheres remarkably with the biblical model of oppression. Indeed, the coherence is precise enough to make the case that a Marxist analysis is not a necessary foundation for a liberation theology; a biblical scaffolding can work equally as well.

This leads to one final methodological observation. I have attempted to identify the theological impasse that the birth of liberation theology has created, an impasse with crucial implications for Christians and non-Christians in the Americas. If we are to move beyond this impasse, we must achieve some minimal consensus about several things: the essence of Christian and biblical faith, appropriate theological and ethical methodology, the nature and operation of ESP oppression, and ultimately in all of this, theological authority must be renegotiated. This is so because the measuring rods used by both sides invoke conclusions about the essential character of those items, conclusions that are problematical from the other side. This can only exaggerate the impasse and end by focusing the debate on each side's assessment criteria and their validation. My defense of liberation theology is, in sum, an affirmation of the *provisional* co-equality of its reading of the good news and its historical experience as we face these life and death matters. This status, I have attempted to show, is not dependent upon whether its reading of scripture and the human situation has been demonstrated to be accurate and adequate. The determination of its measure of truth must await the historical resolution of the logically prior questions advanced here as the focus of the coming debate.

Notes

1. Frederick Herzog, *Liberation Theology* (New York: Seabury Press, 1972), viii.
2. S. Paul Schilling, *God Incognito* (Nashville: Abingdon Press, 1977), 120–1.
3. Juan L. Segundo, *Liberation of Theology* (Maryknoll, New York: Orbis Books, 1976), 9.
4. Lewis Carroll, *Through the Looking Glass*, in *The Complete Works of Lewis Carroll* (New York: Random House, 1949), 214.
5. Jose M. Bonino, *Doing Theology in a Revolutionary Setting* (Philadelphia: Fortress Press, 1975), 89.
6. Segundo, *The Liberation of Theology*, 5–6.
7. "By emphasizing the complete self-giving of God in Christ . . . the oppressors can then request the oppressed to do the same for the oppressors. If God gives himself without obligation, then in order to be Christian, individuals must give themselves to the neighbor in like manner. Since God has loved us in spite of our revolt against him, to be like God we too must love those who . . . enslave us. . . . This view of love places no obligation on the white oppressors. . . . In fact, they are permitted to do whatever they will against black people, assured that God loves them as well as the people they oppress." James Cone, *A Black Theology of Liberation* (New York: Lippincott, 1970), 133–4.
8. Major Jones, *Christian Ethics for Black Theology* (Nashville: Abingdon, 1974), 16–19, adapted.
9. Consider what Helder Camara in *The Spiral of Violence* calls the "second violence," a violence initiated and designed to thwart the oppressor's "first violence." This violence is justified according to the classical criteria for the just war. Given this perspective, "no practical distinction can be made between the right of governments to use force to maintain order and the right of armed revolution to overthrow those governments when the order they maintain is anti-human." J. Andrew Kirk, *Liberation Theology: An Evangelical View from the Third World* (Atlanta: John Knox Press, 1979), 31.
10. "When someone is asked how he would behave under certain circumstances, the answer he usually gives is his espoused theory of action for that situation. This is the theory of action to which he gives allegiance and which, upon request, he

communicates to others. However the theory that actually governs his actions is his theory-in-use, which may or may not be compatible with his espoused theory. Furthermore, the individual may or may not be aware of the incompatibility of the two theories. We cannot learn what someone's theory-in-use is simply by asking him. We must construct his theory-in-use from observations of his behavior." Chris Argyris and Donald Schon, *Theory in Practice: Increasing Professional Effectiveness* (San Francisco: Jossey-Bass Publishers, 1975), 6–7.

11 See Richard Wentz's chapter, *"The Liberationist Spirituality of the Republic."*
12 I interpret these as different sides of the same coin; one should not designate one as the chicken and the other as the egg. This point is crucial since many of the critics of liberation theology see it as a theological justification for ESP, especially Marxist, conclusions draw from a non-biblical and non-Christian source. José Comblin correctly identifies liberation theology's basic argument to which its critics must respond: a biblically referenced—and therefore an internal criticism—of traditional theology. "In some sense, all the sources of the theology of liberation or freedom are biblical. On going back to the traditional [theologies], I am always struck by the modest importance attributed to freedom. It is even more amazing when contrasted with the prominence of freedom in the Bible. . . . The rediscovery of freedom by theology is a return to the Bible." José Comblin, *The Church and the National Security State* (Maryknoll, New York: Orbis Books, 1979), 41.
13 Gustavo Gutierrez, *A Theology of Liberation* (Maryknoll, New York: Orbis Books, 1973), ix.
14 James Cone, *God of the Oppressed* (New York: Seabury Press, 1975), 81–2.
15 Robert McAfee Brown, *Is Faith Obsolete?* (Philadelphia: The Westminster Press, 1974), 120–1.
16 Benjamin Mays, *The Negro's God* (New York: Atheneum, 1969), 155.
17 M. A. Stodart, *Quarterly Review, 84* (December 1848), 173–4.
18 Peter Berger, *The Sacred Canopy* (New York: Doubleday, 1969), 33.
19 Jacob Burkhardt, *Force and Freedom* (Boston: Beacon Press, 1943), 184.
20 Paul Tillich, *Love, Power, and Justice* (New York: Oxford University Press, 1960), 87.
21 Romano Guardini, *Power and Responsibility: A Course of Action for a New Age* (Washington, DC: Regnery, 1961).
22 Elsa Támez, *The Bible of the Oppressed* (Maryknoll, New York: Orbis Books, 1982).
23 Julio de Santa Ana, *Good News to the Poor: The Challenge of the Poor in the History of the Church* (Maryknoll, New York: Orbis Books, 1979).

Chapter 11

MORAL DECISION-MAKING IN THE POST-MODERN WORLD

IMPLICATIONS FOR UNITARIAN-UNIVERSALIST
RELIGIOUS EDUCATION

William R. Jones

It is a distinct honor to be invited as the Sophia Fahs Lecturer. All those like myself, who are honored to be a part of this distinguished lectureship, are asked to address an issue of significant impact on religious education in our denomination. For my contribution to the series, I want to focus on the next battle zone that we as religious liberals and religious educators will face.

Whether of our choosing and whether we like it or not, it should be clear to each of us that we are engaged in a fundamental battle over the role and value of liberalism and pluralism in the life of our nation. Prayer in the public schools, ERA, abortion, creationism, and so on immediately come to mind as places where we are already shooting from the trenches. And though on the surface, these are separate squabbles, they are manifestations of a single and fundamental conflict that is widening. It is this fact that I want to discuss with you this evening.

Character Education: The New Battleground

What is the next battle line in this growing religious warfare? I am convinced that it will be the issue of the content and method of moral education in the public arena. Perhaps the easiest way to get at the heart of this issue is to highlight some significant developments that were reported the week before this conference. Mike McManus, a syndicated writer of religious news, asks: "What would you rather have in the public schools—the moment of silence struck down recently by the Supreme Court or the teaching of character education in which students learn to appreciate basic Judeo-Christian values?"[1]

The article goes on to describe the almost unanimous preference for the teaching of character education or what can also be called: value indoctrination. The article, for instance, calls our attention to a law, recently enacted in Tennessee, that mandates character education. "The course of instruction in all public schools in Tennessee shall include character education to help students develop positive values and improve student conduct."[2]

Add to this the new diagnosis of the Secretary of Education, William J. Bennett, that recommends character education as the preferred solution to the ills of public education and the moral malaise of the nation. "Character education," Bennett affirms, "is as necessary to the improvement of education as medical attention is to the treatment of physical ailments. Our society's future depends heavily upon the successful blending of character education with cognitive learning."[3]

The article also informs us of the phenomenal success of teaching materials published by the American Institute for Character Education, now being used in 16,500 classrooms. Special note is made of its success "in Chicago's tough South Side where two-thirds are on welfare." And let us not forget the final line of the article, that all of this costs only "one dollar per kid!"[4]

And Jerry Falwell's endorsement—"While institute materials aren't religious, they are certainly compatible with the moral perspective of Judeo-Christian ethics and helpful in teaching moral principles in public schools"[5]—is an ominous portent of a battle strategy we liberals will have to counter.

Value Indoctrination: Saint, Satan, or Scapegoat?

Let me say in advance that I personally welcome the idea of character education. I say this because I believe that education is never value-neutral and that our public institutions are already engaged in value indoctrination and moral education. For instance, the very design of the institution and especially its power configurations express precise value commitments. Even value clarification is not neutral. It affirms the freedom of the child as moral evaluator and not required, as a matter of course, to conform to norms umpired by others.

What is at stake in all of this for religious liberals? It is not, as is often believed, the fact of character education itself. Value indoctrination—let us not fear the term—is inevitable as every society and every parent recognize. Once we acknowledge that toilet training and teaching the use of silverware are instances of value indoctrination, we must also recognize that it is the content and method of character education, not its actuality, that should concern us as religious educators. Indeed, when we examine character education more carefully, we will see that it affords several attractive possibilities for liberals, in particular, to insert into the public domain key liberal values that are trans-cultural.

To get a proper fix on all of this we should recall that the impetus for prayer in the public schools was the conviction that our national morals had deteriorated and that it was necessary to return America to its proper moral anchor. Linked to this was a precise understanding of the cause of our decline, namely, that America had abandoned its belief in the biblical tradition of moral absolutes as the necessary, the one and only one, ground for our public ethic. According to the religious right, if America is to regain its moral sanity, it must return to these moral rules that are universally valid for all times, all places, and all individuals. It must, in short, embrace moral absolutism as the framework for the life of our nation. Any other choice, we are warned, leads inevitably to moral nihilism, the belief that nothing is wrong, everything is permitted.

Listen to the diagnosis of Francis Schaeffer, the leading theologian of neo-fundamentalism.

> Nobody has ever discovered a way of having real "morals" without a moral absolute. If there is no moral absolute, we are left with hedonism (doing what I like) ... without absolutes, morals as morals cease to exist, and humanistic man starting from himself is unable to find the absolute he needs. But because the God of the Bible is there, real morals exist. Within this framework I can say one action is right and another is wrong without talking nonsense.[6]

The consequence of these developments is unobscure. If character education is the coming trend, then religious liberals will soon be confronted with different programs of value indoctrination to which we must respond; our response must be both critical and constructive.

Given that the content and method of character education or value indoctrination is constructed on a specific moral pedagogy, that is, a particular catalog of values and instructional techniques, we must critically assess the adequacy and accuracy of these models in light of our own faith commitments and our pedagogical inclinations. For religious liberals in this historical period, it means that we must launch a sustained attack on absolutism as the foundation for character education. My purpose this evening is to supply the rationale for this claim and to outline a model for moral instruction that seeks to avoid the quicksand of an absolutist ethic.

The Religious Right: Unacknowledged Situation Ethicists

Let me begin by sharing with you an anonymous letter I received several years ago in response to a lecture, "Bibliocracy, Hypocrisy, or Democracy? Questions to the Moral Majority," that criticized its method of moral legitimation. (Let me digress for one moment and also share with you a methodological principle that I have found invaluable for isolating the core of one's moral system: Do not focus initially on the content of someone's moral code. Rather, rivet your attention on the reasons given for the rightness of the actions. In short, unpack the method of moral legitimation.)

Based on this principle, I examined the religious right and only one conclusion was permitted: the claim about the foundation of their ethics was suspect. One did not uncover the absolutes they claimed as the ground for the moral imperatives. Instead, what stared one in the face was the same relativity and subjectivity that they denounced in others. In point of fact, I found that they were unacknowledged situation ethicists—what they identified as the source of liberalism's immorality.

Consider the following statements from Jerry Falwell, one of the leaders of neo-fundamentalism.

At a conference on the family, an Alabama minister asked Falwell to square his position on abortion with his stand against the nuclear freeze, intimating that if the sanctity of life demands that we outlaw abortion, should not our concern for the dignity of innocent life likewise direct us to ban the use of nuclear weapons.

This is Falwell's response: "I wish there were no nuclear bombs, but we must all face reality, and the Soviet Union is not going to disarm." But another member of the audience quickly said, "I think that reply is an example of situational ethics." Falwell, who criticized situation ethics as a dogma of secular humanism, hesitated, then responded, "The United Nations is not the Prince of Peace. Jesus is. Until he comes back, there will be no lasting peace on earth."[7] Also consider the following transcription from Jimmy Swaggart's TV Bible study that affirms even more explicitly the doctrine of situational ethics, the very opposite of the absolutism that Falwell and Swaggart espouse.

> There is no set rule that one can go by. . . . You can't draw a fast line and say: "if you do this, you are able to do thus and so." It can't be done that way. Each situation has its own set of circumstances and would have to be dealt with accordingly.
>
> The only answer I can give is this: Once again, each situation is different. Once again, I as a minister of the gospel—and I don't think any preacher can—can not draw a line and make a firm and fast rule and say that this applies to any and all cases. The only answer I can give, and it may seem that I am backtracking or I'm trying to close the door and get out and not have to answer—but it is the only answer that I can give and it is this: that the lady whoever it may be—would have to seek God and get God's direction and guidance and do what she feels in her heart that the Lord would want her to do. That's about the only answer that I can give. I think it would be improper for me to go further than that. I think I would be dealing in an area that only God should deal in. That's about all I know to say.

If this is not an affirmation of situational ethics, I don't know what is.

But to return to the anonymous letter. Based on the volume of calls and letters received, one illustration—actually a minor point in the overall argument—seemed to ruffle a lot of feathers. The background is important here. Several local ministers at the time had argued that gays were unfit to hold offices of public trust or service, and this was sanctioned on the basis of selected biblical passages. Given this use of the Bible as an absolute norm, as well as the fundamentalist claim to follow in Jesus's footsteps, it appeared to me that minimal consistency required that the religious right should have publicly raised the question about Ronald Reagan's moral fitness to be president.

Let me refresh your memory. Jesus says nothing for or against homosexuality. He simply doesn't discuss it as a discrete moral issue. But he is very specific about divorce. "Whosoever divorces his wife and marries another commits adultery against her; so too if she divorces her husband and marries another, she commits adultery."[8]

The unobscured formula that I extra here is divorce + remarriage = adultery. And given further the religious right's praise of the Ten Commandments that also condemns adultery, why did Falwell and Swaggart fail to link the problems plaguing America with the possibility that we have an adulterer in the White House and that divorcees may be holding public seats of power?

The foregoing argument prompted this anonymous letter.

> You have absolutely no business giving out interviews on your opinion of the Moral Majority, the bible or God. . . . How blasphemous you are, speaking out against God and his children who are trying to do God's leading, following the New Testament teachings, also knowing God's moral laws have never been revoked. Why you as an obvious atheist chose to teach religion is quite a mystery. True, anyone can be an authority on the different religions in the world, but just because you have studied religions, you are not an authority on the word of God which is without error.
>
> Another sad situation is your being a religious humanist, thereby approving all the ungodly textbooks and persons who are ungodly in our schools and government, causing many to stumble and perhaps be lost, dying without Christ, suffering forever in the lake of fire, which is no myth.
>
> Thank God that you no longer preach; but how sad that you even teach. May God have mercy on your soul.

I sincerely regret that the writer did not enclose a return address for I would have wanted to relay that I once held the same point of view. As a teenager in Louisville, Kentucky, the city of my birth, my idol was Billy Graham. I went around announcing that we were living in the last days, that Armageddon was upon us, all the while dragging in alleged absolutes to justify what, why, and when of my moral decisions. I finally had to admit that I was cheating. I had to confess that I was using a subjective principle, which was to acknowledge that I had not gleaned an infallible or omnicompetent guide from the Bible, nature, reason, science, or computer as I had claimed. The more I struggled to escape from subjectivity and relativity, the more I resembled the unhappy stork that Rabbi Nahman of Kossov describes:

> A stork was stuck in the mud and was unable to pull out his legs until a bright idea struck. "Don't I have a long beak," he said? So he stuck his beak into the mud, leaned upon it and pulled out his legs. But then he said: "What's the use.

My legs are out, but now my beak is stuck." So another idea came to him. He stuck his legs back into the mud and pulled out his beak. But again what was the use?[9]

The Evolution of Moral Decision-Making

This parable of the stork helps us to introduce a brief account of the evolution of absolutism in the West. For purposes of our discussion, it is important to differentiate between three periods in our intellectual development: pre-modern, modern, and post-modern—and relate each to a specific understanding of the role of absolutism in moral legitimation.

The preeminent foundation of morality in the past has been absolutism. When called upon to justify our moral codes—and the same is true for our economic, social, and political practices and institutions—the human bias is to appeal to the fundamental structures of reality, to nature or nature's God. To convince others that what we say is right and what we do is morally correct, we refuse point blank to ground our morality in our own, our human, authority. Rather—and there is a clear-cut reason for this that we will identify—the entire rule of ethics in the pre-modern period reduces to this: eliminate as much as possible, the human, the subjective factor.

The story of the Ten Commandments, one of the indispensable texts for the religious right's character education in the public schools, helps us to understand that almost universal method of moral legitimation. The biblical account of the Ten Commandments' origin seeks to reduce the human input to zero. Moses, the human agent involved here, is not God's stenographer, writing down what God dictates. Rather, God is her/his own stenographer, thus avoiding any potential errors in dictation. Moreover, God chisels the Commandments in stone, thus eliminating the need for delete buttons, "white out," and erasers. In short there is no filtering of the Commandments through the human heart, mind, or hand. Moses's function, in the final analysis, is that of a pack horse.

The pre-modern period, for our purposes here, the medieval, carries forward this model of the Ten Commandments, invoking supernatural authorities: Bible, church, and pope. These sources of revelation illumine the divine, the ultimate source, and foundation of the absolute. Through these sources of revelation, a channel to objective certainty was established.

The modern period is often contrasted with the medieval, but in terms of the history of moral absolutism, they have much in common. Though there is a distinct shift from the Bible, the book of supernatural revelation, to a book of nature as the source for the absolute, both continue the traditional view that without the absolute there is no morality. They differ primarily in terms of the particular absolute that is advanced and how we come to know it.

In addition to nature and science, human reason was also advanced in the modern era as a way to get beyond subjectivity in the moral sphere. However, the results, as with the Bible and nature, were the same. Because of the exalted status that Unitarian Universalists assign to reason, let me dwell here on the failure of reason to provide a foundation of objective certainty for morality.

The Demise of Moral Absolutism: The Plucked Chicken Fallacy

Liberals were in the vanguard of those seeking to establish moral absolutes grounded on reason. In this regard they were able to clear the field by removing the absolute authority of supernatural revelation. But having cleared the field, the absolutes spawned by reason suffered the same fate as its predecessors. A simple illustration should persuade you that reason is incapable of resolving fundamental ethical conflicts of the kind we face daily.

Various Eastern religions draw the boundary between human and sub-human life in a manner that includes the cow as a member of the human family. Our view of human nature affirms the opposite. Not only do we slaughter the cow, we barbecue it. From the Hindu perspective, our actions are tantamount to murder and cannibalism. Using reason—throw in science, Bible, whatever you want—demonstrate that we are right and the Hindus wrong or vice versa. You will fail.

In point of fact, it is easy to show that the elevation of reason in the modern period has actually enlarged the area of human choice. We need only note that the development of reason as an alternative authority automatically enlarges the number of possible authorities. Having undermined the infallibility and omnicompetence of its rivals, for example, revelation and the Bible, any failure of reason to demonstrate its own infallibility simply exaggerates the objective uncertainty and increases the scope of human subjectivity.

The evolution of moral absolutism instructs us that the Bible, nature, and reason have not yielded the elusive absolute. From the ashes of the old "absolute" that the new "absolutes" seeks to replace, we get not the proverbial sphinx but the plucked chicken.

In one of his lectures, Plato is reported to have defined the human being as a two-legged animal without feathers. After the lecture, one of his pupils went out, found a chicken, plucked it, labeled it HUMAN BEING, and placed it on Plato's desk. THE ABSOLUTE turns out to be the plucked chicken, a counterfeit absolute that is absolute in name only.

Let us move to the post-modern period, and here we must examine two significant factors: the loss of faith in absolutes and, following from this loss, the enlarged role and responsibility of human choice as moral evaluator. First, we must ask: Why the loss of faith? What has caused it? Several developments can be cited, and these I suggest should guide us in our search for the proper model of character education.

If we listen to the religious right and its effort to reestablish the absolute as norm, we hear the following scenario: the blame is placed on the doorsteps of secular humanism and liberalism. But this is a classic case where the beam is in the critic's—here absolutism's—own eye.

The most cursory examination will easily absolve religious liberals and humanists of this charge. The real culprit responsible for the quickened demise of the absolute is absolutism itself. Note first that competing absolutes dethrone each other. Consider the situation where Roman Catholicism is the single authority, drawing its absolutes from the sacred text and lips of the pope. Along comes Protestantism, drawing its authority and absolutes from the same sacred book. The logic of absolutism affirms that both cannot be right; one is the plucked chicken masquerading as the absolute, but which? If the sacred text itself were an absolute and infallible guide, the contest between the absolutes would never surface. Indeed, the presence of competing interpretations of the absolute immediately calls into question not only the authority and absolute character of the sacred text but also that of the competitors themselves. And need I remind you that all of this is occurring and "ain't" no humanists around anywhere.

Another scenario that is replicated over and over again helps to explain the demise of the absolute. To decide between two rival interpretations of the same sacred text, we move outside the text to another authority: reason, holy spirit, science, and so on. But as history documents, these "outside" authorities spawn rivals, and then the vicious cycle starts anew.

Let us consider quickly one other scenario. The inner logic of absolutism forces it to establish that rival absolutes are absolutes in name only. This leads to a strategy of showing that the human factor that it has avoided contaminates the absolutes of its rivals. But this strategy involves a boomerang effect that potentially deabsolutizes all absolutes. And here too, like the stork in the mud, the best efforts of the absolutist to escape subjectivity it dreads, catapults her/him back into it.

There is one final factor leading to the demise of the religious and moral absolute that falls outside the scope of our analysis here: the linkage between oppression and absolutism. If one examines the mechanism of oppression carefully, one will discover absolutism as essential to its operation. What one does not uncover is the humanism and relativism that apostles of absolutism, like Francis Schaeffer,[10] incorrectly identify as the cause of dehumanization.

Nature as Moral Absolute: Problems and Prospects

Besides the substantial difficulty in identifying the real absolute, there is the equally menacing problem of practicing the absolute. Consider the embarrassing predicament of the absolutist who sincerely attempts to follow the dictates of the Bible or nature as an absolute norm. Where is the person who consistently treats these as absolutes in a literalistic way? What I always discover is that the Swaggarts and Falwells preach the morality of absolutism but practice the morality of situation ethics and relativism.

It is childishly easy to show that the absolutist is guilty not only of the PC (the plucked chicken) fallacy but also another type of PC casuistry, the pick and choose fallacy. As the moral majority's unequal and inconsistent condemnation of homosexuality and Ronald Reagan's divorce illustrate, the disciple of absolutism picks and chooses in a manner that the alleged absolute does not explicitly direct or allow. Whether the alleged absolute is a sacred text or the book of nature, or some other norm, the actual practice of the absolutist is clear; there is always a process of selection and rejection that evidences the operation of human choice, the omnipresence of human subjectivity.

An extended examination of absolutism based on the natural order argument will help us understand the embarrassing problematics of absolutism. The appeal to the natural order as the ultimate foundation for social and moral legitimation is one of the most general patterns of human reasoning. Historically, the authority of the natural order in human affairs is outranked only by an appeal to the supernatural realm, the divine order of reality. And in point of fact, these twin authorities have usually been linked like two sides of the same coin.

The natural law theory in moral legitimation parallels the familiar proof-text approach to sacred scripture. Nature functions as the "sacred text" that is scrutinized and then taught as a catechism. Nature's activities, its pattern of birth and death, ebb and flow, and in particular, its hierarchical patterns are probed from top to bottom so that we can formulate a "Ten Commandments" for governing the society. These "Commandments," based on the natural order, become our favored principles of social organization and morality, principles to which we must conform if we are to realize our true ends as human beings.

Let us reflect on why the appeal to nature and the divine reality have and continue to monopolize moral legitimation. Advocates of the natural order position seek to coerce conformity to their understanding of the Good and the True by investing their imperatives with the authority of ultimate reality itself. Given that what some humans have created, others can change or destroy, societies are loath to ground morality on human authority. The need to protect the moral code from whim and caprice recommends the strategy of the divine logo or the authority of natural order. Given this understanding, we arrive at the following formula to enhance the survival of our moral codes and institutions.

> How can the future of the institutional order be best ensured . . .? Let the institutional order be so interpreted as to hide as much as possible its constructed (human) character. Let the people forget that this order was established by men and continues to be dependent upon the consent of men. Let them believe that, in acting out the institutional programs that have been imposed upon them, they are but realizing the deepest aspirations of their own being and putting themselves in harmony with the fundamental order of the universe.[11]

The Pick and Choose Fallacy

What is illicit about this commonplace operation of moral legitimation that authorizes the label "fallacy"? The illicit feature is visible once we consider some "case studies" drawn from well-documented responses to the natural order as a moral absolute. Let us start with the cockroach, that "detestable creature that defies all our efforts to exterminate it." Scientists tell us that these life forces—note I use a neutral term that does not reflect our normal superior-inferior, human-sub-human categories—were on the scene millions of years before us, and it is predicted that they will likely be around when we are gone. While we are both here, sharing this planet earth, our efforts to exterminate the cockroach have not succeeded. What does this failure tell us about nature's value system? Are we, or is the cockroach, nature's darling? What does conformity to nature dictate in this context: continuing our "genocidal" practices against the cockroach, adopting a policy of co-existence, of "live and let live," or withdrawing and letting the cockroach have its uninterrupted day in the sun?

Other common human responses to the natural order raise a similar dilemma. Take crabgrass, another "devil" that resists our policy of extermination. Look at cancer, from the perspective of nature rather than our own; on what grounds do we label cancer as "bad"? Given that humans differ from most other life forms in that our sex life is not restricted to specific seasons or times, demonstrate that the natural order mandates human sex as procreation, recreation, or both. If both, where is the guide from nature that identifies a given option on a particular occasion?

Several issues and questions become clear in all of this: Is it not the case that we label as good those features of nature that conform to our understanding of what is good and condemn those that we judge to be bad. But in light of the actualities of the natural order, our norms are self-established and self-validated. They are, accordingly, immediately suspected as question-begging.

Does not our attitude toward the cockroach, for instance, indicate that we humans approach the natural order with a preestablished norm, a norm that we cannot document to be affirmed by nature itself. Is it not the case that when the absolutist testifies that nature is her/his final norm, the actual practice, when all is said and done, demonstrates that some other norm—not nature—is functioning as the absolute.

Can we, in matters of morality, move from the "is" to the "ought," from the natural world to the level of governing rules for human society—without the intermediate operation of human evaluation, human choice, and human subjectivity? The evolution of absolutism suggests that we cannot. If this is the case, then the appeal to the absolute in moral discourse is a mystification to camouflage a subjective principle of authority that is not acknowledged. Several observations help us to get to this particular point. First, one should note that the cloak of the absolute allows a human voice to masquerade as God. Need I remind you that each time we hear: "Thus, sayeth the lord," or that "This is the will of God" it is always some human allegedly speaking for God.

Moral Decision-Making: Guiding Principles for the Post-Modern Liberal

With the foregoing analysis as background, let me isolate some of the basic principles that should control our quest for a moral system in the post-modern world.

1. Generally speaking, the parameters that define moral decision-making must accommodate both the particularities of the human situation and the historical context in which we have our being. Our historical situation appears to be this: whereas the modern and pre-modern periods sought to establish an objective certainty as the foundation for morality, the postmodern world operates with objective uncertainty as the context for our moral decision-making. We must recognize that though various traditions advance themselves as absolutes, none has been able to certify this exalted status without begging the question or appealing to an internal faith claim that is not self-validating.

What this suggests is that the failure of absolutism to validate its claims has created a situation of objective uncertainty, where the so-called objective methods of truth seeking—science, reason, and revelation—do not demonstrate the ultimacy of their conclusions or produce the certainty that their inner logic demands. Having reached an impasse at the objective pole, we are pushed to the subjective pole, to human choice and decision, as the determinative factor that weights the case in favor of a given possibility.

For this reason religions and moralities now move, live, and have their being within an environment of relativity and pluralism. The sheer existence and number of competing faith communities and socially powerful rivals force each to revalidate the content of its faith and morality under the close scrutiny of its rivals. If we look at the actual results, accomplishing this with objective certainty is exceedingly difficult; no one has yet executed this feat. Rather, the end product has been an atmosphere that relativizes the content of these religions and moralities.

2. All of this says to me—and here the objective uncertainty of the historical context and the human condition coalesce—that rather than the transcendent absolute outside of the human as the foundation for morality, we are in a situation where human choice becomes the functional foundation for morality. I know this sounds arrogant and nihilistic. But I think that if you look carefully at Van Cleve's discerning understanding of the role of human choice in morality, can we reach any other conclusion?

> At the very core of the human being, there operates the power of choice. And it is this power of choice that sets us off as men. It is this power of choice which must decide not only what is true but what criteria should be used to determine the truth, and what standards shall be used in deciding between competing criteria, and what judgments shall be employed in deciding on the standards, ad infinitum. Human choice is the ultimate court of judgment both in morals and in practical judgment; it rules between competing choices of moral action. But it also rules on what moralities shall be used in making judgments, and what meta-moralities shall be used in deciding which morality is best, ad infinitum. Ultimately when all the sham of Reason, Nature, Science and God have

been stripped away, there stand you and I, our choosing selves, naked before a cosmos of alternatives, trying to plot our way through it and thus to give substance and essence to the idea of Man.[12]

In this sense, our values consist of our choices.... If I really believe myself to be a human being, in all cases, I must be the final arbiter of what is good and true—it doesn't matter what the external thing is—a God, a Nature, a doctrine, or even the uncoerced community of persuasion. Many people do not want this responsibility. They want to be told what to do; they want to be told what to be. Yet even in wanting to be told they are expressing their essence; that is, they want to be a creature who needs to be told what to do or what to be.[13]

I take all of this to mean that Abraham's situation, when he is commanded to slay Isaac, represents the human situation. Faced with the command: "Slay thy son," he is immediately forced to function as ultimate valuator or final arbiter of right and wrong. Without a method of objective certainty, he is forced to decide who is speaking to him. Is it Yahweh, Lord of the universe, testing Abraham's faith? Or is it Moloch, the deity who demands human sacrifices, arranging his next meal? Or is it Moloch masquerading as Yahweh or vice versa? Or is it Abraham's unconscious desire to be relieved of the burdens of parenthood? If Abraham cannot demonstrate who is speaking to him, if he cannot demonstrate the validity and ultimacy of any criteriology he introduces to settle the issue, he is functioning as ultimate valuator. He must decide the source of the command, and in making this judgment, at the same time, determine the values of the command. If he concludes that the decree is from Yahweh, the command is morally imperative. If, however, he concludes that the voice is Moloch's or Satan's, the order must be rejected. But clearly only Abraham can make this decision.

Likewise with humankind: forced by virtue of our freedom and the existential situation of objective uncertainty, we cannot escape the necessity to be the measure of even that higher reality that created us. There is no way to escape this responsibility short of denaturing humanity, for it is a factor of the freedom that is our essence.

3. Post-modern developments have shown that if one rejects absolutism as the foundation for morality, one cannot avoid the question posed by nihilism, is everything permitted?

It all depends on where you are,
It all depends on when you are,
It all depends on how you feel,
It all depends on what you feel,
It all depends on how you're raised,
It all depends on what is praised,
What's right today is wrong tomorrow,
Joy in France, in England sorrow.

> *It all depends on point of view*
> *Australia or Timbucktoo,*
> *In Rome do as the Romans do,*
> *If tastes just happen to agree,*
> *Then you have morality.*
> *But where there are conflicting trends,*
> *It all depends, it all depends.*[14]

Given this understanding, how does one show that killing 6 million Jews is no worse than wearing mismatched socks. Or, as Francis Schaeffer has posed the issue:

> With nothing higher than human opinion upon which to base judgments . . . the justification for seeing crime and cruelty as disturbing is destroyed. The very word *crime* and even the word *cruelty* lose meaning. There is no final reason on which to forbid anything—"If nothing is forbidden, then anything is possible."[15]

When each of us is forced to rebut nihilism without begging the question, when we expose the full impact of absolutism's as well as rationalism's failure to move beyond human subjectivity as their inner logic demands, Dietrich Bonhoeffer's portrait of the responsible moral agent will be accepted as an appropriate model for post-modern ethics.

Bonhoeffer, you recall, was a Lutheran minister who had to answer the agonizing question of whether he could participate in the assassination of Hitler, the nation's leader. As you recall, he did participate, was caught, tried, and placed in prison where he eventually died. Every time I read this passage I sense that it perhaps controlled his conscience when he made his fateful decision.

> The responsible man acts in the freedom of his own self, without the support of men, circumstances, or principles, but with a due consideration for the given human and general conditions. . . . The proof of his freedom is the fact that nothing can answer for him, nothing can exonerate him, except his own deed and his own self. It is he himself who must observe, judge, weigh up, decide, and act. It is man himself who must examine the motives, the prospects, the value and the purpose of his action. But neither the purity of the motivation, nor the opportune circumstances, nor the value nor the significant purpose of an intended undertaking can become the governing law of his action, a law to which he can withdraw, to which he can appeal as an authority and by which he can be exculpated and acquitted. . . . The action of the responsible man is performed . . . wholly within the domain of relativity, wholly in that twilight which the historical situation spreads over good and . . . evil. . . . It has to decide not simply between right and wrong and between good and evil, but between right and right and between wrong and wrong. . . . It is performed without any claim to a valid claim to a valid self-justification, and therefore, without any claim to an ultimate valid knowledge of good and evil.[16]

If we as religious liberals can incorporate this understanding of moral decision into modules of value indoctrination and programs of character education, the future should give us no headaches that a few UU Tylenol cannot handle.

Notes

1. Mike McManus, "Teaching Ethics in Schools Aids Basic Parental Goal," *Tallahassee Democrat*, June 15, 1985.
2. Ibid.
3. Ibid.
4. Ibid.
5. Ibid.
6. *The Complete Works of Francis Schaeffer: A Christian Worldview* (Westchester, IL: Crossway Books), Vol. 1, *The God Who Is There*, 1982, 117.
7. Sue McInnish, "Conference Seeks To Strengthen Families," *The Montgomery Advertiser*, April 3, 1982.
8. Mk 10:11-12.
9. Abraham Heschel, *The Insecurity of Freedom* (New York: Farrar, Straus & Giroux, 1966), 140, adapted.
10. "Because the Christian Consensus has been put aside, we are faced today with a flood of personal cruelty.... The Christian consensus gave great freedoms without leading to chaos, because the society in general functioned within (absolute) values given in the Bible.... Now that humanism has taken over, the former freedoms run riot, and individuals ... increasingly practice their cruelties without restraint. And why shouldn't they? If the modern humanist view of man is correct and man is only a product of chance in a universe that has no ultimate values, why should an individual refrain from being cruel to another person, if that person seems to be standing in his or her way?" Schaeffer, *Whatever Happened to the Human Race?* 287.
11. Peter Berger, *The Sacred Canopy* (New York: Doubleday, 1969), 33.
12. Van Cleve Morris, *Philosophy and the American School* (Boston: Houghton Mifflin, 1961), 76.
13. Ibid.
14. Quoted in Abraham Edel, *Ethical Judgment: The Use of Science in Ethics* (New York: Free Press, 1955), 16.
15. *The Complete Works of Francis Schaeffer: A Christian Worldview* (Westchester, IL: Crossway Books, 1982), Vol. 5, *Whatever Happened to the Human Race?* 290.
16. Dietrich Bonhoeffer, *Ethics* (New York: Macmillan, 1955), 87.

Part III

THE POLITICS OF RACE

Chapter 12

POWER AND ANTI-POWER

William R. Jones

Unitarian Universalists as a group have neglected the fundamental issue of the role, status, and value of *power* in human affairs. Unfortunately, we do not have a viable theology of power to undergird our social ethics, and this absence not only renders us ineffective but often places us on the wrong side of ethical issues. We have advanced glowing and commendable resolutions on the pressing social issues of the day; we do not lack the sensitive eye and heart to see what needs to be done; but we too often flounder when we reach the question of how: the question of strategy. And this, I suggest, is because we are confused and deluded about the appropriate place of power in human affairs.

This problem was impressed upon us most vividly some years ago when Unitarian Universalists were trying to work their way through the perplexing Black caucus movement and its slogan, "Black power." My subsequent study in liberation theology has confirmed my conviction that there is a clear-cut connection between oppression and the endorsement of the position I want to challenge here, namely *anti-powerism*.

Anti-Powerism

This distinction between power and anti-powerism is no academic matter. I boldly state that unless you adopt the position of powerism you will come out with an inaccurate analysis of the racial problem and an ineffective resolution of the same. As a Black man, I am concerned that Black leaders, especially those whom whites advance as Black leaders, too often advance anti-powerism. Consider Booker T. Washington for instance, who made this claim: "The opportunity to exercise free political rights will not come to the black in any large degree through outside or artificial forcing, but will be given to the Negro by the Southern White people themselves, and they will protect the Negro in the exercise of these rights." Booker T., and Martin Luther King also, felt that it was only necessary to dramatize the undemocratic and immoral nature of discrimination and racism, and equal justice would gradually become a reality. Force was deemed neither necessary nor desirable. Black leaders today are not strikingly different from Booker T. Recall the initial response of Black leaders to the slogan, *Black power*. Roy Wilkins complained, "We of the NAACP will have none of this. It is the father of hatred and the mother of violence." (I still believe that what really disturbed Roy and others was the emphasis on power, not the emphasis on Blackness.)

The position of anti-powerism regards ethics and power as incompatible. It wants to separate love and power as far as possible. It sees the quest for power, not in neutral, but always in negative terms. The essence of this position is best expressed in Jacob Burckhardt's description: "Now, power in its very nature is evil, no matter who wields it. It is not stability but lust, and ipso facto insatiable; therefore it is unhappy in itself and doomed to make others unhappy." Those who advocate anti-powerism conclude that we have a moral situation only when we can push power outside or to the periphery of the ethical circle. Making power central, according to this view, leads to ethical nihilism, the contradiction of ethics, for it is assumed that to make power central in ethics requires that we affirm the principle, "Might makes right", and no one wants to claim this as the foundation to morality.

A Force for Ethics

It is this basically negative view of the role of power that must be corrected. Power must be rehabilitated as central and controlling, a legitimate force in social ethics. One can say with confidence that a constructive social ethics will be impossible as long as we continue to look at power with distrust.

My concern is to rehabilitate the concept of power, to make it a respectable religious and ethical option among Unitarian Universalists.

It is not difficult to show that power is in fact the superstructure of religion and ethics. Romano Guardini, for instance, concludes that "Every act, every condition, indeed even the simple fact of existing is directly or indirectly linked to the conscious exercise of power." Or take Paul Tillich: "In any encounter of man with man power is active, every encounter, whether friendly or hostile, whether benevolent or indifferent, is in some way a struggle of power with power." Or take Reinhold Niebuhr's short but pregnant "Life itself is power." Are not the fundamental differences in the status of human beings differences in the possession of power? What is the difference between master and slave, parent and child, teacher and student, male and female, Black and white, rich and poor but the disproportionate amount of power that each has at his disposal?

If you look at the Black situation—the racial situation—again I would contend that only an analysis in terms of power provides an accurate description. The primary obstruction to Black humanity is not Blackness but *powerlessness*; the Black is powerless because a stronger power, white power, looms over the crucial areas of his existence. One could increase statements of this type ad nauseum, but let me simply summarize the point, namely that power appears to be a central category of human and ultimate reality. To remove it, therefore, or to make it peripheral to ethics is impossible.

The Source of Law

Let me hasten to my second point. Can the advocate of anti-powerism point to an actual ethical system where power is not central? I agree it is possible to talk about such a system without contradiction, just as I can talk about a Black president of the United States, but I cannot isolate such a creature. Two models have been set forth as examples of anti-powerism in ethics—non-violence and the Christian ethic of love. When we turn to the Christian ethic of love it is, I think, an illusion to conclude that power is absent or not central. Consider the *source of values*, that is, God, the omnipotent, the sovereign. God in his role or sovereign serves as the maintainer of the law, the judge, and punisher of violators of the law. Power is implicit and explicit in God as the source of the law, as an expression of his sovereign will.

Nor does non-violence differ here. Non-violence is affirmed because it is considered to be that which is most powerful, that which will endure and withstand time and change and the activity of hostile forces. You do not understand Gandhi, I insist, if you do not see in his practice a way of *associating yourself with that which is most powerful*.

Consider Gandhi's statement, in which he assigns to the law of love the same status as a law of nature: "The law of love will work," he says, "just as the law of gravitation will work, whether we accept it or not." In this sense, the person who tries to defy the law of love is analogous to one who tries to defy the law of gravitation. What we have in the Christian and Gandhian approaches is, then, not the absence of power but different roads to power, different definitions, different understandings.

I think it is possible to see that the category of power is overlooked in other parts of the Christian and biblical heritage. Consider, for instance, the concept of humility which is usually interpreted in terms of anti-powerism. But according to the New Testament, at least as I understand it, a precondition for humility—is not weakness but strength, *power*. Consider Philippians, when God empties himself of his power and his majesty, humbles himself and becomes obedient unto death. Humility designates a power that one has but refuses to use, not a weakness where one is forced to submit to a higher power. Humility involves putting aside one's power for a special purpose, bringing oneself to a level that is less than one is actually able to occupy. The point appears to me to be obvious: if you want me to be humble, first give me power.

Power Is Neutral

Finally, I argue, anti-powerism constructs an illegitimate equation between power and violence. It equates an excess of power with power itself. It is blinded by the excess of power to eliminate power in its entirety. It holds that because power leads to violence, power should be eliminated. But the error of this view is obvious. You could use the same principle to say that fire should be eliminated because it leads to destruction; or sugar should not be used because it causes diabetes or bad teeth; rivers should be eliminated because they cause floods; life itself should be done away with because it involves suffering or pain. I think it is a mistake for us to try to see power as intrinsically evil, for once we do this we have to regard life itself as evil. Power itself is neutral. The quality of power is determined by the one who employs it and for what purposes. And what is violence, in the final analysis, but an excessive or illegitimate use of power, a power that has gone too far?

I have learned that one cannot respect all freedoms equally at the same time. To act on behalf of the freedom of the oppressed involves acting against the freedom of the oppressor. No action can be generated for one person without its being immediately applied against other persons. It is impossible for me not to act against the freedom of some persons. If I do nothing I act in opposition to the freedom of those who are oppressed. If I do nothing, I act at the same time in favor of the status quo and in favor of the oppressor. If I act on behalf of the oppressed, then I must deny, in part, the freedom of the oppressor. As one put it, we do not have a choice between purity and violence, but only between different forms of violence.

Co-equal Power

If I am correct in my analysis of power, it is not possible to eliminate it from ethics or from human life. The only solution I see is this: to establish a situation where any one power is confronted by a co-equal power. It is this balance of power which to me is the most perfect. I would suggest that the history of what you regard as moral advancement involves the same situation, creating a situation of co-equality of power. And what you would designate as the most inhuman situations are those which involve gross or the greatest inequality in the distribution of power.

Let me conclude. The future lies open to those who see clearly what is true about themselves and the reality in which they live. The future belongs to those who forge new forms of political and social life based on these truths. I am calling Unitarian Universalists to travel a new road, one previously undiscovered and believed impossible. I suggest that we tread this way: Do not fear power but fear its misuse; do not damn power, but condemn its inordinate concentration. Use the power that you have to enlarge the power of all oppressed people and seek no power which you do not want to grant to your fellows. As Hosea Ballou affirmed, if we agree in brotherly love, there is no disagreement that can do us any injury; but if we do not, no other agreement can do us any good.

Chapter 13

RELIGION AS LEGITIMATOR AND LIBERATOR

INSIGHTS FROM THE UNDERCLASS FOR PUBLIC POLICY

(A Worm's Eye View of Religion and Contemporary Politics)

William R. Jones

By way of introduction, let me connect my topic to the general purpose of the conference, outline the framework of my analysis, and identify some of the presuppositions that you will detect in my analysis.

For my contribution to these proceedings, I want to examine the role, status, and value of religion in contemporary politics from the viewpoint of those who are labeled variously as the oppressed, the wretched of the earth, and the underclass. These are the people who occupy the lowest rung of the economic, social, and political (ESP) ladder; these are the groups who by virtue of their ESP condition are confined to the worm's eye view of life, seeing the parade of history from that place where the "trickle down" reaches its final destination.

Liberation Theology as a Worm's Eye View

Most of us are already familiar with the proverbial bird's eye view. But far fewer of us recognize as well the importance and necessity of a worm's eye view to obtain an accurate picture of whatever topic we are discussing. Let us unpack some of the important meanings inherent in these contrasting images of the worm and the bird and reflect on why a worm has been chosen to represent the underclass. In making a contrast between a worm's and a bird's eye view of things, one is in fact forcing this question. Is there a correlation between one's ESP *context* and the *content* of one's politics, ethics, and public policies—especially where the issues of the need and the method of social change are concerned? To affirm a worm's eye view of things is to remind us that there are, in fact, important differences in the political perceptions, goals, and strategies of the upper class and the underclass.

In addition to raising the question of the correlation between one's ESP context and one's values and deeds, there are other important reasons for selecting the worm to symbolize the oppressed rather than, for instance, the snake or any other creature that lives on the ground and has to see things from the ground up, rather than from the sky down. The worm, unlike the snake, symbolizes the essence of defenselessness against a more powerful, wide-ranging, and far-seeing predator. From the vantage point of the worm it appears that not only the early bird gets the worm but the late bird as well. Looking at the matter politically and sociologically, the superior armaments of the bird—its talons, beak, superior size, speed, and so on—signify the gross imbalance of power associated with one's position as underclass. We see in the worm the quintessence of a deficit of power. Only in death, perhaps, when the body turns to the dust from whence it came, does the worm have its day in the sun.

If one approaches the question of the religious dimension in public policymaking from a worm's eye perspective in today's culture, we are forced to rivet our attention on the phenomenon called liberation theology, the most recent effort by the oppressed to relate religion to the political arena. A product of the Third—but what Hoyt Fuller contends should be called the First—World, liberation theology self-consciously seeks to advance the agenda of the underclass and to express its worldview. We have already witnessed its critical influence and importance in South America, for example, El Salvador. Within our own national boundaries, liberation theology is a generating force in such movements as Black, feminist, and native American theology. Though today a still small voice, there should be little doubt liberation theology is emerging as a prominent and inescapable ingredient in the politics of God and the politics of wo/man. Whether it is saint or sinner, savior or subversive, must await the future verdict of history. But until that verdict is announced, liberation theology cannot be ignored by those in the religious and political arenas; it represents too many, too long voiceless, and too long powerless in the unfolding human drama.

Using the Afro-American expression of liberation theology as a backdrop, I want to analyze the religio-political motifs of liberation theology in a way that will decipher for us its inner logic. My concern throughout will be to treat those insights that a liberation theologian would most likely want an audience of this type to understand and appreciate, precisely because these are the most often misinterpreted and misunderstood, for example, its advocacy of violence as a religio-political strategy. A concluding section will spell out what I see as the most significant impact of liberation theology upon contemporary politics. My basic conclusion is that in the short run, liberation theology will exacerbate the difficulties of reaching political consensus. In the long run, however, I regard its impact as fundamentally salutary.

Religion and Politics: The Not-So-Odd Couple

Before launching into a discussion of the why, what, and how of liberation theology, let me identify my understanding of our purpose for coming together and spell out some of the presuppositions involved in this undertaking that cannot be treated in sufficient detail in this lecture. Implicit in the topic of our conference is the belief that religion is an influential, if not indispensable, personage in the drama of politics—past, present, and future. Sometimes as actor, on other occasions as producer, frequently as agent, repeatedly as director, and habitually as playwright, the impact of religion on politics is unobscured. Whether off-stage in the wings or on center stage as star actor, the involvement of religion in politics is such that any understanding of the political realm that omits the religious dimension can only be regarded as "sound and fury, signifying nothing."

Having said this, let me hasten to add another dimension that is not readily apparent from the title of the conference. Though the title accents the impact of religion on the political realm, this should be understood as affirming a dialectical relation between religion and vice versa. Based on this understanding, I stand before you today as an eager participant in a dialogue, anticipating that your expertise will assist me and my colleagues to understanding better the role, function, and value of religion, while trusting that our insights about religion may illuminate some of the hidden corners that effective policy-makers and judicious statespersons must know if they are to avoid being boxed into them.

Beyond the dialectical relation of religion and politics, we must treat several other matters as background for our analysis. These can best be described and understood by examining some recent cartoons and an article from *The Plain Truth*. There are several unstated meanings in the cartoon that I want to spotlight. Matters that appear to be solely political or economic in nature and thereby deal purely with practical matters are in fact linked to deeper religious, moral, and philosophical affirmations. That is to say, political policy inevitably points back to what Alvin Gouldner terms "background assumptions"; that is, a logically prior level of affirmation about general theories of human nature, the nature of reality, the working of the universe, and wo/man's place and power within it, and so on. It is easy to show, for instance, that policies and theories in economics and politics are not ends in themselves but means to a higher ideal, for example, the common good, the summum bonum for humanity. Moreover, it can be shown that each political and economic system is in fact an effort to manufacture the good society which, in turn, presupposes very specific understandings about the nature and destiny of humanity.

Our policy decisions in sum are built upon an unconscious worldview, a hidden and usually unconfessed, unacknowledged metaphysics of religious perspective. It is this level of background assumptions that structures both our consciousness about life and colors, in turn, our policy decisions and options.

Two crucial corollaries follow from this understanding: (1) when two individuals or groups disagree, what is at the root of these disagreements are our background assumptions; (2) we determine the worthiness of political theories and their resulting policies by judging the accuracy and adequacy of its philosophical and religious underpinnings.

A recent article, "Humanity Won't End in a Nuclear Holocaust," illustrates the connection between our policy blueprints and background assumptions that I want to highlight. In response to the suspicion of Dr. Helen Caldicott, president of Physicians for Social Responsibility, that nuclear warfare may annihilate humanity, an editorial writer for *The Plain Truth* counters: "God will intervene and forcibly *stop* man at the last possible moment from destroying himself. The Bible reveals (it is further argued) that man will use nuclear weapons before God steps in to save man from total nuclear destruction."[1] Let us reflect for a moment on some of the implications of this understanding for the policymaker. Given this scenario, it would appear that (a) limited nuclear warfare is not only possible but inevitable; (b) the scenario that pictures human annihilation as the fallout of "limited" nuclear warfare is blatantly inaccurate; (c) efforts such as the nuclear freeze movement are doomed to failure if the goal is to eliminate nuclear blasts totally; and (d) given President Reagan's recent announcement that the nuclear freeze works against the best interests of the United States, should we now add to that that advocates of the nuclear freeze are ultimately working against God's will as well?

Because of the illustrations that I have used, several points must be made clear to avoid a misunderstanding here. Many of you, no doubt, think that my purpose is to castigate the position of *The Plain Truth*, and to ridicule those policies mentioned in the cartoon where sacred texts become a spiritual Ouija Board for clues to the future of the human race and policies to direct us there. Though I continue to harbor the gravest reservations about such approaches to public policymaking—primarily because they hide the actual authority that is being invoked, an authority that is more subjective than is suggested by appeals to the sacred text or to the word of God—I am not concerned here to register these criticisms. Rather, my purpose is to illuminate this level of analysis and affirmation that the cartoons make explicit but which our reporting and background analyses for public policymaking usually overlook. My purpose ultimately is to force the conclusion that in making the most prosaic political and economic decisions, we are at the same time involved in a general debate about, for instance, different theories of human nature and the working of the universe and our place within it. I want further to suggest that when we rivet our attention on this logically prior level of policymaking, it will be clear that the crucial issues and nagging conflict confronting us often have their rootage within the religious arena.

The virtual invisibility of this level as a religious dimension except, perhaps, by cartoonists and conferences like this, requires explanation. I would say that we tend not to be aware of this level of analysis as religious because we operate on a dictionary definition that equates religion and theism. Within this framework, systems that do not explicitly advance a belief in or affirm the necessity of worship of God consistently escape the level of religious. A different approach that interprets religion in terms of its function, I would suggest, provides a more accurate description of the actual state of affairs and a more adequate base for policy decision-making. Within the functional approach, whatever is advanced as ultimate for human well-being—be it a political system, such as capitalism or communism; a specific lifestyle, for example, vegetarianism, jogging; a philosophical perspective, for example, humanism or atheism—must be regarded as religious. Accordingly, the more sensitive we are to the religious dimension and the more accurate is the understanding of religion that we bring to the policy arena, the more effective and adequate will be our decisions and our policies.

The foregoing understanding of what is at stake is fraught with implications for the policymaker and the reporter. It suggests that the reporter, for instance, must illuminate and make explicit this level of thought and activity for the readers and for the citizens' inspection and assessment. It is to suggest for the policymaker that by virtue of the concrete decisions that he or she makes, especially decisions where competing perspectives are at stake, the "neutral" politician and policymaker is inadvertently enhancing or undermining particular religious perspectives. Though he/she may wish to be, she/he cannot be simply a neutral participant.

The Context and Purpose of Liberation Theology

Liberation theology is a most attractive model to illustrate the central theme of this conference: the interplay of religion and politics. The value of examining liberation theology in this regard is the fact that it explicitly links the religious and political. Indeed, we are constantly reminded of this linkage through its various labels: political theology, the politics of God. An additional value lies in the fact that liberation theology highlights two radically different kinds of linkage between the religious and the political order, between the pulpit and the parliament. I will designate these two roles of religion in the political sphere as religion as legitimator and religion as liberator. These two ways of interpreting religion suggest that religion operates in the political sphere as a Dr. Jekyll and Mr. Hyde. An accent on the legitimator functions sees religion as the unflinching bulwark for the existing social order, as its sanctifier and sacred religion. To emphasize the role of liberator, contrastingly, sees religion as subversive relative to the present order, concerned to radically modify the existing ESP configurations.

To clarify these contrasting functions of religion and their respective impact upon the political realm, it is necessary to draw our attention to the following: (a) the context of liberation theology, (b) its purpose, and (c) its understanding of oppression.

Liberation theology surfaces both as a diagnosis of and prescription for a specific ESP situation, namely, a context of gross ESP inequalities that last from generation to generation. Robert McAfee Brown has accurately described the context as a world where

> 20 percent of the people control 80 percent of the world's resources, where two-thirds of the human family goes to bed hungry every night, in which the economic disparities between the rich nations and the poor nations are mammoth, in which there is a clear and ugly equation that goes: rich = white, poor = non-white and in which, despite occasional pockets of poverty in the former and pockets of affluence in the latter, there is a further equation that goes: affluent white nations = northern hemisphere, poor non-white nations = southern hemisphere. . . . The context is a history in which the powerful rich minority has been increasing its power and riches . . . and a history in which, with very few exceptions, the church has been on the side of power and wealth.[2]

An Anatomy of ESP Oppression

With an understanding of the context of liberation theology, its purpose can be specified. Speaking politically, the raison d'être of liberation theology, whatever its geographical location, is to eradicate ESP oppression. Its primary purpose, speaking religiously, is to demonstrate that this eradication is a moral, spiritual, Christian, and biblical imperative. What this means and what this entails, both for the religious and the political spheres, becomes clearer once we understand the nature and the mechanism of the oppression that liberation theology seeks to eradicate. For our purposes, I want to reduce the structural framework of oppression to the following features:

(1) Oppression affirms a two-category system, a division of the human family into at least two distinct groups. These groups are arranged

(2) in a hierarchy of superior and inferior, for example, in-group, out-group; rich, poor; master, slave; male, female; white, Black; and so on. This hierarchical arrangement is

(3) correlated with a gross imbalance of power and privilege. The alleged superior group possesses the unobscure surplus of power and privilege, the alleged inferior group, the unobscure and grossly disproportionate deficit. (Below, this uneven distribution of power becomes the focus of another aspect of religion as legitimator: its sustaining support for our structural aspects of oppression—quietism and anti-powerism).

(4) The alleged superior group will also have the *most* of whatever the society defines as the *best* and the *least* of the *worst*. In contrast, the alleged inferior group will have the *least* of the *best* and the *most* of the *worst*.

(5) This hierarchical division and the pervasive ESP inequalities it expresses are *institutionalized*. The primary institutions that operate to maintain an unequal distribution of power, resources, and privilege. It goes without saying that when we talk about the connection between religion and oppression, we are treating the impact of religion on the ESP structures that comprise the institution in question.

(6) Grounded in ultimate reality—nature or supernature (God). From a worm's eye view, the intimate linkage between the political order and religion means this: any effort to alter the political order must initially or concurrently radically restructure the religious order as well. In other words, the function of religion as liberator requires an undermining of religion as legitimator.

(7) The oppressed are oppressed, in fundamental part, because of the beliefs they hold. They adopt, or more accurately, are indoctrinated and socialized to accept a belief and value system that motivates them to confirm to the social order, embrace its inequalities as good or inevitable, thus stifling their desire to attack the foundation of these ESP inequalities. Put in other words, the oppressor must persuade the oppressed to act in a way that preserves and conserves what is already present, to refuse to take corrective action where basic institutional structures and cultural patterns are involved. In this

regard, the inner logic of oppression requires an attitude of quietism and a philosophy of anti-powerism *for the oppressed.*

Oppression and Quietism

How is this accomplished? Liberation theology's answer implicates the religious tradition of the culture in a manner that inaugurates a "rotten-apple-in-the-basket" examination of the tradition—an examination, as will be shown, with grave consequences for the political order.

An early book review of *The Autobiography of Jane Eyre* gives an insight into the process by which quietism is generated.

> Altogether *The Autobiography of Jane Eyre*, the reviewer tells us, is preeminently an anti-Christian proposition. There is throughout it a murmuring against the comforts of the rich and against the privations of the poor, which as far as each individual is concerned is a murmuring against God's appointment.[3]

This review illustrates the inner logic and mechanism of oppression. Oppression maintains itself by claiming that its fundamental structures and values are the product of and in conformity with the structure of reality itself. It is here that the function of religion as legitimator becomes apparent. By invoking the supernatural/divine order—one could as well appeal to the natural order—as the foundation for the oppressive institutions, several things essential to the maintenance of oppression are accomplished. We immediately establish a superhuman foundation, which, by virtue of its alleged ultimacy and power, compels our acceptance, our obedience, in sum our conformity. If it is believed that the social and political order expresses God's will and purpose, corrective action to change the society would be impossible. Human power could never hope to win against God's omnipotence: "Our arms too short to box with God." In addition, corrective activity would be inappropriate. Even if we had the power to change our ESP position, clearly it would be blasphemous to do so. Whatever status we have is the status that God intends for us to have; what is, is what ought to be. A similar conclusion would follow from the belief that our ESP inequality is the consequence of divine punishment.

Peter Berger has accurately isolated a general and historical function of religion that is central to liberation theology's understanding of religion as legitimator.

> The historically crucial part of religion in the process of legitimation is explicable in terms of the unique capacity of religion to "locate" human phenomena within a cosmic frame of reference. . . . The *efficacy* of religious legitimation can be brought home by asking a recipe question. . . . If one imagines oneself as a fully aware founder of a society . . . how can the future of the institutional order be best ensured. . . . Let the institutional order be so interpreted as to hide as much as possible, its constructed character. Let the people forget that this order was established by men and continues to

be dependent upon the consent of men. Let them believe that, in acting out the institutional programs that have been imposed upon them, they are but realizing the deepest aspirations of their own being and putting themselves in harmony with the fundamental order of the universe. In sum, set up religious institutions.[4]

Central to its critique of religion as legitimator of the status quo is the claim that core beliefs and values of the religious tradition are essential props for oppression. This has been and continues to be the principal feature of the Afro-American variety. Benjamin Mays's criticism of religion as a prop for oppression, though advanced decades ago, is a classic statement of this theme. Blacks, he claimed, conform to or rebel against their oppressive situation by virtue of the concept of God they hold.

> The Negro's social philosophy and his idea of God go hand in hand. . . . Certain theological ideas enable Negroes to endure hardship, suffer pain and withstand maladjustment, but . . . do not necessarily motivate them to strive to eliminate the source of the ills they suffer.
>
> Since this world is considered a place of temporary abode, many of the Negro masses have been inclined to do little or nothing to improve their status here; they have been encouraged to rely on a *just* God to make amends in Heaven for all the wrongs they have suffered on the earth. In reality, the idea has persisted that hard times are indicative of the fact that the Negro is God's chosen vessel and that God is disciplining him for the express purpose of bringing him out victoriously and triumphantly in the end. The idea has also persisted that "the harder the cross, the brighter the crown." Believing this about God, the Negro, in many instances, has stood back and suffered much without bitterness, without striking back, and without trying aggressively to realize to the full his needs in the world.[5]

Oppression and Anti-Powerism

Religion, according to liberation theology, has been invoked in another substantial way to instill an attitude of conformity in the underclass. Part of the mechanism of oppression is to motivate the oppressed to adopt a philosophy of anti-powerism, whereas the oppressor lives by the opposite philosophy of powerism. The consequence of all of this is to keep gross imbalance of power, privilege, and resources intact. Let us clarify the distinction between these antithetical philosophies.

Anti-powerism and powerism represent contrasting beliefs and attitudes about the role, status, and value of power in human affairs. Anti-powerism regards power as essentially negative or evil. The essence of this position is best expressed in Jacob Burckhardt's description: "Now power in its very nature is evil, no matter who wields it. It is not stability but lust, and ipso facto insatiable. Therefore, it is unhappy in itself and doomed to make others unhappy."

Anti-powerism regards ethics and power as incompatible. It seeks the quest for power, not in neutral, but negative terms. Those who advocate anti-powerism conclude that we have a moral situation only when we push power outside or to the periphery of the ethical domain. According to this view, making power central leads to ethical nihilism and affirming the concept that "might makes right."

In contrast, the position of powerism affirms power as a central and indispensable religious category. Power becomes a controlling concept for describing and interpreting the basic categories of religion and morality. Powerism seeks ultimately to advance power as the preeminent interpretive framework for all aspects of human affairs, as well as the natural and supernatural world. Power, from this perspective, is neutral, neither inherently evil nor good; rather its quality depends upon who wields it and for what purpose.

Advocates of powerism would consider the following as appropriate descriptions of their position. "In any encounter of man with man, power is active, every encounter, whether friendly or hostile, whether benevolent or indifferent, is in some way, a struggle of power with power." Or the equally comprehensive scope of power that is affirmed by Romano Guardini. "Every act, every condition, indeed, even the simple fact of existing is directly or indirectly linked to the conscious exercise of power."

Since oppression involves a gross imbalance of power, the underclass can be kept "in its place" to the degree that it adopts the inner logic of anti-powerism. If anti-powerism is right, in its characterization of power, then the oppressed, "in their place," are, indeed, in the *best* place. To persuade the oppressed to move from a situation of gross imbalance of power to co-equality of power s/he must, subjectively, define the objective situation of a deficit of power as negative, as detrimental to one's well-being; religiously speaking, as sin. Obviously, this understanding of one's situation is thwarted if anti-powerism is the operative philosophy.

Black liberation theologians see the perpetuation of anti-powerism in the white endorsement of Black "heroes" who advance anti-powerism over those in the camp of powerism; the elevation of Martin L. King, Jr. over Malcolm X, of George Foreman over Muhammad Ali, the rejection of the Black athletes at the Olympics who gave the "Black power" sign, and, perhaps the most familiar case, Booker T. Washington over W. E. B. DuBois. Washington's statement still remains a classical description of anti-powerism. "The opportunity to exercise free political rights will not come to the black in any large degree through outside or artificial forcing, but will be given to the Negro by the Southern white people themselves, and they will protect the Negro in the exercise of these rights."

It is instructive to consider another area of religion to which liberation theology has applied the "rotten-apple-in-the-basket" approach: the liturgical life of the oppressed. What was uncovered can best be illustrated by a comparison of the liturgical calendar of Judaism and Afro-American Christianity.

The most cursory examination of the Jewish liturgy reveals a dimension that is curiously absent from the Afro-American liturgy: The religious celebration of ESP liberation. (This absence, however, is not baffling, if one understands the mechanism of oppression.) One is struck by the way the Jewish calendar revolves around historical events that commemorate their release from bondage, the defeat of a despot practicing cultural genocide, and so on. Passover, Purim, and Hanukkah immediately come to mind. Nor is the theme of ESP liberation absent from the rest of the liturgical calendar; many interpreters extract this theme, for instance, from the sabbath observance.

With this understanding of the Jewish liturgy as background, turn to the calendar of the Black Christian church and identify comparable celebrations of ESP liberation. You would search in vain; there are none. Nor has the Black church paid tribute to its own heroes, to Martin Luther King Jr., Malcolm X, Sojourner Truth, Nat Turner, as other ethnic communities have honored their heroes, for example, St. Patrick's Day.

Liberation Theology and the Logic of Ethnicity

The final dimension of liberation theology that should receive our attention is its elevation of the category of ethnicity and cultural pluralism as controlling norms for the underclass. A proper understanding of these categories is essential if we are to grasp the mission and function of the Black church and its impact on the social sphere.

The mission and function of Black religion from the perspective of liberation theology has been captured in two statements—one from W. E. B. DuBois many decades ago and the other from Lerone Bennett, Jr., the dean of Afro-American historians. DuBois argued:

> We Negroes form and long will form a perfectly definite group, not entirely segregated and isolated from our surroundings, but differentiated to such a degree that we have largely a life and thought of our own. . . . This fact in itself has its meaning, its worth and its values. . . . And it is this fact that [Black religion] has got to take into account and make [its] major problem.

In more recent times, Lerone Bennett, Jr. has advanced a parallel admonition:

> The overriding need for the moment is for us to think with our own eyes. We cannot see now because our eyes are clouded by the concepts of (the oppressor). We cannot think now because we have no intellectual instruments save those which were designed expressly to keep us from seeing. It is necessary for us to develop a new frame of reference which transcends the limits of the oppressor's concepts. The oppressor's concepts have succeeded in making black people feel inferior. The oppressor's concepts have created the conditions that make it easy to dominate a people. The initial step towards liberation is to abandon the partial

frame of reference of our oppressor and to create new concepts which release our reality.

Liberation theology seeks to translate the DuBois-Bennett prescription into concrete programs for the different areas of the life of the Black community, including social, political, and cultural arenas.

To reduce the misinterpretations and misunderstandings that usually accompany this part of liberation theology's agenda, let us attempt to reduce the DuBois-Bennett prescription to certain basic propositions as these relate to religion and theology, the focus of this conference.

(1) An ethnic approach to theology is both legitimate and necessary because all theologies are particular. We can agree that the intent of theology is universal, that is, to provide a description of reality that is not simply the idiosyncratic viewpoint of the theologian or her/his community. Yet the basic particularity of theology cannot be ignored.

A simple illustration on this point should be persuasive. If I send you on a scavenger hunt and ask you to bring back F-L-O-W-E-R, you will fail. You can bring me back the word, "flower," but any flower you bring back will be a concrete flower—a rose, a dandelion, an orchid, and so on. Likewise with theology, you will discover only particular theologies—Jewish, Christian, American, the theology of X, a theology that enhances oppression, a theology that enhances liberation. It would appear that only the individual who is willing to endorse the exaggerated realism of the universale ante rem position can avoid this conclusion.

To accept particularity in this fashion is not to reduce theology to ideology or "blackology." Nor is it to argue that a given theology only mirrors the subjective perspective of a particular party at a specific time. Rather it is to assert such commonly warranted principles as the following: every affirmation is also a negation; each concrete expression of a cultural reality posits specific questions and answers and thereby effectively excludes the opposite answers; no single tradition or perspective has demonstrated the totality of human knowledge. Finally, it is to demand from those who challenge the preeminence of particularity that they present to us the alleged universal that does not require supplementation or modification in light of opposing viewpoints.

Given this understanding of particularity, several things follow that we want to examine in sequence.

(2) The failure of a particular community to express and advance its own cultural perspective is, in fact, a form of self-dehumanization. Blacks say, in effect, that it is not necessary for them "to do their thing" because it is unimportant in comparison with the other theological systems. Blacks say, in effect, that the existing theologies have already captured the quintessence of truth and any Black input is now redundant. In sum, Blacks forge their own chains if they fail to demand co-equal authority for their vision of reality.

Several things follow from the particularity of theology which we want now to examine in sequence. The category of particularity leads to the affirmation of authentic pluralism. Because of the confusion that clouds this term, let us examine its inner meaning and logic by comparing and contrasting it with assimilation and integration. Let me begin with an anecdote from Moms Mabley that illustrates a common misunderstanding about these three models for social interaction. In her inimitable fashion, Moms describes a scene in a lunchroom in Mississippi that had just been desegregated. An elderly Black lady sat down at a convenient table and asked to see the menu. After scanning it from cover to cover, she asked the waitress, "Do you have chitterlings?" The waitress responded, "No." The elderly Black lady asked, "Do you have collard greens?" Again, the response was no. She inquired about several other items that are staples on any "soul food" menu but every time the response was no. Finally, the elderly Black lady said indignantly, "You ain't ready for integration."

What she was saying was that the restaurant, at least at the menu level, was still operating on an assimilationist model. That is, a one-category model or a single theme is advanced as the norm or the ideal and everything else is forced to conform to it.

Contrastingly, integration is a two-category model. At least two things are regarded as co-equal and co-significant; neither is superior to the other. Accordingly, both must be included to obtain the ideal situation. Beyond the affirmation of the co-equality of the items, however, integration adds another dimension: it blends or combines the co-equal items such that the product is different from the individual character of the original components.

Cultural pluralism is different from both assimilation and integration. Like integration, it affirms a two- or multi-category model. At least two things are regarded as co-equal and co-significant. But there the similarity ends. Rather than blending the items, as integration does, pluralism asserts that each should retain its distinctive character, its individuality, its uniqueness. The end result of pluralism—if we use a culinary metaphor—is a cultural smorgasbord.

If these distinctions are accurate, then we must say that liberation theology is committed to cultural pluralism at this phase of its history. Its inner logic does not eliminate the integration model, but it does appear to insist that the merger of Black and non-Black perspectives can authentically occur only after the Black perspective has been appropriately articulated. In sum, the phase of comprehensive articulation of cultural perspectives that is correlated with the logic of pluralism must precede the merger phase, that is, integration.

To address other misunderstandings about the heightened ethnicity associated with liberation theology, we must make it clear that cultural pluralism is not an argument for Black racism, nor is it a call for racial separatism. What cultural pluralism affirms has been appropriately expressed, for instance, by Michael Novak and Oscar Wilde. Novak perceptively argues: "To be faithful to our own personal vision is not to deny the truth of the vision in others." In a similar vein, Oscar Wilde correctly identifies the precise difference between authentic pluralism and a despotic, assimilationist doctrine. "A red rose," he insists, "is not selfish because it wants to be a red rose. But it would be horribly selfish if it wanted all other flowers in the garden to be both red and roses." In summary, cultural pluralism is an attempt to establish the co-equality of different cultural perspectives—not the superiority of a Black one.

Implications for Politics and Policymaking

With the previous discussion as background, we can now draw together some of the implications of our analysis for the political arena and those individuals actively engaged in the formation and implementation of public policies.

A major problem area—forging a consensual base for adjudicating issues in the public interest—will no doubt be exacerbated *in the short run*, to the degree that liberation theology is successful in articulating and implementing its program. The liberationist dichotomy between religion as legitimator and religion as liberator is obviously a distinction between authentic and inauthentic religions. The social and political structures formally legitimated by those religious authorities now called into question as inauthentic will require a new source of legitimation for the political and social sphere.

The hegemonic authority of religion will be further undermined in the sense that liberation theology furthers the scope of secularization. Here again, the distinction between authentic and inauthentic religion reduces the authority of religion in general relative to other competing authorities in the culture.

The liberation theology makes political and moral consensus more difficult to obtain in the short run. Its societal impact as a whole, I suggest, will be salutary. Liberation theology, as the name suggests, accents the role of religion as liberator, as avant-garde of fundamental political and social change. I see in its birth pangs a continuation of that spirit and dedication that marked the birth of our own nation: "the last great hope of mankind."

Notes

1   Michael A. Snyder, "Humanity Won't End In A Nuclear Holocaust!," *The Plain Truth* 47, no.7 (August 1982): 19–21.
2   Robert McAfee Brown, *Is Faith Obsolete?* (Philadelphia: Westminster Press, 1974), 35.
3   Lady Elizabeth Eastlake, "Vanity Fair—and Jane Eyre," Review of Jane Eyre, by Charlottee Bronte. *Littell's Living Age*, March 17, 1849, 497–511.
4   Peter L. Berger, *The Sacred Canopy* (New York: Doubleday & Company, Inc. 1967), 33.
5   Benjamin Mays, *The Negro's God*, (New York: Atheneum, 1969), 155.

Chapter 14

HYPOCRISY, BIBLIOCRACY, AND DEMOCRACY

IMPLICATIONS FOR GAYS AND LESBIANS IN THE MILITARY

William R. Jones

Whether of our choosing and whether we like it or not, the gay/lesbian issue (GLI) forces you, our congressional and military leaders, and us, your constituents, to revisit this contentious debate, and to choose and incarnate our foundational values for America, the last best hope for humankind.

To understand the GLI it is necessary to decode the historical and ideological situation that spawn the GLI as a "problem" and a "threat." We will misread the situation if we fail to see that the GLI is a manifestation of a more fundamental conflict that is actually widening in our nation, a continuing conflict that is also evident in the unresolved controversy about racial and sexual discrimination, prayer in the public schools, abortion, and so on.

Recall that the impetus for prayer in the public schools and the anti-abortion movement was the conviction that our national morals had deteriorated and that it was necessary to return America to its proper moral anchor. Linked to this was a precise understanding of the cause of our decline, namely that America has abandoned its belief in our biblical tradition of moral **absolutes** as the necessary, the one and only one, ground for our public ethic. According to this religious perspective, if America is to regain its moral sanity, it must return to these moral rules, grounded on nature or God, that are universally valid for all times, all places, and all individuals.

In all of this we see a defense of some variation of Francis Schaeffer's position, the leading theologian of neo-fundamentalism. "Nobody has ever discovered a way of having real 'morals' without a moral absolute. If there is no moral absolute . . . morals as morals cease to exist. . . . With nothing higher than human opinion on which to base judgments . . . the justification for seeing crime and cruelty as disturbing is destroyed. The very word crime and *cruelty lose meaning*" (Adapted).

The deed and creed of my faith community, the Unitarian Universalist Association, toward lesbians and gays differ conspicuously from the policy and procedures of congressional military leaders. It has corrected its discriminatory and oppressive policies to provide gays and lesbians unrestricted access to our ministry and administrative hierarchy as *co-equals*. For my contribution to these proceedings I want to explain the "how" and "why" of this stark difference in philosophy and practice.

Given our commitment to democratic principles in our denomination and our nation, we could do no other. And given our philosophy of pluralism we could do no less. We also found that those who were opposed to admitting lesbians and gays to our ministry could not defend their opposition without blatant hypocrisy and an appeal to question-begging stratagems. In sum, the opposition to gay/lesbian rights based on moral absolutism is highly problematic. This is what I want to share, along with some principles that will illuminate some of the hidden corners that congressional and military policy makers must be aware of—if they want to avoid being boxed into them. These are principles that we already acknowledge and that I have found advantageous for conflict resolution in similar contexts.

First Principle

It has not gone unnoticed that economic, social, and political policies inevitably point back to what Alvin Gouldner terms "background assumptions," that is, a logically prior level of faith affirmations about human nature, the nature and working of the universe, woman's place and power within it, and so on. Matters that appear to be solely political or economic in nature and thereby assumed to deal purely with practical matters are in fact linked to deeper religious, moral, and philosophical affirmations that constitute very specific beliefs and values about, for instance, the nature and destiny of the human species. This usually unstated worldview, this particular belief and value system is present—regardless of which position one adopts on a given issue and operates as the scaffolding for our policy decisions.

What is at stake here for the congressional and military public decision makers? (1) Though the policy maker may aspire to be a neutral participant with regard to these faith issues where competing commitments are at stake, the concrete decision that she or he makes means that she or he is inadvertently defending or attacking one particular side of the religious debate. Accordingly, this level of thought and commitment should be made visible for each citizen's inspection and assessment. (2) We are forced to admit that our policies—be they economic, social, political, or military—are never ends in themselves; they are means or blueprints to erect the good society, to establish the common good and summum bonum for humanity. (3) When individuals and groups disagree on policy matters, the root of the conflict is usually this level of background assumptions. (4) In the final analysis, we must judge the validity and merit of our policies by its underpinnings, the accuracy and adequacy of its background assumptions.

Second Principle

The DDT principle-diagnosis determines therapy. As an illustration: I have a headache, so I go to a doctor for treatment who diagnoses why I have a pain. The diagnosis, whatever it is, identifies a particular cause for my headache, and the therapy, in turn, is linked to that causality. If, for instance, the diagnosis/causality is constipation, you can predict the likely therapy: Ex-lax, more bulk, water, or exercise. Suppose, however, a second medical opinion indicates that I have a brain tumor. Same therapy? No! Because this diagnosis identifies a different cause, it prescribes a radically different therapy.

The therapy-diagnosis principle obliges us to incorporate the concept of "false causality" in our analysis and assessment of issues. To illustrate: a suburbanite on Long Island dug a huge hole in her/his backyard, 90 by 90 feet. An alarmed neighbor asked for the "why" and "wherefore" of that gigantic crater, and received this answer: "To keep the elephants away." The neighbor now even more disturbed, retorted: "There aren't any elephants within 10,000 miles of this neck of the woods," and the hole-digging suburbanite came back with: "See how effective it is."

Several implications follow from this understanding for our assignment. Any corrective that you may propose for a problem—be it a policy, program, or curriculum—will be grounded on your particular diagnosis of the situation and its implicit causality. In this sense, every policy recommendation is an implicit demonstration and endorsement of the accuracy and adequacy of the diagnosis/causality to which it is a response. Accordingly, the merit or demerit of any therapy or policy that is presented to us should be judged on the validity of *its causal* analysis, its successful avoidance of a false causality. The implication of this is clarified once we consider our human proclivity to legitimation and hypocrisy.

Third Principle

Give attention to the hypocrisy implicit in the following anecdote that illustrates our third principle: *expose our hypocrisy.* A Roman Catholic priest was conducting a catechism class on heaven which involved a series of five questions. Question one: "How many of you believe in heaven?" All raised their hands. Question two: "How many of you believe that heaven is a good place?" All raised their hands. Question three: "How many of you believe that heaven is the best place?" Again, all raised their hands. Question four: "How many of you want to go to heaven?" All raised their hands again, but this time, most raised both hands. His final question: "How many of you are willing to die tomorrow and go to heaven?" Not a single hand was raised. If their answer to the first four questions represented their actual belief, their answer to the fifth question should have been either "Yes," or if "No," they should add quickly "I don't want to wait until tomorrow. I want to die right now." This anecdote recommends a critical method that compares and contrasts our *announced* belief—what we preach—with our *actual* belief, the belief that underlies what we practice. This tactic effectively uncovers our inconsistencies and hypocrisy. When hypocrisy is present, that is, when actual practice does not dovetail with announced beliefs, our announced beliefs are *absentee* beliefs. Our actual belief is Absent Without Leave (permission) (AWOL), and we conceal this absence by using a replacement belief to answer the roll call for our actual belief. Directing our attention to the human activity of legitimation clarifies all of this and also exposes the hypocrisy of neo-fundamentalism.

What is legitimation? It is that human activity whereby we justify whatever we do, when we do it, where we do it, how we do it, and why we do it. Legitimation operates as a powerful form of social control, particularly through an appeal to moral absolutism. To secure conformity to our understanding of the Good and the True and the social institutions we construct, we seek point blank to eliminate as much as possible, the human, the subjective factor. Given that what some humans have created, others can change or destroy, societies are loath to ground morality on human authority. The need to protect the moral code from whim and caprice recommends the strategy of the divine logo or the authority of natural order.

To ensure the survival of our moral code and institutions, Peter Berber provides this recipe:

> Let the people believe that, in acting out the institutional programs that have been imposed upon them, they are putting themselves in harmony with the fundamental order of the universe. Let the institutional order be so interpreted as to hide as much as possible its constructed [human] character. Let the people forget that the order was established by men and continues to be dependent upon the consent of men. (Adapted)

The story of the Ten Commandments follows this recipe. The biblical account seeks to reduce the human input to zero. There is no filtering of the Commandments through the human heart, mind, or hand. Moses, the human agent, is not God's stenographer, writing down what God dictates. Rather God is her/his own stenographer, thus avoiding any potential errors in dictation. Moreover, God chisels the Commandments in stone, thus eliminating the need for delete buttons, "white out," or erasers. Moses's only function is that of a pack horse.

My life history also illustrates these insights. I was born and raised a fundamentalist. As a teenager, I went around teaching biblical prophecy. Billy Graham was my idol. I could skillfully go to one chapter, splice from another and paste them together as "the word of god." But, I finally had to admit that I was cheating. I could not identify "chapter and verse" in the test that directed me to splice in the precise way that I did.

Another example: No one literally conforms to each of the Bible's directives or follows in Jesus's footsteps without some adjustment. Otherwise, we would all be carpenters, and we would not marry. An example that relates to the GLI. Some six years ago, several local ministers argued on the basis of selected biblical passages that gays were unfit to hold offices of public trust or subjective. Given this use of the Bible as an absolute norm, as well as their announced claim to follow in Jesus's footsteps, is it not hypocritical and inconsistent that they never questioned Ronald Reagan's moral fitness to be president?

Let me refresh your memory. Jesus says nothing for or against homosexuality. He simply doesn't discuss it as a discrete moral issue. But he is very specific about divorce. Divorce + remarriage = adultery (Mark 10). And given their praise of the Ten Commandments that also condemns adultery, why did they fail to link the problems plaguing America with the possibilities that an adulterer was in the White House or that divorcees were holding public seats of power?

Moral absolutism, at base, is a hypocrisy. It does not practice what it claims: strict conformity to an alleged absolute. We all operate on what I term the PC fallacy, we pick and choose among options that we did not create. We approach nature's "absolutes" and life styles as a menu from which we pick and choose according to our tastes. We then legitimate our choice by claiming that nature has established one and only menu item as the piece de resistance.

The evolution of moral absolutism instructs us that neither the Bible, nature, nor reason has yielded the elusive absolute; from the ashes of the old "absolute" that the new "absolutes" seeks to replace, we get not the proverbial sphinx but the plucked chicken.

In one of his lectures, Plato is reported to have defined the human being as a two-legged animal without feathers. After the lecture, one of his pupils went out, found a chicken, plucked it, labeled it HUMAN BEING, and placed it on Plato's desk. THE ABSOLUTE turns out to be the plucked chicken, a counterfeit absolute that is absolute in name only.

Consider the embarrassing predicament of the absolutist who sincerely attempts to follow the dictates of the Bible or nature as an absolute norm. It is childishly easy to show that the absolutist is guilty not only of the PC (the plucked chicken) fallacy but also another type of PC casuistry, the pick and choose fallacy. As the moral majority's unequal and inconsistent condemnation of homosexuality and Ronald Reagan's divorce illustrate, the disciple of absolutism picks and chooses in a manner that the alleged absolute does not explicitly direct or allow. Whether the alleged absolute is a sacred text or the book of nature, or some other norm, the actual practice of the absolutist is clear; there is always a process of selection and rejection that reveals the omnipresence of human subjectivity and human choice.

An extended examination of absolutism based on the natural order argument will help us understand its embarrassing problematics. The appeal to the natural order as the ultimate foundation for social and moral legitimation is one of the most general patterns of human reasoning. Historically the authority of the natural order in human affairs is outranked only by an appeal to the supernatural realm, the divine order of reality. And in point of fact these twin authorities have usually been linked like two sides of the same coin.

The natural law theory in moral legitimation parallels the familiar proof-text approach to sacred scripture. Nature functions as the "sacred text" that is scrutinized and then taught as a catechism. Nature's activities, its pattern of birth and death, ebb and flow and in particular its hierarchical patterns, are probed from top to bottom so that we can formulate a "Ten Commandments" for governing the society. These "Commandments," based on the natural order, become our favored principles of social organization and morality-principles to which we must conform if we are to realize our true ends as human beings.

What is illicit about this commonplace operation of moral legitimation that authorizes the label "fallacy"? The illicit feature is visible once we consider some "case studies" drawn from well-documented responses to the natural order as a moral absolute.

Let us start with the cockroach, that "detestable creature" that defies all our efforts to exterminate it. Scientists tell us that these life forces—note I use a neutral term that does not reflect our normal superior-inferior, human-sub-human categories—were on the scene millions of years before us, and it is predicted that they will likely be around when we are gone. While we are both here, sharing this planet earth, our efforts to exterminate the cockroach have not succeeded. What does this failure tell us about nature's value system? Are we, or is the cockroach, nature's darling? What does conformity *to* nature dictate in this context? Continuing our "genocidal" practices against the cockroach, adopting a policy of co-existence, of "live and let live," or withdrawing and let the cockroach have its uninterrupted day in the sun?

Other common human responses to the natural order raise a similar dilemma. Take crabgrass, another "devil" that resists our policy of extermination. If we look at cancer, from the perspective of nature rather than our own, on what grounds do we label cancer as "bad"? Given that humans differ from most other life forms in that our sex life is not restricted to specific seasons or times, demonstrate that the natural order mandates human sex as procreation, recreation, or both. If both, where is the guide from nature that identifies a given option on a particular occasion?

Also note the different implications for the GLI issue when we direct attention to the different causalities for homosexuality and the specific causality that opponents of gays and lesbians' rights must defend. God or nature can be the cause in the sense that left-handed is an "abnormal" life style that is genetically determined. On the other hand, gay/lesbianism can be regarded as a chosen life style and here the causality resides within the choice of the individual person. To justify their position, opponents of gay/lesbian rights must successfully rebut a genetic determination for homosexuality on scientific grounds or else god or nature is accountable and responsible and gays/lesbians are not. Also, the fact that left-handed individuals can be trained to operate in a right-handed life style does not rebut the genetic determination of left-handers. Once it is allowed that left-handers can morally defy and overrule the life style that nature and nature's god has recommended, how can natural law theorists overrule a similar option for gays and lesbians without exposing their hypocrisy?

Several issues and questions become clear in all of this: Does not our attitude toward the cockroach, for instance, indicate that we humans approach the natural order with a preestablished norm, a norm that we cannot document that nature itself affirms? Is it not the case that when the absolutist, for instance, testifies that nature is her/his final norm, the actual practice, when all is said and done, demonstrates that some other norm—not nature—is functioning as the absolute?

Is it not the case that we label as good those features of nature that conform to our understanding of what is good and condemn those that we judge to be bad? But in light of the actualities of the natural order, our norms are self-established and self-validated. They are, accordingly, immediately suspect as question-begging and grounded on hypocrisy.

Chapter 15

THE DISGUISES OF DISCRIMINATION

CIVIL RIGHTS, 1954–65

William R. Jones

The opinions which men and groups hold of each other and the judgments which they pass upon their common problems are notoriously [self] interested and unobjective. These judgments . . . are biased . . . because there is no strong inclination to bring all relevant facts into view. While the ideological taint upon all social judgments is most apparent in practical conflicts of politics, it is equally discernible, upon closer scrutiny, in even the scientific observations of social scientists. The latter may be free of conscious bias or polemic intent. Yet every observer of the human scene is an agent in, as well as an observer of, the drama which he records.

We . . . look at history from some locus in history . . . [We are] engaged in its ideological conflicts, and [we] use [our] intellectual processes to justify [our] own ends.

—Reinhold Niebuhr, *Ideology and the Scientific Method*, 1953.

This chapter is a "cuss and discuss" effort in the public humanities. As a contribution to current discussions about moral leadership in Florida—particularly in the public and private sphere—it may well be controversial. It argues that our interpretation of the civil rights era is fundamentally flawed and informed by a method of mislabeling and misdiagnosis that legitimizes and continues the uncorrected discrimination against Black Americans. It shows that America's ongoing game plan is not to correct but to continue the defects, deficits, and disadvantages [those terms will be used interchangeably] that its laws and policies of racial discrimination created and maintained. It looks at the roles of three prominent Floridians in the civil rights era—Governor LeRoy Collins, Governor Claude Kirk, and the Reverend C. K. Steele—through this lens. This chapter argues too that white America is in denial—like the denial of the addict—about its controlling causality and culpability for these defects.

This chapter relocates the debate about the moral leadership of political figures in the civil rights era and where each belongs on the scale of moral leadership. For instance, Collins's superior moral leadership is often taken for granted and characteristically opposed to Kirk's. Here, it represents a different variety of moral *mis*leadership, thus blurring the conventional distinction between them.

Finally, this chapter suggests a different methodology, a "look in the mirror" method, for decoding moral leadership—yesterday, today, and tomorrow. This approach directs attention away from the object and its objective features—here the actions and attributes of Collins, Kirk, and Steele—to the subject, your and my response to their creeds and deeds, your and my self-interested strategies of survival and well-being.

That is the critical variable of Reinhold Niebuhr's biblical and prophetic realism and Carter G. Woodson's insightful concept of miseducation. "The so-called modern education . . . does others so much more good than it does the Negro," Woodson wrote in *The Miseducation of the Negro* in 1933, "because it has been worked out in conformity to the needs of those who have enslaved and oppressed weaker people." What he identifies here is the omnipresent ideological tilt that is expressed when you and I, for instance, make a choice between rival leaders or when we rank those we label moral leaders.

The reliable testimony of Niebuhr's biblical realism also reinforces the suspicion expressed in this chapter. "Judgments in the field of history," he reminds us,

> are ultimately value judgments in . . . that they do not intend merely to designate the actions which lead to desired ends, but seek to give guidance on the desirability of the ends. . . . Human beings have a penchant for masking what *they* desire under the idea of the desirable . . . [confusing] what *they* desire and the desirable [and thereby] . . . pretend[ing] a greater value for an act than merely its gratification of the desires of the agent. (Emphasis added)

The most fruitful categories for understanding the civil rights era are protest and counter protest. These counter actions include white efforts to thwart, to accommodate and absorb, to roll back the changes effected by Black protest. The purpose of the counter action is to reestablish—in a changed but *uncorrected* form—the surplus and deficit of power and privilege that characterized American society before the Black protest of the civil rights movement. In the interpretation I outline here, C. K. Steele represents protest, the response of Collins and Kirk, varieties of counter actions. The respective visions and strategies of the latter two are strategically linked to the nation's objectives regarding the questions of race.

As protest, the objectives and strategies of Steele and his contemporaries in the movement were to replace racial oppression—here white supremacy and its institutions and worldview—with a new world order. Steele and others ground their struggle on the very principles that the white founding fathers of America invoked in their liberation from Great Britain's tyranny—life, liberty, and the pursuit of happiness—rejecting only their philosophy and practice of counter*violence* that was the heart and soul of the American Revolution.

The controlling value of the civil rights protest was the affirmation of Blacks as *co-equal* centers of freedom, authority, and value; their co-humanity; their equal humanity relative to whites. In this sense, the civil rights movement incarnated the logical, political, and moral priority of *human* rights over *civil* rights. For this reason, *civil* rights is an inaccurate and deceptive label that is too often used to direct attention away from what the Kerner report identified as the object of Black protest in the late 1960s: white racism and white hypocrisy. Giving priority to civil rights presupposes a situation where human rights are already in place. Black protest affirmed this had not yet occurred; *human* rights were still a dream. Whites still held the master key to the original chains involved in defining Blacks as property; and whites continued Black enslavement through policies of *indirect* discrimination that did not establish a level playing field or correct for the disadvantages still in place as a result of the discrimination that was never corrected.

To clarify this distinction and demonstrate the linkage between mislabeling and maintaining oppressive social policies, let us analyze America's history of uncorrected racial discrimination in education. Four periods are instructive: slavery, post-slavery, the 1954 Supreme Court decision, and today's attack on affirmative action.

During slavery it was illegal to teach Blacks to read and write, a policy that was tantamount to total exclusion. Can anyone question that this exclusionary policy created fundamental educational inequalities (deficits) that gave whites an institutionally based advantage?

Moving to the post-slavery period we find a new strategy: the separate-but-equal doctrine that, at first glance, appears a total reversal. This policy abandoned exclusion for partial inclusion, suggesting thereby an evolution in moral leadership, a more moderate position standing against those who advocated total exclusion.

But as history informs us, the tilt of this leadership was to continue and preserve a system that guaranteed whites the most of the best and the least of the worst in education, while legitimizing a most of the worst and least of the best arrangement for Blacks. Retrospectively, we see clearly what the new policy amounted to moral misleadership. It continued and perpetuated the defects, deficits, and disadvantages created by the prior discrimination based on exclusion by race.

The 1954 Supreme Court decree is often heralded as a death blow to racial discrimination in education. But a closer scrutiny of what it proscribed and what it allowed gives us a quite different picture. It was a landmark decision only for equal access, not for equal opportunity. Let me illustrate and explain.

Diagrammatically, the separate-but-equal doctrine, which the Supreme Court outlawed, is accurately represented by a circle with a line drawn down the middle; Blacks occupy one side and whites the other. What the Supreme Court did was to erase, to remove, the line down the middle, thus constitutionally prohibiting the direct use of race. Hope Franklin, David Colburn, and David Garrow have all noted, the movement thrived on segregationist white counter protest and, paradoxically, was defused, on occasion by accommodationists, who gave a little ground. Collins's supporters would classify him a progressive not an accommodationist. But from this writer's perspective—that is a distinction without a difference, validated by the outcome of his and the nation's policies regarding discrimination.

We today will be convicted of moral misleadership if we fail to apply to Collins, to our assessment of him and ourselves, the closer scrutiny that the US Civil Rights Commission advocated: "The blatant racial and sexual discrimination that originated in our conveniently forgotten past . . . continues to manifest itself today in a complex interaction of attitudes and actions of individuals, organizations, and the network of social structures that make up our society. Past discrimination continues to have present effects." The task today is to identify these effects and correct the forms and dynamics of the discrimination that produced them.

Chapter 16

TOWARD A NEW PARADIGM FOR UNCOVERING NEO-RACISM IN AMERICAN INSTITUTIONS

William R. Jones

Where justice is denied, where poverty is enforced, where ignorance prevails, and where any one class is made to feel that society is an organized conspiracy to oppress . . . and degrade [it], neither persons nor property will ever be safe.

—Frederick Douglass

Our nation is moving towards two societies, one black, one white, separate and unequal. . . . Racial prejudice, discrimination and segregation have shaped our history, decisively, they now threaten the future of every American.

—The Kerner Report

Beyond my conception of ignorance and deliberate ill-will as causes of race prejudice, there must be other and stronger and more threatening forces, forming the founding stones of race antagonisms, which we had only begun to attack or perhaps in reality had not attacked at all.

—W. E. B. DuBois, *Dusk of Dawn*

There is considerable debate about the continued presence, scope, and influence of racial discrimination in American institutions. The debate has been particularly fierce and heated, for instance, as regards the legal and criminal justice systems, generating studies, for example, *The Myth of Racism in the Criminal Justice System*, that affirms the presence of racial discrimination in America's past but denies its current influence or presence.

The trend of interpretation from the federal judiciary and the Supreme Court also suggests that racial discrimination is no longer detected by judges and juries to a degree that redress is morally or legally ordered—hence the cascading charge of reverse discrimination and the growing acceptance of the validity of this charge for overturning previous "special interests" decisions that were installed as acknowledged correctives to the perceived presence of racism.

Whether of your choosing or not, you are actively engaged in this ongoing debate, and whether you perceive the presence of racial discrimination as you examine this issue will depend upon your understanding of racial discrimination and how it manifests itself in our society today.

Whether something is visible or invisible to us depends upon the sophistication and accuracy of our viewing instruments. An inaccurate understanding of racial discrimination will yield the conclusion that it is not present nor prevalent. But, as the new Hubbard telescope reminds us, the fact that something is invisible to us does not mean that it does not exist. This new telescope did not create the stars that we are seeing for the first time. They were there all along, but our instruments were too crude to make them visible for our inspection. Invisibility, alone, is insufficient grounds for establishing non-existence.

Unfortunately, this unsettling fact is increasingly ignored in societal audits that address the situation of African Americans. To those societal diagnosticians who now control the discipline and ESP policies, racial discrimination is virtually invisible—not as they mistakenly affirm because of substantial success in eradicating racism, but because they choose to utilize an inaccurate and confusing picture of racism.

Given this state of affairs, I would advance methodological directives that would reopen this debate and challenge the trend that affirms the declining influence of race and historic discrimination in American life. These directives are more accurate and sophisticated instruments that will enable you to determine whether racial discrimination is in fact present. These instruments, I confidently predict, will demonstrate the continued presence, pervasive scope, and controlling influence of racism in American society, in general, and the particular object of our investigation.

Examine any aspect of the African American situation in America and you will inevitably encounter the SS phenomenon. It does not matter if you analyze the family, crime, or players in the NBA, sooner or later you come face to face with some "startling statistics" that identify a striking disproportionality between the ratio of African Americans in the general population and a given social index. For example: "There can be little doubt that blacks commit a disproportionate number of FBI Crime Index offenses, and are in turn, disproportionately victimized by crimes involving physical contact."

Often described as "the American Dilemma," the SS phenomenon and its causality lie at the center of the unresolved debate about the continued presence and scope of racial discrimination in American institutions. Your assignment, whether you like it or not, draws you into this debate. Your task, as you have already discovered, is (a) to examine the why and wherefore of this phenomenon as it relates to the legal justice system and (b) to determine if racial discrimination is an essential determinant of its causality. It will also become clear to you that any policy recommendations you advance will inevitably commit you to a specific conclusion about the causality of the SS phenomenon, as well as your dismissal of alternative causal hypotheses. Moreover, it will become apparent to each of you that in determining causality you are, at the same time, assigning responsibility, and ultimately, who or what is morally culpable.

The grid that I advance here for critical review of the SS phenomenon is customarily designed as structural discrimination or institutional oppression. Its point of departure is the institutional portrait of America that is outlined when one lists the basic institutions in America that:

1. Black Americans created and/or controlled for 4 generations (200 years);
2. white Americans created and/or controlled for 6 generations (300 years);
3. Black Americans created and controlled for ½ generation (25 years) under which white Americans had to live;
4. white Americans created and controlled for 6 generations (300 years) under which Black Americans had to live.

When you draw up these lists, invariably, you are forced to conclude that whites, not Blacks, have created and/or controlled the basic institutions in America under which our two societies, "separate and unequal," have lived. Yet when we consider the definitions of social reality that hold sway, this simple fact of causality and accountability is invisible. It is replaced by other definitions of social reality that place accountability and responsibility elsewhere, usually upon the shoulders of the victim.

This erroneous understanding is now dominant by virtue of the surplus of power that enables the majority group to define social reality and pick and choose between competing causalities of that reality in such a way that racial discrimination is rendered invisible. In this way the majority group's hierarchical status is legitimated as just, and proper—not grounded on oppressive social structures and not reflecting injustice. Accordingly, corrective measures that restructure the status quo are neither necessary nor desirable.

Given this understanding, the causality question is the logically prior, the threshold issue for your professional organization to consider. Hence, my primary recommendations:

- Familiarize yourself with the category of institutional oppression/racism and its analysis of the causality of the SS phenomenon.
- Make explicit the causality that underlies your analysis of existing geriatric policy and forthcoming policy recommendations.

The application of this grid to your task will materialize the invisible racism from its spectral mode, forcing you to raise fundamental questions about the very foundation of your society and its role in economic, social, and political oppression. Unpleasant though it may be, this is the task that confronts each of us now and tomorrow.

What follows are some of the concepts and analyses, drawn from Robert Blauner's *Racial Oppression in America*, that inform the perspective and methodology of institutional oppression.

* * *

Historically, discrimination against minorities and women was not only accepted but it was also governmentally required. Overt racism and sexism as embodied in popular notions of white and male supremacy have been widely repudiated but our history of discrimination based on race, sex, and national origin has not been readily put aside. The blatant racial and sexual discrimination that originated in our conveniently forgotten past, however, continues to manifest itself today in a complex interaction of attitudes and actions of individuals, organizations, and the network of social structures that make up our society. Past discrimination continues to have present effects. The task today is to identify these effects and the forms and dynamics of the discrimination that produced them.

> The process of discrimination involves many aspects of our society. No single factor sufficiently explains it, and no single means will suffice to eliminate it. Such elements of our society as our history of de jure discrimination, deeply ingrained prejudices, inequities based on economic and social class, and the structure and function of all our economic, social, and political institutions must be continually examined in order to understand their part in shaping today's decisions that will either maintain or counter the current process of discrimination.[1]

The most common understanding of discrimination rests at the level of prejudiced individual attitudes and behaviors. Although open and intentional prejudice persists, discriminatory conduct is often hidden and sometimes unintentional. It may be difficult to identify precisely all aspects of the discriminatory process. But understanding discrimination starts with an awareness that such a process exists and that to avoid perpetuating it, we must carefully assess the context and consequences of our everyday actions.

Although discrimination is maintained through individual actions, neither individual prejudices nor random chance can fully explain the persistent national pattern of inequality and underrepresentation. Nor can these patterns be blamed on the persons at the bottom of our economic, political, and social order.

Discrimination against minorities and women must now be viewed as an interlocking process involving the attitudes and actions of individuals and the organization and social structures that guide individual behavior. That process, started by past events, now routinely bestows privileges, favors, and advantages on white males and imposes disadvantages and penalties on minorities and women. This process is also self-perpetuating. Many normal, seemingly neutral, operations of our society create stereotyped expectations that justify unequal results; unequal results in one area foster inequalities in opportunity and accomplishments in others; the lack of opportunity and accomplishment confirms the general prejudices or engenders new ones that fuel the normal operations generating unequal results. United States Commission on Civil Rights, adapted.

* * *

Prejudiced attitudes are not the essence of racism. Racism is unfortunately too often equated with intense prejudice and hatred of the racially different—thus with men of evil intent. This kind of racial extremism is not necessary for the maintenance of a racist social structure. The men of goodwill and tolerance who identify racism with prejudice (thereby) exempt themselves from responsibility and involvement in our system of racial injustice and inequality by taking comfort in their own favorable attitudes toward minority groups.

The error in this point of view is revealed by the fact that such men of good will help maintain the racism of American society and in some cases even profit from it. This takes place because racism is institutionalized. The processes that maintain domination—control of whites over non-whites—are built into major social institutions. These institutions either exclude or restrict the participation of racial groups by procedures that have become conventional, part of the bureaucratic system of rules and regulations. Thus there is little need for prejudice as a motivating force. Because this is true, the distinction between racism as an objective phenomenon, located in the actual existence of domination and hierarchy, and racism's subjective concomitant of prejudice and other motivations and feelings is a basic one.

* * *

> One day Brother Fox caught Brother Goose and tied him to a tree.
> "I'm going to eat you, Brother Goose," he said. "You've been stealing my meat."
> "But I don't even eat meat," protested Brother Goose.
> "Tell that to the judge and jury," said Brother Fox.
> "Who's gonna be the judge?" asked Brother Goose.
> "A fox," answered Brother Fox.
> "And who's gonna be the jury?" inquired Brother Goose.
> "They all gonna be foxes," said Brother Fox, grinning so that all his teeth showed.
> "Guess my goose is cooked," sadly acknowledged Brother Goose.

This familiar anecdote from Afro-American folklore aptly describes the relocation of the analysis of social reality and the moral picture that results when we shift from the interpretive model of prejudice to that of institutional oppression.

Given the fact of the majority's group institutional control, s/he, it can establish a moral base by proudly and openly affirming an explicit doctrine of racism, arguing that Blacks are in an unequal situation by virtue of natural or supernatural forces that lie outside its control. Accordingly, it cannot be held morally accountable for these inequalities.

However, given this justification for ESP oppression, the only remaining option whereby the majority group can escape moral responsibility is to blame the victim for the "startling statistics" and the "undesirability" to which the prejudice is a "reasonable" response.

Whereas both of these options are attractive moral loopholes for the advocate of the prejudice model, neither of these moral escape routes is available if institutional oppression is our diagnostic norm. The diagnostics of prejudice draw attention away from the majority group's control, and by the same logic, the institutional area escapes the demand for ESP correction. It is important to note that the ideology of prejudice does not force the issue of societal control and the concomitant responsibility for the ESP results of the institutional system. Rather, Blacks are counseled to pull themselves up by their bootstraps and thereby demonstrate that the racist's portrayal of Blacks is a grotesque caricature. In this way Blacks will neutralize their "undesirable" characteristics and the prejudice that is a response to these traits will quickly vanish. A classic catch-22 remedy.

The disadvantages of this diagnosis are readily apparent; this analysis of the racial problem does not generate effective ESP change. The basic institutions of the society, with their ESP inequalities, remain essentially intact; institutional change is put in the deep freeze.

Note

1 John Lescott-Leszczynski, 1984, *The History of US Ethnic Policy and Its Impact on European Ethnics* (First published by Westview Press, 1984 and republished by Routledge in 2019), 13.

Part IV

CRITICAL REFLECTION ON JONES'S WRITINGS

Essay 1

THE DEBATE THAT SHAPED A FIELD

WILLIAM R. JONES AND DEVELOPMENTS IN BLACK THEOLOGY

Anthony B. Pinn

Black theology developed during the late twentieth century as a professionalization of religious thought embedded in social justice work and the more "progressive" Black churches. It marked an aggressive critique of white Christianity and its links to injustices in the United States. And, it sought to reclaim the Christian story as one of an ontologically "Black" God committed to the well-being of those who suffer the most—that is, Black people.

Black Theology and Its Critics

Black theology made a significant splash in both academic and popular arenas—and fostered a fair amount of critique from white scholars. However, its advocates encountered little critique within African American circles that wasn't easily dismissed by its founders as forms of "Black face" appeasement to whites. That is, with a few exceptions. As James Cone, the acknowledged founder of academic Black theology, attests, four Black scholars offered critical engagement that demanded response. "As for my critics," Cone writes, "[Charles] Long, [Gayraud] Wilmore, [J. Deotis] Roberts and [William R.] Jones also transformed my intellectual life with their challenges, questions, and critiques."[1] This statement warrants some unpacking. Wilmore and Roberts raised, in respective order, questions concerning the adequacy of Cone's attention to Black culture and Cone's disconnecting of liberation and reconciliation. Yet, both critiques maintained the integrity and necessity of the assumed theistic underpinning of any proper understanding of Black liberation—both assumed the dominance of a Christian orientation.[2] Long exposed the flaw in this assumed necessity of a Christian orientation through his turn to religion as fundamental "orientation" expressed through the church and also through "extra-church" orientations.[3]

With all three of these thinkers, there seems a common assumption of theism as viable if not vital for understanding Black religious thought and praxis. This assumption is where Jones differs, and it is through this difference that he offered what I would argue is the most important critique of Black theology's assumptions, content, and aims measured against evidential-existential considerations. To this challenge, Cone responded that Jones offered an "external" critique, which is to say Jones's critique required limited attention because it failed to hold as true the same religious claims as Cone.[4] This is because, according to Cone, "to do internal criticism is to think as others (i.e., committed, Black Christians) think and to criticize on the basis of their presuppositions."[5] This is not to suggest Cone argues Jones should be ignored but rather that his critique fails to understand (because he does not embrace?) the fundamental logic of Black Christian commitment. With the others, Black theology—at least as done by its founder—responded through counter-theological argument. The critique offered by Jones cut too deep and took away too many of the assumptions held by Black (Christian) theologians—and foregrounded an earthy ethics.[6]

In presenting Black humanism as a critique of Black theism and a religious position, he "elevates the theodicy question to first rank."[7] Jones, in part, points out the shortcomings of a God concept—that is, a God concerned with the well-being of Black people—without verifiable evidence. In making this argument, Jones, by extension, advocated for the ability of humanism to offer both a community of response and a mode of thought suitable for liberative activity that is dependent on what we know to be real—human effort.[8] With Jones, there wasn't simply an effort to "think" Black humanism—although his intellectual contributions to our understanding and framing of Black "freethought" are without question—he also developed strategies for organizational structures as well as modes of practice. One sees this in his involvement with the Unitarian Universalist Association as well as his use of Black humanism as a hermeneutic by means of which social injustice could be analyzed and addressed.

While the impact of Black humanism on Black theology is important, there are also theoretical shifts fostered by Jones's debate with Cone that merit consideration. That is not to say such considerations aren't part of the current work in the study of African American religion, but rather that they aren't often recognized as in part stemming from the philosophical challenge offered by Jones. Which is to say, Jones's question to liberation theology required conceptual reformulations and shifts in source material represented, for instance, in the recent turn to the nature and meaning of the Black body, and the more open sense of what I will call "theological doubt." To restate the case, what I have in mind are two conceptual shifts: (1) the central nature of materiality—for example, Black embodiment and (2) the theological significance of "doubt."[9]

Materiality and Black Embodiment

Black theology, while having a rhetorical concern with Black embodiment, gave little "weight" to the actual materiality of Black bodies as evidenced by its willingness to posit responses to suffering that privileged the integrity of the God concept over the physical well-being of Black people. Black life is clouded by the mystical workings of a figure—Jesus the Christ—whose value involves an escape from the body. Thereby dynamics of suffering are hidden when they can't be turned into an ultimate theological good. This failure to adequately address the nature and meaning of suffering is pointed out by Jones as he calls for an alternate approach. He writes, "in sum, blacks today should be asked to conform only to those aspects of the tradition whose proliberation impact has been clearly established."[9] Maintaining the faith-based assertion of God's goodness despite unresolved Black suffering speaks to the centrality of a certain metaphysics over the materiality of the Black condition and the sociality of Black possibility. Then, to draw from Jones, "functional ultimacy" of the human with respect to the existential conditions of life implies what it doesn't explicitly name—the centrality of embodied existence as the geography of these conditions and the way in which those conditions are understood and measured. Black humanism, as a hermeneutic, serves to privilege materiality over assumptions couched in faith.

The question—"Is God a White Racist?"—has an impact in part because it ties together, without theological sleight of hand, claims and embodied consequences of those claims. Jones opens recognition of the degree to which Black theology has tended to be about "no" body—that is to say, they fail to render central to analysis the manner in which material bodies occupy time and space. Instead, religious necessity—that is, the demands of Christian commitment—trumps what the physical body says about the ongoing injustice marking Black experience of the world. Early modes of Black theology, one can reasonably claim, involved truth loosely tethered to embodied circumstances but with a firm commitment to a vertical arrangement of evidence that often blocked the ongoing consequences of material life by alluding to *Truth*. Jones pushes for truth(s) as grounded—verifiable and conditioned by material experience. Jones raises questions concerning the certainty of historical evidence for God's involvement in Black liberation—arguing that the historical record suggests just as easily the idea that God is a white racist concerned with the destruction of Black people. And, the claim of Jesus as the answer to Black suffering and God's position regarding this suffering isn't an answer based on material evidence but is rather a faith stance?

Doubt

By doubt here, I don't mean agnosticism pushing its way into Black theologizing. Rather, I mean to highlight engagement with evidential speculation that holds upon the plausibility of success or failure conditioning theological claims—that is, a taming of faith-fueled assumptions.

One shouldn't lose sight of the value in the questions Jones pushed—questions that cut against longstanding theological assumptions/arguments through evidential doubt and the Janus-like quality of so many theological assertions concerning God and Black people. These are clear-eyed questions. Much of Black theology, and I have noted this elsewhere, works along a model reminiscent of the geometric proof: the answer is known (i.e., God loves Black people and is committed to their liberation and well-being), and what remains is to outline the steps used to reach this conclusion.[10] Theologizing *qua* the geometric proof approach involves what I would call disingenuous probing—which is a rather hollow call for evidence.

Doubt, as evidenced in Jones's work, took the form of a question regarding the proper evidence for claims of liberation—and a turn toward human accountability and responsibility for the shape of freedom. Is struggle ongoing, perpetual? Does the concept of God need to be rethought in light of ongoing Black misery? Does it enhance Black suffering, or does it challenge Black suffering—and is the claim to either position authenticated through encounters in the space and time of our social world(s)? Such questions are theoretically buttressed by his turn to Existentialism (e.g., Sartre)—or what I would note as his appreciation for Black Moralism vis-à-vis figures such Richard Wright, who was seldom employed in Black religious thought, and Albert Camus for whom doubt is a condition of life. This is not to say the first generation of Black theologians—for example, Cone—were not aware of Black Moralism and didn't engage it. Cone certainly does from his first published books through his last but, with Cone, Camus became only a way to measure Black experience and the social world framing it as opposed to a means by which to challenge and refine theological claims in light of the pounding presence of absurdity. Put another way, unlike Jones, Cone and other Black theologians couldn't hear Wright's and Camus's call for the end of hope and "future" speculations in large part because they couldn't get beyond their bias against the secular humanism of both figures. Through his philosophical turn, Jones highlights the manner in which doubt can serve as a theological-philosophical tool within the study of Black life that exposes a range of narratives (including Black humanism) as opposed to it being perceived simply as a rejection of the only viable posture—faith as evidence. As a tool, doubt doesn't consume possibility; rather it tames claims made concerning possibility by filtering them through the existential dilemmas and material conditions associated with life in an anti-Black social world.

While ignored by some because of his secular humanism, those within the first generation of Black theologians who sought to respond to Jones's challenge did so while preserving a foundational assertion of faith. More recently, there has been some movement in Black theology tied to the debate between Jones and Cone—played out through thinkers informed by that debate and its call to alternate cultural sources. For example, developments in some dimensions of womanist theology speak to a creative and forceful recognition of an internal flaw—the overlap of oppressive tendencies and liberative desires. And the use of Black literature, particularly that of Zora Neale Hurston, for instance, served as a way to frame and think through both internal and external modalities of suffering—and to project a mode of possibility that doesn't resist this materiality but instead centers on the struggle against oppression as liberative by the very way in which it resists the normalizing of Black pain. Laced throughout much of this thinking is a sense of vulnerability that awakens but doesn't destroy. It urges doubt—for example, of social world regulations, of popular perceptions of freedom, and of a future that is radically different. This taming of expectation through an appeal to the embodied connotations of Black life serves to soften some claims made. This is not to suggest theistic Black and womanist theologians have forgotten God, no; but, rather, "God-talk" has gained a greater appreciation for materiality and historical circumstances as "truthful" depictions of life not countered by faith alone. That is to say, it seems, there is a greater concern with checking claims about God in light of the ongoing attention to physical conditions—and greater explicit attention to human accountability and responsibility. Put another way, for some, the Christ Event represents a moral example, not the historical answer to Black suffering. This shift in important ways owes much to William Jones.

Notes

1 James H. Cone, *Said I Wasn't Gonna Tell Nobody* (Maryknoll, NY: Orbis Books, 2018), 102.
2 See, for example: Gayraud Wilmore, *Black Religion and Black Radicalism* (Maryknoll, NY: Orbis Books, 1983); J. Deotis Roberts, *Liberation and Reconciliation: A Black Theology* (Philadelphia: Westminster Press, 1971).
3 Charles H. Long, *Significations: Signs, Symbols, and Images in the Interpretation of Religion* (Philadelphia: Fortress, Press, 1986).
4 This claim regarding the nature of Jones's critique, however, fails to account for Jones's call for an internal critique as the required mode of engagement. He makes this claim in 1972, three years before Cone charges him with offering an external critique because, he argues, Jones's doesn't work from a solid understanding of what the Christ Event means for Black Christians. See: Jones, "Toward an Interim Assessment of Black Theology," *The Christian Century*, May 3, 1972, 513–17.
5 James H. Cone, *God of the Oppressed* (New York: Harpers, 1975), 267–8.
6 One gets a sense of this, for example, in his effort to describe ethics within Black theology through a comparative discussion of Mao, King, and Malcolm X, in which he critiques King's non-violent direct action approach and its assumptions concerning the moral and ethical capacity of whites and the tenacious nature of white supremacy. See: "Liberation Strategies in Black Theology: Mao, Martin, or Malcolm?" in *Philosophy Born of Struggle: Anthology of Afro-American Philosophy from 1917*, ed. Leonard Harris (Dubuque, Iowa: Kendall/Hunt Publishing Company, 1983), 229–41.
7 William R. Jones, "Religious Humanism: Its Problems and Prospects in Black Religion and Culture," *The Journal of the Interdenominational Theological Center*, Vol. 7, No. 2 (Spring 1980): 182.
8 Ibid.
9 William R. Jones, "The Case for Black Humanism," in *Black Theology II*, ed. William Jones and Calvin E. Bruce (Lewisburg: Bucknell University, 1978), 226.
10 See, for example: *Why, Lord? Suffering and Evil in Black Theology* (New York: Continuum Publishing, 1995); and *The End of God-Talk: An African American Humanist Theology* (New York: Oxford University Press, 2012).

Essay 2

NEO-RACISM AND THE SHORTCOMINGS OF RELIGIOUS LIBERALISM

Jamil W. Drake

Today, we're [humanists] operating with an inaccurate diagnosis of the racial problems in America. We have a distorted, outdated view that informs our response.[1]

... my diagnosis of this social reality and demonstrate its superior merit for producing a preventive/corrective therapy.[2]

William R. Jones is mainly remembered for his noteworthy critique of Black liberation theology in his 1973 classic text, *Is God a White Racist: A Preamble to Black Theology* (IGWR). Jones challenged the theism of Black theology that he felt reified the divine racism of "whiteanity." His critique of Black theology extended to American Christianity more broadly and the "holy symbiosis" of the Right-winged Evangelicals in particular.[3] Moreover, he posited that the "functional primacy of the human" was the most effective way to account for Black suffering and consequently the possibilities of liberation.[4] Contemporary scholars often overlooked that his humanocentric and secular theodicy in *IGWR* were inseparable from his affiliation and interaction with Unitarian Universalism (UU). At the time of the 1973 publication, he was a minister of the Unitarian Universalist Association (UUA) and would actively be part of its organizations for racial and social change in America and abroad (e.g., South Africa) until his death.[5] Thus, at the same time he critically engaged Black theologians, he was also engaged in a serious "internal critique" of the Unitarian Universalist Association's "Universalists, Unitarians, and Humanists." Highlighting his affiliation and interaction with the Unitarian Universalist Association also captures his larger lifelong quest to properly diagnose neo-racism/neo-oppression that informed his "internal critiques" not only of Black theology but also of religious liberalism. The analysis he provided in *IGWR* of Black liberation theology also structured his critique of Unitarian Universalism and religious liberalism more broadly. This edited volume of his writings situates his Black and religious humanism within his broader intellectual and political project to understand the complexities of neo-racism/neo-oppression in his commitment to Black liberation.

Essay 2. Neo-Racism and Religious Liberalism 197

Jones noted that Unitarian Universalists faced the same problems as Black liberation theologians. With the unification of the Universalist Church of America and American Unitarian Association in 1961, Unitarian Universalism not only came to represent a liberal religious tradition that had roots in its anti-Calvinistic in eighteenth-century America but also included a deep respect for individualism, freedom, equality, human agency, and openness to change. Yet, his orientation represented the gradual humanistic strand that had gained traction with the 1930 publication of the *Humanist Manifesto* that "fostered religious values apart from any notion of divine [sovereignty]."[6] Like many Unitarian Universalist post-Christians in American history, he became an affiliate of the Unitarian Universalist Association after he left his predominantly African American Baptist denomination in Louisville, Kentucky, in the late 1950s.[7] For Jones, Unitarians, Universalists, and Humanists had failed to properly diagnose the neo-racism that blinded them from understanding their own complicity in its perpetuation. Thus, his early critique of the Unitarian Universalism (and Black liberation theology, too) was predicated on what he took to be the "mutation" of racial oppression in the aftermath of the two 1964 and 1965 Civil Rights policies. By the late 1960s, he called for a theoretical distinction of neo-racism from "classical racism." According to Jones, "neo-racism" was an intricate and "indirect, institutionally-based and maintained dynamic of discrimination" that structured the economic, social, and political institutions.[8] Like other African American intellectuals in post-Civil Rights, he was painstakingly seeking to make the invisibility of whiteness visible.[9]

We must historically situate Jones's response to Unitarian Universalism (and also Black theology) and his determination to identify neo-racism within the political eddies of the intensification of neoliberalism through its draconian social and economic policies around taxes, law and order, and welfare cuts that disproportionately affected African American and low-cash populations in the last three decades of the twentieth century.[10] Additionally, the rise of the Christian Right and color-blind neo-conservatism (with moderate Democrats!) contributed to his internal critiques of the Unitarian Universalism as well. The chapters in this edited volume highlight the effects of the social world in the immediate aftermath of the Civil Rights bills on his unending quest to develop a "phenomenology of oppression" with his assessment of the various mutations and modifications of racism. In the end, his lifelong intellectual project of understanding racial oppression for the sake of Black liberation was founded on what he called the "DDT principal"—or the premise that "diagnosis dictates the therapy."[11]

"Divine racism" prevented Black theologians from understanding the virus of neo-racism and consequently its cure. In his estimation, Black liberation theology had misdiagnosed neo-racism and obscured its vision of liberation (i.e., cure). Similarly, the Unitarian Universalist Association prevented liberal "Unitarians, Universalists, and Humanists" from developing a vaccine to combat neo-racism/neo-oppression.[12] The liberal social ethics of Unitarian Universalism contributed to its misdiagnosis of neo-racism. Although Jones championed Unitarian Universalism's nontheistic "functional ultimacy of the human" perspective, he questioned its democratic commitments on the grounds that their "espoused theory (or ethical commitments) did not align with applied or theory-in use in politics."[13] Moreover, Jones often addressed the Unitarian Universalist as an insider by self-identifying as a "religious liberal" and affirmed their egalitarian ideals of individualism, pluralism, and freedom.[14] At the same time, he was also aware of his "outsider" status as he often interacted with predominantly white Unitarian Universalists as a *Black* humanist who sought to show how their aforementioned democratic social ethics reified the logics of anti-Black neo-racism. He leveraged his insights into neo-racism to strongly encourage the Unitarian Universalist Association to be more self-reflective of their liberal ethical commitments in post-modern America.

William Jones had often challenged the Unitarian Universalist Association for its failure to understand racism beyond its classical or traditional iterations. He claimed that the church had a static view of race that confined racism to direct enslavement, segregation signs, and burning crosses. On the other hand, the Unitarian Universalist Association's static view also confined racism to the subjective level of "individual attitudes and behaviors."[15] His challenge did not allow Unitarians, Universalists, and Humanists to bask in the glory of their liberal social ethics while distinguishing themselves from the "deplorable" or "overt practices of contemporary hate groups like KKK, skinheads, [and David Dukes]." Moreover, the subjective view of racism of Unitarian Universalism's social ethics actually fed into the logics of neo-racism that posited a "false causality" of the socio-economic status by shifting the blame to Blacks for their plight. Thus, the extraction of "racism" from the broader social structures of dominance privileged a neoliberal and individualistic model of race where specific attitudes, behaviors, and values were the source of social bigotry and/or strivings. Such an extraction manufactured specific moral and civic behaviors that rendered Black and lower-class communities as a pathological, lazy, uncontrollable, lascivious sub-human mass. Neo-racism worked through the moral framework of the right, just, and good that sanctioned racial inequality. Unitarian Universalism's cherished egalitarian ideals of individualism, equality, and pluralism obscured the more subtle structural forms of racism entrenched in the American social apparatus. According to Jones, Unitarian Universalism needed to disabuse themselves of the notion that individual prejudice was the impetus of racism.

Unitarian Universalism's preoccupation with individual prejudice as the primary element of neo-racism significantly obscured the significance of power in social life. On the one hand, he understood that Unitarian Universalism developed its social ethics devoid of an analysis of power. For Jones, the inaccurate understanding of power in neo-racism led religious liberals to concentrate their energies on fostering rational, deliberative, and persuasive democratic methods to appeal to the "conscience" of the dominant group for the sake of Black freedom. By Jones's lights, power was a fundamental aspect of neo-racism. Filtered through his "anatomy of oppression," he posited that neo-racism highlights a dominant raced, classed, and gendered group that had an "overwhelming surplus of power that provides monopolistic access to the society's life-sustaining and life-enhancing resources."[16] Thus, the absence of an analysis of power fails to come to terms with how the dominant group (the nice and earnest ones) benefited from the surplus of power and privilege of racial and economic oppression. He noted that Black "powerlessness" was the "primary obstruction to black humanity."[17] From the vantage point of Unitarian Universalism, Jones felt that relinquishing social and institutional power was a right step in the direction of Black liberation.

Not only did it fail to understand power reify neo-racism, but it also ran the risk of fostering what he called "anti-power" or "quietism" of Black communities. The anti-power at the root of Unitarian Universalism's liberal social ethics compelled them to misrepresent other Black liberation movements outside of their perceived ethical framework of democracy and freedom. Essentially, Unitarian Universalism's anti-power placed them on the "wrong side of social issues."[18] Unitarian Universalism's anti-power impacted what non-Unitarian Universalist political and grassroots movements it supported, endorsed, and aligned within its collective struggles for Black liberation. It also caused the Unitarian Universalist Association to criticize and denigrate other Black political organizations that they considered not aligned with their ethical principles. Jones considered anti-power to be the Unitarian Universalism's separation of social ethics from power. This separation was due to what he took to be the Unitarian Universalism's pejorative view of the power that they replicated in their criticisms of Black political organizations that called for socio-economic (and psychological) power in post-Civil Rights America. Prior to his publication of *IGWR*, Jones had started to call out Unitarian Universalism's response to different Black political and leftist organizations (e.g., The Black Power Movement) whom it felt jeopardized its democratic ethical codes and customs. Not only did he understand power as neutral, but he also argued that equating power(s) of the dominant and dominated group within structural inequality and violence was a false one. He urged the Unitarian Universalist Association to develop a "theology of power" to guide their social ethics, and consequently, align with other organizations in the struggle for using power for the purpose of eliminating its excessive abuse or misuse by the dominant few. Unitarian Universalism's goal should be to create "a situation of co-equal power."[19]

Additionally, eliminating the "structures of dominance" helped the Unitarian Universalist Association rethink its commitments to pluralism, individualism, and freedom. An understanding of neo-racism would prevent masking pluralism and freedom in the anti-Black logic of assimilation. Assimilation and freedom rehearsed the individualistic view of race that blamed Black and low-income people for their inability to be part of American mainstream society. In particular, assimilation (and integration, too) revealed a complete disregard for individual and collective differences in the name of a moral, social, and cultural *absolute* or standard that all *should* adhere. For Jones, true pluralism and freedom required creating life-sustaining institutions and resources that protect and embolden individual and collective difference. Here, Jones alerts us to a critique of democracy and freedom that operated on the basis of exclusion and unfreedom for different populations.

To be sure, neo-racism initially developed in the aftermath of the Civil Rights bills. Jones shows us that identifying the mutations of race and oppression is arduous. It demands unending work and concentration. His critique of Unitarian Universalism and broader religious liberalism still resonates among today's liberal contingent and its quick disassociation from white and Christian nationalism in the United States and abroad. How might we undermine our ethical work for a just society and reify racial oppression today? We must properly diagnose the complex mutations of racism, so we do not replicate racial oppression. I am happy for this collection of Jones's writing that reintroduces the public to this brilliant mind and internal critique.

Notes

1. William Jones, "Oppression, Race, and Humanism," *The Humanist* 52, no. 6 (November/December, 1992): 8.
2. William Jones, "The New Three R's," in *The Transient and the Permanent in Unitarian Universalism*, ed. Jan Seymour-Ford, Vol. II (Boston: Skinner House Books, 1995), 162.
3. It is clear that Jones's critique of Christian theism was against the historical backdrop of the rise of the Christian Right. For his challenge to the Christian Right, and in particular theologian Frances Schaffter's call for the holy symbiosis of Protestant and Catholics to mobilize establishing a backlash against civil rights, see: William R. Jones, "Moral Decision-Making in the Post Modern World: Implications for Unitarian-Universalist Religious Education," in *Unitarian-Universalism: 1985: Selected Essays*, ed. Wayne Arnanson (Boston: Papercraft Printing Co., 1985), 1–20. Here, Jones argues that the Christian Right's theistic absolutism falls prey to situational ethics.
4. The "functional ultimacy of wo/man" captures the UU concept of authority. This concept understood that the human individual is a "co-equal center of freedom, authority, and value." Thus, God, freedom, value, truth, and knowledge developed from human choice and interpretation.
5. William Jones seems to have become affiliated with the UUA while he was a divinity student at Harvard Divinity School in the late 1950s.
6. Daniel McKanan, "Unitarianism, Universalism, and Unitarian Universalism," *Religious Compass* 7, no. 1 (2013): 18. Here, McKanan is building on the work of William F. Schulz on religious humanism in the UUA. See: http://archive.uuworld.org/2003/06/feature3.html.
7. For brief discussion of his religious upbringing, such as his family of pastors and early love of Billy Graham, see William Jones, "Preface," *Is God a White Racist? A Preamble to Black Theology* (Boston: Beacon Press, 1978).
8. He discussed neo-racism within the acceleration of neoliberalism with Reagan to Clinton. For instance, we find that Jones discussed neo-racism in light of the policy debates regarding the (Black) underclass. Additionally, he discussed it with special attention to the ways in which the US government favored welfare for the rich through tax cuts and other incentives. See: Jones, "Oppression, Race, and Humanism," 10.
9. George Lipsitz, "The Possessive Investment in Whiteness: Racialized Social Democracy and the White Problem in American Studies," *American Quarterly* 47, no. 3 (September, 1995): 369.

10   Ibid.
11   William Jones, "The New Three R's," 170.
12   I do not think Jones shared the liberal optimism that racism would end. Anthony Pinn noted that one of the central elements of humanism is a "constrained optimism regarding humanity's creative and destructive tendencies." Jones's objective uncertainty coupled with his secular theodicy reflects this constrained optimism. See: Anthony Pinn's *Humanism: Essays on Race, Religion, and Popular Culture* (New York: Bloomsbury, 2015), 3.
13   William Jones, "The New Three R's," 172.
14   Jones self-identified himself as a religious liberal in his "Toward a New Paradigm for Uncovering Neo-Racism/Oppression in UUism" speech.
15   William Jones, "Towards a New Paradigm for Uncovering Neo-Racism in American Institutions," in *Soul Work: Anti-Racist Theologies in Dialogue*, ed. Marjorie Bowens-Wheatley and Nancy Palmer Jones (Boston: Skinner House, 2003).
16   William Jones, "The New Three R's," 168.
17   William Jones, *Power and Anti-Power, Kairos: An Independent Quarterly of Liberal Religion* (Spring, 1977), 66.
18   Ibid., 65.
19   Ibid.

Essay 3

EXPANDING THE ALTAR: TRANSGRESSING AND TRANSFORMING CONVENTIONAL BOUNDARIES IN BLACK LIBERATION THEOLOGY

Brittany L. O'Neal

The legacy of William R. Jones has until recently been under-represented in the larger Africana philosophical tradition and canon. The role of trailblazer is not always met with open acceptance or favor. When Dr. Jones published his magnum opus, *Is God a White Racist?: A Preamble to Black Theology*, in 1973, he was met with silence from his interlocutors, including those discussed in the text. Additionally, Jones claims, "In fact, they found it [*Is God a White Racist?*] to be a fraudulent traitor to these traditions" of liberation theology's cultural representation and Black religious traditions.[1] Jones dedicated his scholarship (and personal life) to determining whether Black theology and Black philosophy had the potential to enact positive economic, social, and political change within society.[2]

This essay will investigate the placement of William R. Jones's humanocentric theism within the ranks of Black liberation theology. In conversation with Dr. Jones's theological and philosophical canon, his work demonstrates the role of critiquing the normative boundaries found in Black liberation theology. Additionally, this essay will address the legitimacy and necessity of Jones's role as a philosophical theologian by transgressing the conventional boundaries of Black liberation theology as a Christian-centric theological system. Through this method, Jones challenges his closest interlocutors to sharp criticism, but offers an alternative religious perspective grounded in the Black historical experience.[3] Jones was a stark critic of conventional Christian theological categories, including what he termed "mis-religion" and "Whiteanity." Jones describes "Whiteanity" as a survival religion characterized by a racist Christian theology that supports the continued oppression of African Americans. Jones prefaces his discussion of "Whiteanity" by asking, "[i]s it authentic liberation theology, or is it Christianity/Whiteanity—a religion of oppression, a species of the slave master's Frankenstein transmutation of biblical religion and Christianity that Carter G. Woodson labels mis-religion and Benjamin Mays, 'compensatory beliefs'?"[4]

Jones's scholarship highlights the complexities of Black liberation theology through an internal assessment of theological claims and beliefs that affirm to be liberatory. Jones's main criticism of Black liberation theology is the narrow Christian-centric focus that denies the inclusion of non-Christian and nontheistic perspectives in the Black historical record.[5] To state it another way, Jones's theological (and philosophical) thought transgressed and transformed the conventional boundaries of Black liberation theology and Black philosophy.[6] His close friend and fellow philosopher Roy D. Morrison aptly notes,

> Jones is probably the only member of the family of thinkers who employs critical philosophical analysis to make a critique of the internal structures of traditional black religion.... In other words, when all of the technical terminology and all of the apologetics arguments have been explored, black theology asks, what if anything, does God do for black people.[7]

By challenging the scope of what constitutes Black liberation theology, Jones was considered an "outsider" and occupied a space "reminiscent to a 'pariah status.'"[8]

By pointing out the "logical potholes" and "unsound detours" found in Black liberation theology's promise of economic, social, and political liberation and the eradication of oppression, Jones openly assesses how certain theological beliefs, values, and attitudes may undergird oppression.[9] Jones's theological stance for challenging normative views in Black liberation theology are best understood through the biblical concept of divine suffering. Jones uses the concept of theodicy, God's suffering-servant model, and the "multievidentiality" of suffering in the Black experience to demonstrate that normative Black liberation theologies are actually theodicies in disguise and may be "working at cross-purposes with their goals," of eradicating oppression.[10]

Jones contests that the theologies of Albert Cleage and James H. Cone are in practice *theodicies*. Theodicy is the explanation of human suffering given God's superlative traits. The possibility of divine racism informs the methodological system in Jones's theology because "God's benevolence is not self-evident."[11] Jones suggests five identifying categories for detailing divine racism: first, God categorizes people into "in" group and "out" group; therefore God does not treat people equally. Second, the "out" group suffers more. Third, the imbalance is dictated on God's will, but humans can be used as an instrument. Fourth, there is a racial component to the categories. Finally, God is part of the "in" group. In Jones's critique of normative Black liberation theology, he clearly demonstrates that the charge of divine suffering will lead to quietism.[12] Briefly put, "[q]uietism results ... when corrective actions are deemed *unnecessary*.... Corrective action is *impossible*. ... That corrective action is *inappropriate*" to eliminate oppressive conditions.[13] To justify the benevolence of God, human expression will force us back to a place where suffering is sanctioned by God and labeled as "positive suffering," resulting in quietism. Jones openly asserts, "[t]he oppressed are oppressed, in fundamental part, because of the beliefs they hold. They adopt or are indoctrinated to accept a belief system that stifles their motivation to attack the institutions and groups that oppress them."[14] Jones haphazardly reduces the material condition of the Black community to a set of ideological beliefs and fails to emphasize the material context of social relations of production and the dialectic relationship of living within a capitalistic society.[15]

Black liberation theologies must be assessed in light of the conceptual and methodological implications of liberation.[16] Antithetical fit is a conceptual yardstick used to determine what ideas are helpful or harmful to actualize material liberation. Antithetical fit is not sustainable on its own accord, but when used in conjunction with "praxis verification" and the virus/vaccine model it acts as a methodological "toolkit" to investigate how oppression operates by isolating those doctrines and creeds that support positive suffering and divine punishment.[17]

Jones's view of humanism, or humanocentric theism, does not support a concept of God from a standpoint of a scientific hypothesis, which subsequently would require scientific proof of the existence of God. Humanism can be described as theistic humanism and secular humanism as well as strong humanism that dismisses God or the existence of God (atheism).[18]

Jones's humanocentric theism is ostensibly grounded in the diverse Black cultural religious experience. Jones notes:

> [r]eligious humanism is a neglected aspect of black culture. In discussions of black religion, humanism of all varieties is virtually ignored, and when it is unexpectedly remembered, it suffers from the unfortunate fate of being misinterpreted and misunderstood. Its situation parallels the predicament of the hero in Ralph Ellison's, *Invisible Man*, who though flesh and blood, living and breathing, is treated as if he did not exist.[19]

Black religious humanism is the dialectical counterpart to Black Christian theism and together they inform the broader arena of Black religious experiences. Jones astutely holds:

> Researchers in black religion characteristically narrow their focus to the history of the black church and its monolithic theological perspective of Christian theism. Because the black church is the major institutional expression of black religion, one can readily acknowledge that its thought and practice should receive preeminent attention. Having said this, however, it must also be allowed that the concern to uncover the rich path of the majority position should not obscure *the full content and scope of black religion*. Nor should the effort to honor the black church and its particular theological tradition obliterate the total spectrum of competing species of black religion, *especially the nontheistic perspective*. Unfortunately, this has occurred. (Emphasis added)[20]

The dialectal offerings of Jones's criticism toward his interlocutors and his presentation of humanocentric theism fall short of developing into philosophical materialism, partly because of Jones's own affinity with religious humanism.

In this sense, Jones openly addresses limitations in Black theological thought by highlighting the inadequacies in the conventional historical descriptions of Black religious traditions. By neglecting to include non-Christian traditions within the ranks of Black religion, normative Christian theologians fail to provide a holistic description of Black religious thought. Thusly, when humanism is mentioned within

Black theological circles, there is a misinformed understanding that humanism is a "white" perspective that does not belong in the Black historical record.[21] As Jones notes, "[t]his stance puts me in opposition to those humanists who regard religion as an illusion, who seek to negate the divine reality as the necessary precondition for affirming the humanist gospel of human freedom, and who interpret the history of religion as only an instrument of oppression and dehumanization."[22]

Jones provides various historical examples of Black nontheistic religious traditions and thinkers who challenged the basic norms and precepts of Christianity, even if these ideas did not influence the masses of African Americans. For example:

> To resurrect black religious humanism requires a second interpretive principle that current researchers in black religion do not sufficiently honor: *The actual origin as well as the current position of black religious humanism must be seen as a response to perceived inadequacies of black Christian theism, its theological rival.* Implicit in this principle is the hypothesis that black humanism emerges as part of a debate that is internal to black life and thought. It is not a spinoff of the enlightenment, the scientific revolution or, as J. Deotis Roberts has suggested, a borrowing from Comte. (Emphasis in original)[23]

From this point, we not only see Jones's view of humanocentric theism as a viable alternative to Christian-centric theologies, but he also expands the horizons of what is included as Black liberation theology. Jones asserts several points that are deemed necessary for a prolegomenon to Black theology, which includes a theology that is part of a monotheistic tradition, upholds God's omnipotence and benevolence, rejects the idea of quietism, and employs the final objective of liberation.[24] His place within this discussion is not from the perspective of atheism or Christophobia, with the objective to eradicate religion, but rather Jones is trying to produce a Black religious perspective with the main purpose of eradicating suffering. Humanocentric theism is a clever maneuver to provide a viable theological framework while critically exploring the material conditions in Black communities.

Dr. Jones is one of the most significant thinkers of the twentieth and twenty-first centuries. *Is God a White Racist?* and many of his other writings have concretely changed the way we think about philosophy and the ongoing concern with corrective action through "rigorous criticism" and practical application.[25] His philosophical theology pushes us past the stagnant boundaries of a Christian-centric, theistic-only Black liberation theology by opening the door for an analytical examination of the religious histories that have been overlooked and overshadowed by the larger, institutionalized Black religious traditions.

Notes

1   William R. Jones, *Is God a White Racist?: A Preamble to Black Theology* (Boston: Beacon Press, 1998), xi.

2   See, "Newsletter on Philosophy and the Black Experiences," *APA Newsletter* 12, no. 2 (Spring 2013).For a detailed historiography of African American philosophy, see John H. McClendon, III and Stephen C. Ferguson, II, *African American Philosophers and Philosophy: An Introduction to the History, Concepts, and Contemporary Issues* (London: Bloomsbury Press, 2019). Also see Lewis Gordon, ed. *Existential Africana: Understanding African Existential Thought* (New York: Routledge, 2000). Gordon dedicated *Existential Africana* to William R. Jones.
3   Jones, *Is God a White Racist?*, 205–14.
4   Ibid., ix–x.
5   For more on the leading Black liberation theologians during the 1960s and early 1970s, see James H. Cone, *God of the Oppressed* (New York: Seabury Press, 1975); Albert B. Cleage Jr., *The Black Messiah* (New York: Sheed and Ward, 1968); Major Jones, *Black Awareness: A Theology of Hope* (Nashville: Abingdon Press, 1971); J. Deotis Roberts, *Liberation and Reconciliation* (Philadelphia: The Westminster Press, 1971); Joseph R. Washington, *Black Religion: The Negro and Christianity in the United States* (Boston: Beacon Press, 1964).
6   William R. Jones, "The Legitimacy and Necessity of Black Philosophy: Some Preliminary Considerations," *The Philosophical Forum, A Quarterly* IX, no. 2–3 (Winter-Spring 1977–8): 117–48. Also, Joyce Mitchell Cook, William R. Jones, and Robert C. Williams, "The Black Philosopher," in *Conversations from Wingspread/Radio Program* (Racine, WI: The Johnson Foundation, 1976).
7   Roy D. Morrison, II, "Self-Transformation in American Blacks: The Harlem Renaissance and Black Theology," in *Existence in Black*, ed. Lewis R. Gordon (New York: Rutledge, 1997), 46.
8   John H. McClendon, with assistance from Brittany O'Neal, *Philosophy of Religion and the African American Experience: Conversations with My Christian Friends* (Boston: Brill, 2017), 287–326.
9   Jones, *Is God a White Racist?*, xix.
10 Jones, *Is God a White Racist?*, 206. Also see, Anthony Pinn, *Moral Evil and Redemptive Suffering: A History of Theodicy in African-American Religious Thought* (Gainesville: University Press of Florida, 2002), 7–8 and fn. 12 of Introduction. The suffering-servant model can be understood as God's good grace, but Jones warns us "[p]rior to the exaltation event and the multievidentiality of suffering, God's favor and disfavor remain equally probable." Jones, *Is God a White Racist?*, 20.
11 William R. Jones, "Theism and Religious Humanism: The Chasm Narrows," *The Christian Century* 92, no. 18 (May 1975): 523.
12 William R. Jones, "Process Theology: Guardian of the Oppressor or Goad to the Oppressed," *Process Studies* 18, no. 4 (Winter 1989): 277; Jones, *Is God a White Racist?*, 21.
13 William R. Jones, "Reconciliation and Liberation in Black Theology: Some Implications for Religious Education," *Religious Education* 67 (September–October 1972): 387.
14 William R. Jones, "Religious Humanism: Its Problems and Prospects in Black Religion and Culture," *The Journal of Interdenominational Theological Center* 7, no. 2 (1979): 181.
15 For more on African American philosophical materialism, see McClendon and Ferguson, *African American Philosophers and Philosophy*. Also, see Stephen Ferguson, *Philosophy of African American Studies: Nothing Left to Blackness* (London: Palgrave Macmillan, 2015). For more on theodicy and the Black experience, see, Stephen

Ferguson, "Teaching Hurricane Katrina: Understanding Divine Racism and Theodicy," *APA Newsletter on Philosophy and the Black Experience* 7, no.1 (Fall 2007): 1–5; Pinn, *Moral Evil and Redemptive Suffering*.

16 William R. Jones, "Theodicy and Methodology in Black Theology: A Critique of Washington, Cone and Cleage," *The Harvard Theological Review* 64, no. 4 (1971): 543.

17 Jones, *Is God a White Racist?*, 207–8. Also see, William R. Jones, "Toward a New Paradigm for Uncovering Neo-Racism," in *Soul Work: Anti-Racist Theologies in Dialogue*, ed. Marjorie Bowens-Wheatley and Nancy Palmer Jones (Boston: Skinner House, 2003), 1–3. By using all three methods of inquiry—antithetical fit, praxis verification, and the virus/vaccine model—it is possible to explore which Black liberation theologies undergird oppression and which support liberation. Antithetical fit is a methodological tool used to determine the liberatory potential of a theological principle. Praxis Verification measures the practical fit of a theological principles ability toward transforming economic, social, and political realities. Lastly, the virus/vaccine model is the practical application of correctly identifying the pathogen that supports oppression and develop a vaccine to immobilize the virus. If the virus is misidentified or mislabeled, the corresponding vaccine will fail to destroy the virus. See, Jones, *Is God a White Racist?*, 206.

18 William R. Jones, "The Case for Black Humanism," in *Black Theology II: Essays on the Formation and Outreach of Contemporary Black Theology*, ed. William R. Jones and Calvin E. Bruce (Lewisburg: Bucknell University Press, 1978). Jones suggests humanocentric theism supports humans as responsible agents for the history of human suffering, and to blame God leads to quietism. For a diverse examination of theological perspectives found in the Black historical record, including death-of-God theologies, pantheism, panentheism, deism, and atheism, see Anthony Pinn, *Varieties of African American Religious Experiences* (Minneapolis: Fortress Press, 1998).

19 Jones, "Religious Humanism," 169.

20 Ibid.

21 For scholarship on Black atheists and the nonreligious tradition, see Juan Floyd-Thomas, *The Origins of Black Humanism in America* (New York: Palgrave, 2008); Douglas Heck, "Humanism: African American Liberation '(A)Theology,'" *Free Inquiry* 21, no. 4 (Fall 2001); Michael Lackey, *African American Atheists and Political Liberation* (Gainesville: University of Florida Press, 2007); Sikivu Hutchinson, *Moral Combat: Black Atheists, Gender Politics, and the Values Wars* (Los Angeles: Infidel Books, 2011); Sikivu Hutchinson, *Godless Americana: Race and Religious Rebels* (Los Angeles: Infidel Books, 2013); Kwasi Wiredu, "Morality and Religion and Akan Thought," in *African-American Humanism: An Anthology*, ed. Norm R. Allen (Buffalo: Prometheus Books, 1991); Kwasi Yirenkyi, "Atheism and Secularity in Ghana," in *Atheism and Secularity*, ed. Phil Zuckerman (Santa Barbara, CA: Praeger, 2010).

22 Jones, "Theism and Religious Humanism," 521.

23 Jones, "Religious Humanism," 178–9.

24 Jones, *Is God a White Racist?*, 174–5. Jones offers twelve key points to be included in a Black liberation theology. I have condensed several of the points earlier.

25 Jones, *Is God a White Racist?*, xxi. Also see, Henry T. Johnson, "Philosophy Religiously Valued," *A.M.E. Church Review* 7, no. 4 (April 1891).

AFTERWORD

Darrell Jones

Christmas Day, 1974.
I was five years old. My brother was fifteen. We had hurried down to the tree to see the bounty of presents that awaited us. As we surveyed the space underneath the tree, all we saw were two large bags of walnuts each with our name on them. My brother started to search for other places where our booty of gifts must be hidden. Were they behind the couch, in the closet? This quickly turned to complaining that this couldn't be all we had gotten.

These are just walnuts, he exclaimed! What are we supposed to do with this?

It was then that my father engaged him in a debate about the multiple uses for nuts, their portability and nutritious qualities. My brother wasn't buying it.

My father's tactic switched to a bargaining methodology. "Okay, well, listen. I'll make you a deal. You can either take your bag of walnuts or I will trade your nuts for these coupons for McDonald's." My brother loved McDonald's at that time, and although he wasn't thrilled about this single gift option, he figured it was better than a bag of walnuts. I was confused by the whole exchange, but my brother being older, I immediately took his cue and said I, too, wanted these things called coupons.

With the exchange confirmed among all parties, my father ceremoniously went over to the dining room table with the two large bags of nuts and started to crack them open. With each nut, he pulled out a dollar bill neatly folded inside the shell casing. Placing the shells on one side and stacking the bills on the other, he proceeded to crack the first, second, third nut, and when he reached the sixth nut, he pulled out a five-dollar bill. This was just too much for my brother to handle. My brother tried to retract the deal stating the inequities of the process to which my father reminded he had the information needed to make a choice, and thus a new debate ensued. At five, it took me a couple of months of questioning to understand that money didn't actually grow in walnuts.

As I got older, I understood the experience in terms of value coming in small packages, and that the exterior of something familiar might not match the inside. On additional replays, the narrative of strategic deceit to purposely shift someone's worldview appeared. For my brother at his age, it was an exercise in critical thinking, the ability to persuade, to make a cogent argument, what is the nature of Christmas, a parent's role and expectations for this holiday. For my father, it was possibly a kind of preparation for us to look closer—a practice as the trickster or the predictive nature of humanity and choice making.

Ingrained in my memory is the amount of labor it took to impart this lesson: breaking open a precarious nut right down the seam, taking out the meat, folding the dollar bill, and carefully gluing it back together.

For the past ten years, I've delved deeply into archiving his intellectual work in conjunction with Florida State University Special Collections Department. During this process, there were over 160 Dole banana boxes filled with his intellectual materials. It was a favorite container for him in its multiple uses and portability. I can't help but notice a similarity between the walnuts and the boxes. Although different in scale, both containers were filled with content to promote learning, debate, and perception. This volume pulls together some of the essays and book chapters that mark out my father's thinking on key issues—and that present some of the lessons I associate with those walnuts and some of the sharp insights found filed away in those boxes.

The chapters in these pages not only speak specifically to a particular time and audience but also touch on his personal lessons, a call to debate and a demand for active performance. As I talk to his colleagues who have been privy to his analyses, they often reiterate the theme that they can never simply look at the surface level of things again. I will never view a box or nut the same way, as I'm continually reminded of him and his work. The analysis is there, ever present, informing our perceptions and making us question simplicity, analyze complexity, and continually look closer at our human condition.

INDEX

3M Company   60

abortion   138, 141, 172
Abraham   24, 25, 149
Adam   23, 24
adultery   142, 176
African concept of time   52, 94–5
Africanism   32, 45
African Methodist Episcopal Church   39
agnosticism   47, 193
Ali, Muhammad   167
"the American Dilemma"   184
American Humanist Association   63 n.1
American Institute for Character Education   139
American Revolution   116, 180. *See also* United States
American Unitarian Association   197
announced, actual and absentee beliefs   174
anthropologian   36
anti-abortion movement   172
anti-apartheid movement   3
anti-Calvinistic   197
anti-powerism   3, 108–14, 130, 132, 133, 155–7, 164–8, 199
antithetical correlation   134
antithetical fit   135, 204, 207 n.17
anti-Unitarianism   13
Aquinas, Thomas   112
"as if" philosophy   20, 24
atheism   44, 47, 48, 162, 204
authority   20, 36, 53, 66, 72–4, 116, 117, 123, 136, 146, 175, 176
Autobiography of Jane Eyre, The   132, 165

background assumptions   161, 173
Ballou, Hosea   158
banking concept, of education   86
Barth, Karl   19, 79, 80

belief and value system   67, 68, 105, 113, 126, 129, 131, 147, 164, 166, 173
Bennett, Lerone, Jr.   168
Bennett, William J.   139, 169
Berger, Peter   70, 73, 132, 165, 171 n.4
Berkovits, Eliezer   21, 22, 72, 73
Bible   119, 122, 128, 141–5, 161–2, 175, 176
Bible of the Oppressed, The (Tamez)   135
biblical faith   29, 73, 102, 103, 107, 119, 121–3, 125, 127, 136
biblical realism   180
biblical scriptures
   Luke 2:38   81
   Rom. 6:22; 8:2   81
   I Cor. 7:20-24; 12:13   81
   Gal. 3:28   86
   Eph. 6:5-9   81
   Col. 3:21-4   81
"Bibliocracy, Hypocrisy, or Democracy? Questions to the Moral Majority" (Jones)   140
Black Americans   41, 42, 58, 179, 184
Black bodies, materiality of   192–5
"black caucus"   11, 13, 17, 155
Black Christian
   church   168
   denominations   27
   theism   29, 31–3, 37, 39, 42, 46–8, 51–3, 55 n.20, 204, 205
Black Christianity   28, 33, 34, 105, 131
Black humanism   1, 4, 37, 192, 193, 196
   alienation to Black religion   31–4
   apologetics/theological construction   27–8
   authentic religious perspective and activity of theology   34–6
   Black church as liberating agent   30–1
   and Black theology   28–30
Black humanist(s)   30, 31, 33, 35, 48–53

theologian 28
theology 37, 55 n.20
Black liberation 29–31, 41, 49, 94, 191, 193
  movements 199
  theologians 167, 197
  theology 28, 79–86, 196, 197, 202–5
Black Man's Volunteer Army of Liberation 12
Black Muslims 68
Blackness 12, 14, 15, 30, 86
Black oppression 33–4, 38, 39, 42–4, 47–51, 55 n.20, 71–4, 79, 81–3, 85, 90–2, 94, 202
Black power and Unitarianism 9–17, 155, 156
  alleged incompatibility 9, 11, 15, 16
  contradictory aspects 9
  definition 9, 11, 15
Black Power Movement 11–13, 199
Black religion 27, 28, 30, 32, 33, 37–9, 42, 44, 45, 49, 52, 53, 94, 168, 192, 204
  definition 46, 47
  experience 33, 39, 45, 46, 204
  heritage 40
  pasts 33, 38, 39, 46
  pluralistic interpretation of 45, 46
  tradition in 41, 45, 204, 205
Black religious humanism 38–53, 54 n.9, 196, 204, 205
  Black humanist perspective 48–50
  cultural matrix of 47–8, 54 n.18
  invisibility 41–4
  as invisible religion 39–41
  liberation theology and theological method 50–3
  methodological and semantic practices 44–7
Black(s)
  churches 28, 30–4, 38, 42, 43, 45–9, 51–3, 80, 168, 191, 204
  co-equality 180
  community 10, 30, 31, 48, 63, 169, 203
  consciousness 45, 51, 52
  contemporary 28
  crime 62
  culture 38–40, 42, 44, 191
  embodiment 192–3
  family 63
  heroes 167
  leaders 155, 156
  PhDs 61
  philosophy 202, 203
  powerlessness 12, 156, 199
  religionists 29, 33, 94
  secular 31
  songs 41
  spirituality 29
  theism/theists 49, 192
  theologians 27, 28, 30, 32–4, 36, 37, 47, 53, 79, 80–2, 89, 90, 92–5, 107, 110, 192, 194, 197
  theology 4, 28–31, 34, 37, 38, 46, 53, 82, 88, 89, 91, 92, 94–6, 100, 119, 191–4, 195 n.6, 197, 205
Black Theology of Liberation, A (Cone) 81
Blauner, Robert 185
blues 32, 41, 43
Blyden, Edward W. 41
Bonhoeffer, Dietrich 19, 150
"both-and" approach 80
Brown, Richard C. 98, 100–2, 112
Brown, Robert McAfee 114, 128, 163
Brown, Sterling 6, 13, 39
Buddhism 35
Burckhardt, Jacob 108, 133, 156, 166
Burkle, Howard 22, 75
Bush, George 61, 62

Caldicott, Helen 161
Câmara, Dom Hélder 110, 136 n.9
Camus, Albert 20, 23, 66, 83, 92, 194
Carmichael, Stokely 12
causality 22, 57–9, 63, 173, 174, 177, 184, 185
character education 138–40, 143, 144, 151
Christ 83–6, 107, 127. *See also* Jesus
Christian
  church 80, 84, 85, 98, 101–2
  consensus 151 n.10
  dogmatics 79, 82
  ethic of love 157
  faith 19, 32, 33, 43, 45, 51, 52, 79, 80, 88, 90, 103, 119, 121–3, 125, 127, 136

freedom 82
missionary 41
nationalism 200
orientation 191
theism 29, 38, 200 n.3 (*see also* Christian theism and religious humanism)
theology 80, 88, 119, 123, 124, 202
tradition 18, 52, 83, 93, 116
Christian-centric theologies 202, 203, 205
Christianity 39, 46, 47, 51, 52, 79, 98, 124, 205
Christianization 107
Christian Right 197, 200 n.3
Christian theism and religious humanism 18–19
    aim and strategy 19–20
    differentiation 22–4
    functional ultimacy 19–22
    future 25–6
    human freedom and divine sovereignty 22
    humanocentric predicament 24–5
Christology 88
Chronicle of Higher Education 60
civil law, violation of 110, 111
civil rights 181
    era 179, 180
    groups 12
    movement 180–1
    policies (1964 and 1965) 197, 199
    protest 98, 180, 181
Cleage, Albert 203
Cobb, William Daniel 21, 22, 72
co-equality 80, 81, 111, 113, 117, 123, 124, 136, 158, 167, 170–2, 180
Colburn, David 181
Collins, LeRoy 179–82
color-blind neo-conservatism 197
Comblin, José 137 n.12
Comte, Auguste 32, 33, 45, 47, 48, 205
Cone, James 29–32, 34, 36, 43, 53, 79–81, 125, 127, 191, 192, 194, 203
Cone, Cecil 46, 47
Conference of Latin American Bishops, Medellín (1968) 101, 102
contemporary politics 159, 160

CORE 31
corn-songs 40
corrective actions 70, 71, 83–5, 91–2, 105–6, 132, 134, 164, 165, 185, 188, 203
cosmological argument 120
counterviolence 100, 103, 104, 108–10, 115, 116, 120, 180
    moral and religious legitimacy of 99, 100, 109, 113, 115–17, 126
    practice of 100
    as self-defense 109, 111–12, 115
Cox, Harvey 88
crime statistics 62
cross-resurrection 83
cultural genocide 86, 168
cultural pluralism 168, 170, 171

death-of-God theologians 27
dechristianizing period 43
defensive violence (self-defense) 12, 13, 86, 99, 111, 113, 115, 118 n.27
dehumanization 66, 145, 205
deism 41
DeKlerk, F. W. 56
democracy 199
    principles 173
    process 10, 13
Denney, James 84
Department of Social Responsibility 17 n.1
Devil and the Good Lord, The (Sartre) 21
devil songs 39, 40
diagnosis determines therapy (DDT) 173–4, 197
discrimination 11, 155, 172
    racial 179, 181–7
    sexual 172, 182, 186
divine 46–8, 67
    freedom 71, 74
    omnipotence 24, 70, 132
    order 70, 106, 132, 146, 165
    punishment 70, 92, 95, 107, 135, 165, 204
    racism 92–6, 196, 197, 203
    reality 19, 21, 48, 146
    sovereignty 21, 22, 72
divorce 142, 145, 175, 176
Douglass, Frederick 6, 58, 183
Du Bois, W. E. B. 6, 90, 96 n.4

Dulaney, Jean   17 n.1
Duméry   19

economic colonialism   102
economic-social-political (ESP)   72–4
　context   159
　inequalities   106, 134, 163–5, 188
　liberation   2, 51, 82, 84, 119, 168, 203
　oppression   64, 67–70, 85, 99, 103–4,
　　109, 112, 127–32, 134–6, 164–5,
　　185, 187
　policies   173, 184
Ellison, Ralph   38, 204
employment   13, 15
enlightenment   47, 48
eschatology   40, 49, 52, 53, 82, 83, 88, 94
espoused theory *vs.* theory in use   62
ethical nihilism   156, 167
ethics   156, 195 n.6
　Christian   125
　force for   156
　Judeo-Christian   139
　post-modern   148
　problems   125
　social   109, 155, 156, 198, 199
　theological/political   126
ethnicism   16, 17
Eve   24
evil   82, 83, 90, 108, 113, 130, 133, 150
Ewald, Russell   60
exaltation event   95
exorcist/castration method   51
extrahuman transcendence   23, 25

Fabio, Sarah Webster   6
Faith after the Holocaust (Berkovits)   21
false causality   174, 198
Falwell, Jerry   139, 141, 142, 145
FBI   62
Fierro, Alfredo   111
Files, The (Sartre)   23
Fire Next Time, The (Baldwin)   17
Florida State University (FSU)   60
Florida State University Special
　　Collections Department   210
Foreman, George   167
Franklin, John Hope   181
Freire, Paulo   86
Fuller, Hoyt   160

full manhood   9, 12, 14
functional ultimacy   4, 19–23, 25, 26, 36,
　　96, 193, 197, 200 n.4

Gandhi, Mohandas   116, 157
Garrow, David   181
gay/lesbian(ism)
　issue (GLI)   172, 173, 175, 177
　in military   172–7
　rights   177
God
　acts of   93–4
　benevolence   1, 23, 33, 47, 51, 52, 90,
　　94, 203, 205
　of Christian faith   29
　concept(s) of   35, 49, 50, 64, 67, 69,
　　71, 166, 192, 194, 204
　death/non-existence   27
　doctrine of   79
　existence   45, 47, 120, 204
　faith in   64–75
　as judge   65, 135, 157
　justice   33, 39, 47, 51, 52, 94
　moral laws   142
　omnipotence   135, 157, 165, 205
　as persuader   22
　politics of   30, 85, 160
　power   21
　reconciliation   85, 86
　revelation   34, 80, 127
　saving work   90
　self-giving of   107, 136 n.7
　suffering   83
　and ultimate reality   35
　as white racist   20, 33, 48, 88, 92, 93,
　　193
　will   70–2, 82, 107, 132, 162, 165, 203
"God Reconciles and Makes Free"
　　(Miller)   81
God-talk   32, 34, 195
*Good News To The Poor: The Challenge of
　　the Poor in the History of the Church*
　　(Santa Ana)   135
Gouldner, Alvin   161, 173
Graham, Billy   2, 56, 142, 175
Guardini, Romano   108, 133, 156, 167
Gutiérrez, Gustavo   112, 127

Hartshorne, Charles   19, 28

Haselden, Kyle 14
Herzog, Frederick 119
Hessel, Dieter 85
Hick, John 96
hierarchical division, of human
    family 68, 69, 106, 129, 130, 164
Hitler 66, 150
homo religiosus 19
homosexuality 142, 145, 175–7
Howlett, Duncan 10, 17
human/humanity 20–4
    brotherhood 10, 11, 16
    choice 24, 144, 146–8, 176
    destiny of 161
    freedom/autonomy 19–23, 25, 26, 43,
        72, 74, 198, 199
    as moral creator 25, 72, 74
    nature 144, 161, 162, 173
    reality 20, 21, 43, 156
    reason 143, 144, 146, 176
    rights 181
    sex 147, 177
    situation 24, 136, 148, 149
    subjectivity 144, 146, 147, 150, 176
humanism 38, 56–63, 145, 162, 204–5.
        See also Black humanism; Black
        religious humanism
    in Greek culture 43
    Jones's view of 204
    and socio-economic context 42–4, 48
    Western 48
Humanist Manifesto 197
humanist theology/theologian 27, 28,
    34, 36
"Humanity Won't End In A Nuclear
    Holocaust!" (Snyder) 161
humanocentric theism/theists 20,
    22, 36, 71, 96, 202, 204, 205,
    207 n.18
    antidote to quietism 72–3
    problems and implications 73–5
human-sub-human categories 147, 177
humility 157
Hurston, Zora Neale 194
hypocrisy 173, 174, 176–8, 181

Identity Crisis in Black Theology, The
    (Cone) 46
ideology 100

Ideology and the Scientific Method
    (Niebuhr) 180
idolatry 34, 120
immortality 65
impregnable argument 10
individualism 15–17, 101, 197–9
inequality 57–8, 67–70, 98, 104–7, 129,
    130, 132, 163, 186
    educational 181
    racial 187, 198
inferior groups 68
initiating cause *vs.* consequent cause 63
injustice, logic of 70–2
institutionalized violence. *See* original
    violence
internal criticism 2, 20, 60, 66, 121–4,
    126, 127, 137 n.12, 192
Invisible Man (Ellison) 38, 204
*Is God a White Racist? Preamble to Black
    Theology* (Jones) 1–4, 20, 196,
        199, 202, 205

Jacobs, Joseph 62
James, William 20
Jane Eyre 69, 70
Jesus 34, 36, 43, 53, 84, 120, 127, 142,
    175, 192, 193. *See also* Christ
    reconciling activity of 86
    resurrection of 85
jig-tunes 40
Jones, Charles C. 41
Jones, Leroi 43
Jones, William R. 1–2, 9, 18, 29, 56–63, 88,
    191–5, 195 n.4, 196–9, 202, 203, 205
Jones Oppression Grid & the Jones
    Analytical Model (JOG &
    JAM) 3–4
Judeo-Christian
    faith 29
    tradition 67
just society 64–75
just war theory 99, 112, 113

Katz, Bernard 40
Kaufman, Gordon 22
Kerner Report 181, 183
Kierkegaard 20, 36
King, Martin Luther, Jr. 56, 58, 65, 100,
    107, 114–16, 155, 167, 168

Kirk, Claude   179, 180
Kolakowski, Leszek   90

Larsen, Nella   47
Latin America   102
Latin American liberation theology
    (LALT)   97, 98, 100, 112, 118 n.27,
    124. *See also* counterviolence;
    liberation theology; oppression
  apologetic norm   103–4
  geopolitical implications of   97, 98
  theology of social change   98–102
  and violence   100–3
law of love   157
legal justice system   183, 184
legitimation, definition   174–5
Leith, John   86
liberalism   138, 141, 144
*Liberation and Reconciliation: A Black
    Theology* (Roberts)   80–1
liberation theologians   50, 51, 72, 91, 92,
    97, 110, 135, 160
liberation theology   4, 28, 33, 37, 47–53,
    64, 66–71, 73, 88, 89, 92, 96–8, 105,
    107, 114, 155, 166, 192. *See also*
    Latin American liberation theology
    (LALT); theology, question-begging
  anti-powerism and oppression   133
  apologetic   99–101, 105, 108, 111
  concept of oppression   103, 104
  context, purpose and method   119–
    20, 127–8, 163
  and counterviolence (*see*
    counterviolence)
  critics/criticisms of   99, 100, 104, 109,
    110, 112, 114, 120–3, 125–7, 134,
    137 n.12
  and ESP oppression   128–32, 134
  existence of   123
  implications   134–6
  interim assessments, logical priority
    and internal criticism   121–4, 131,
    134, 135
  and logic of ethnicity   168–71
  moral imperatives   101, 103, 107, 113,
    125
  moral legitimacy   97, 98, 109, 119
  norms of   102, 121, 123–6
  quietism and oppression   132–3

theology of social change   98, 100,
    101, 110
theory of revolutionary change   99
and violence (*see* violence)
as worm's eye view   159–60
Lincoln, Abraham   56
Long, Charles   191
Los Angeles   56, 59, 61
Lovell, John   39, 40, 46
Lucretius   35

Mabley, Moms   170
MacInnis, Donald   26
McKnight, William   60
McKnight Black Doctoral
    Fellowship   60
McKnight Foundation   60
McManus, Mike   138
Macquarrie, John   27, 28
Malcolm X   6, 57, 100, 114, 115, 167, 168
Mao   114
Marshall Plan   62
Marxism   97, 101–3, 112, 120, 135
Marx   103
Mater et Magistra   101
Mays, Benjamin   32, 33, 47, 49, 69, 105,
    131, 166, 202
Mbiti, John   52, 94
meta-moralities   148
Metz, Johannes   82, 83, 88
Miller, Donald G.   81, 82, 84, 85
minority education   60
miseducation   4, 180
Miseducation of the Negro, The
    (Woodson)   180
mis-religion   2, 4, 202
Moltmann, Jürgen   83
monotheism   35–6, 44, 120, 205
moral absolutes/absolutism   139, 140,
    143–6, 172, 173, 175–7
  demise of   144–5
  evolution of   176
  nature as   145–6
moral code   65, 73, 143, 146, 175
moral decision-making   151
  evolution of   143–4
  guiding principles   147–51
  in post-modern period   143, 144,
    147–51

moral education   138, 139
morality   12, 23–5, 65, 73, 98, 143–5, 147, 148, 175–6
moral leadership   179–80
moral legitimacy   98–100, 109, 140, 143, 146
moral misleadership   181, 182
moral nihilism   65, 66, 74, 140
moral theology   111, 112
Morris, Van Cleve   24, 148
Morrison, Roy D.   203
Moses   143, 175
Moynihan, Daniel   63
Muhammad, Elijah   68–9
Myrdal, Gunnar   108

NAACP   31, 156
National Council of Churches   11
National Organization of Social Work   11
National War College   97
Nation of Islam   68, 69
natural law theory   146, 176
natural order   71, 146–7, 175–8
Negroes. *See* Black(s)
Negro's God, The (Mays)   32, 49
neo-fundamentalism   140, 141, 172, 174
neoliberalism   197, 200 n.8
neo-racism   56, 61, 183–8, 196–200, 200 n.8
New England Protestantism   41
New Testament   82–4, 142, 157
Niebuhr, Reinhold   156, 179, 180
non-Christian
    theism   18, 38
    traditions   204
Non-Existence of God, The (Burkle)   22
non-religious songs   40
nontheism   38, 39, 44–6
    Afro-American   48
    component   44
    contemporary   19
    model   28
    religions   36
non-violence   98, 105, 109, 110, 112–14, 125, 126, 157
    and its ideological
        manipulation   114–16
    techniques   12
North America   98, 107, 110

Novak, Michael   19, 170
nuclear freeze   141, 162
nuclear weapons   141, 161–2

objective reality   66, 70
objective uncertainty   24, 25, 143, 144, 148, 149
offensive violence   13, 14
ontology   22
    absolutes   73, 74
    Lucretius's   35
    priority   25, 74
    ultimacy   23, 24
oppressed/oppression   3–4, 111, 116, 126. *See also* Black oppression; economic-social-political (ESP), oppression
    and anti-powerism   108–9, 133, 166–8
    binary logic of   104–6
    ideological perpetuation of   112–14
    inner logic of   68, 72, 106, 129, 132, 133, 165
    institutional   185, 187, 188
    liberation theology's concept of   103, 104
    liturgical life of   167–8
    maintenance structures of   116, 125
    mechanism of   106–8, 145, 165, 166
    post-enlightened   68, 129
    pre-enlightened   68, 129, 130
    and quietism   165–6
    racial   180, 197, 199, 200
    religious legitimation and   132
    transgenerational   67, 93, 131
    worm as symbol of   104, 128–9
Oppression Grid and Analytical Model   4
Orestes   23, 24
original violence   99, 107, 108, 110

Pacem in Terris   101
pacifism   13, 113
papal encyclicals   101, 102
Pascal   66
Payne, Daniel Alexander   39, 47
Philosophy and the American School (Morris)   24
philosophy of power   10–13
pick and choose fallacy   145–7

pie-in-the-sky eschatology   34, 53,
    55 n.20, 91
Pius XII   102
Plain Truth, The   161, 162
Plato   144, 176
plucked chicken (PC) fallacy   144–5, 176
pluralism   19, 29, 46, 138, 148, 170, 173,
    198, 199
political policy   161, 173
political theology   163
"The Politics of God"   30
Populorum Progressio   101
poverty   102
power   116, 117, 123, 124
    vs. anti-powerism   155–6
    category of   157
    co-equal   158, 167
    concept of   156
    economic, social, and political   12,
        108, 111, 113, 115, 117
    as evil   108, 130, 133, 158
    gross imbalance of   68, 81, 104, 106,
        111, 113, 128–31, 160, 163, 164,
        166, 167
    institutionalization of   69
    moral   10–13, 72
    non-moral   10, 13
    objective   110
    and violence   157–8
powerism   108–10, 133, 155, 166, 167
praxis verification   204, 207 n.17
Prometheus   23, 38, 47
proof-text approach   146
property rights   123–4
Protagoras   20, 22, 23, 36
Protestantism   145
Protestant theologian   29
Publications Committee   17
public policy   159, 160, 171
public policymaking   160, 162
public schools
    character education in   138–40, 143
    prayer in   138, 139, 172

Quicksand (Larsen)   47–8
quietism   3, 20, 26, 33, 51, 69–73,
    83–5, 88, 90–2, 105, 106,
    112–14, 117, 132–5, 164–6, 199,
    203, 205

Rabbi Nahman of Kossov   142
race   10, 11, 15, 56–63
    injustice   187
    prejudice   59, 186–8
    problems   14, 59, 155, 188
    relations   9
    separatism   15, 170
racialism   68, 69
Racial Oppression in America
    (Blauner)   185
*Racial Problem in Christian Perspective,
    The*   15
racism   10, 11, 14–17, 33, 68, 79, 82, 115,
    155, 170, 181, 183–7, 198, 200
    anti-racist   15–16
    classical   197
    involuntary   16
    voluntary   16, 17
radical human creativity   19
radical theological left   41
rational persuasion   10
Raymond B. Bragg Symposium   56
Reagan, Ronald   142, 145, 162, 175,
    176
Rebel, The (Camus)   23
reconciliation   79–86, 191
Reconciliation and Conflict (Hessel)   85
relativism   145
relativity   148
religion(s)   19, 25
    authentic *vs.* inauthentic   171
    checkered history of   107, 109
    Eastern   144
    freedom   16
    groupings   16
    ideological use of   113
    as legitimator   164–6, 171
    as liberator   163, 164, 171
    life   28
    Mays's criticism of   166
    models   18
    philosophy of   28, 36, 120
    and politics   160–4
    right   139–44
    as soteriology   35
religious education/educators   79–86,
    138, 139
religious legitimation   75 n.14, 99, 100,
    106–8, 132

religious liberals/liberalism   138–40, 145, 151, 196–200
religious traditions   18, 38, 165, 166
   Black nontheistic   205
repressive violence   110
revolutionary violence   97–101, 111
Roberts, J. Deotis   29, 32, 47, 80, 81, 191, 205
Roman Catholicism   102, 145
root-and-branch approach   51, 52

Sabbath songs   40
sacred text   145, 146, 162, 176
"Saint and Satan" approach   100–2, 110
St. Patrick's Day   168
salvation   23, 29, 35, 83, 90, 91, 103, 117, 134
Santa Ana, Julio de   135
Sartre, Jean-Paul   15, 20, 21, 23, 25, 194
"Sartre's Ethics in Relation to His Philosophical Anthropology: A Criticism of Criticism" (Jones)   2
Schaeffer, Francis   65, 140, 145, 150, 172
Schillebeeckx, Edward   23
Schilling, S. Paul   122
scientific humanism   48
scientific revolution   47, 48
secular humanism   141, 144, 194, 204
secularism   31, 37
secularization   171
seculars   39–41
secular spirituals   43
Segundo, Juan L.   122, 124
self-determination   9, 12
sin   67, 81, 85, 92, 134, 167
Sisyphus   23–4
situational ethics   141, 145
skepticism   41
slave music   40
slavery   38, 39, 42, 63, 81, 94, 109, 181, 198
slave seculars   47
slave songs   43
slave spirituals   46
SNCC   31
social change   98–103, 110, 114, 159, 196
social philosophy   69, 105, 131, 166
social reality   185, 187
social structures   5, 80, 182, 185–7

Society for the Study of Black Religion   32
soteriological singular   36
soteriology   22, 23, 90, 134
Spiral of Violence, The (Camara)   136 n.9
spirituality   29, 125, 126
spirituals   39, 40, 43
Spirituals and the Blues, The (Cone)   32
SS phenomenon   184, 185
State of the Union Address   61
Steele, C. K.   179, 180
Strategic Studies Program   97
structural violence. *See* original violence
suffering
   Black   33, 43, 50, 54 n.19, 88, 91–6, 193–6
   divine   203
   ethnic   2, 4, 26, 88, 93, 130–1
   human   83, 89, 90, 95, 203
   multi-evidential   90, 92, 95, 203
   negative and positive   90, 91, 203, 204
   ontological status of   89, 92
superior groups   68
Supreme Court decree (1954)   181
Swaggart, Jimmy   141, 142, 145

Támez, Elsa   135
taxes   62
Ten Commandments   142, 143, 146, 175, 176
theism   30, 41, 42, 44, 45, 47, 65, 66, 162, 191, 196. *See also* Christian, theism
   contemporary   19, 20
   monolithic   29, 30
   theocentric   70–2
theodicy   2, 4, 37, 50, 82–3, 88–96, 135, 203
   biblical insights   95
   Black   95–6
   and divine racism   92–5
   oppression, quietism and   90–2
   theological preeminence   89–90
theology   18, 25–6. *See also* Black(s), theology
   congeniality   41
   contemporary   19, 20, 85
   deconstruction   67
   doubt   192–5

as eschatology 82, 88
God-centered 40
method 50–3
monolithism 29, 38
question-begging 19, 35, 44, 64–6, 100, 110, 111, 120–7, 135
tradition 33, 38, 41, 47
Third World 98, 99
Tillich, Paul 19, 134, 156
Torres, Camilo 97
Transcendent 20–3, 25, 66, 74
Truth, Sojourner 168
truth as subjectivity 20, 36
Tubman, Harriet 4, 57–8
Turner, Nat 6, 168

ultimate reality 22–4, 35, 49, 50, 69, 70, 74, 84, 91, 92, 105, 106, 129, 131, 132, 146, 156, 164
"Uncle Toms" 11
underclass 159, 160, 166, 167
Unitarianism 9–17, 41
Unitarian Universalism/Universalists (UU) 144, 155, 156, 158, 196–200, 200 n.4
Unitarian Universalist Association (UUA) 2, 17 n.1, 172, 192, 196–9
The Unitarian Universalist Response to the Black Rebellion (UURBR) 10, 17 n.1
United States 58–62, 98, 100, 162, 172, 179, 191, 200
  democracy 11, 12
  geopolitical policies in 116
  liberationists 126
United States Commission on Civil Rights 182, 186
universal brotherhood 10, 16
universalism 41
Universalist Church of America 197
unjust society 66–71, 73, 74

urbanized economy 42
Urban League 31

Vaihinger, Hans 20
value indoctrination 138–40, 151
Vietnam 13, 114
violence 97–103, 105, 107–8, 110, 116, 117, 126, 157, 158
  anatomy of 110–11
  Christian legitimacy of 126
  Malcolm on 115
  and moral legitimacy 109
  quietism, anti-powerism and 112–14
  types of 109, 110
virus/vaccine model 204, 207 n.17
voluntary associations 16
voluntary ethnicism 16

Washington, Booker T. 155, 167
Washington, George 56
Washington, Joseph 28, 30
welfare vs. subsidy 61–2
Wells-Barnett, Ida B. 6
Weltanschauung 91
Western Europe 62
Western religious philosophy 88
white America 13–15, 56, 63, 69
  Negro's image of 13–14
white Americans 12, 58, 185
Whiteanity 6, 51, 52, 79, 196, 202
white Christianity 28, 33, 191
white supremacy 2, 180, 186
Wilde, Oscar 170
Wilkins, Roy 156
"the will to believe" 20
Wilmore, Gayraud S. 41, 43, 191
womanist theology 194
Woodson, Carter G. 6, 180, 202
Wright, Richard 194

Yahweh 149